Ladybucks

Ladybucks

Valerie Bohigian

Dodd, Mead & Company
New York

First Edition

1 2 3 4 5 6 7 8 9 10

Library of Congress Cataloging-in-Publication Data

Bohigian, Valerie.
Ladybucks.
1. Self-employed women—United States.   2. Women
executives—United States.   3. Success in business—
United States.   I. Title.
HD6072.6.U5B64   1987   650.1′024042   86-29227
ISBN 0-396-08852-X

ISBN 0-396-08852-X

To Melanie Lisa Winn—
a stunning winner
who knows how to get and give
the joys and toys of life.

Contents

Ladybucks

Introduction

A girl in her twenties invents exotic natural sodas. A divorceé in her thirties relocates employees for a large corporation. A doctor in her forties reconstructs faces, bodies, and images. A grandmother in her fifties sells franchises that provide quality care for the elderly. A lady in her sixties manufactures curative cosmetics. These women are part of a small but growing group of American females who earn over $50,000 a year.

Today there are 53 million working women throughout the United States. Their average annual salary is under $15,000. Approximately one out of five hundred earns over $50,000 a year. In this latter group are entrepreneurs, executives, and professionals. All are doing what millions of other women would like to do—cashing in big on ideas, talents, skills.

Why do so few women manage this? What does it take to turn work into wealth, ambition into affluence, passions into profits? Where and when is it most likely to happen? Who are the women who win in the money game, who bring in revenues in the millions, who earn salaries of at least $50,000? What do they sell? What are their backgrounds? What common traits unite them, assist their ascents? How are they different from the women who never go from wishing to winning? What are the facts and the myths? This book answers these questions. It covers topics ranging from capitalization to masturbation, location to procrastination, imagination to devastation. It concludes with a quiz for those who want to know how likely they are to earn exceptional amounts of money. Also provided is an Appendix listing sources of help toward this moneymaking end.

Here is a celebration of creation—the creation of wealth by women. The dozens of female moneymakers discussed in this book are

1

subordinate to the theme of dreams coming true, of wanting and getting, of financial supersurvival.* Alone, none of these women are significant—this is not a book of profiles. Collectively, they are very important. They tell an enlightening, encouraging story of persistence and prosperity, grit and glory, fantasy and fortune.

In our society, where earnings are a major measure of success, such women are winners. They dare to dream. They play out their own dreams and the American Dream. They represent all that this book is about—everything that turns a lady's ideas into income, big bucks—*Ladybucks.*

---

*In instances where first names only are given they are pseudonyms used to protect the privacy of the women discussed.

CHAPTER **1**

Location and Ladybucks

The college lecture hall is packed. Dozens of business majors are trying to absorb information that they hope will turn them into tycoons. "What are the three big things a business *must* have in order to succeed?" asks the professor. Hands go up. A good product or service? Owner commitment? Cash flow? Customers? The professor shakes his head, turns to the blackboard, and writes *Location, Location, Location*. A discourse follows on "the essentiality of correct business placement—choosing a site where the potential for success is maximized."

Fortunately, Annie Hurlbut never attended this lecture. Annie runs a million-dollar alpaca importing business from her parents' farmhouse in Tonganoxie, Kansas—not a textbook location where "the potential for success is maximized." To Annie, who began her business in the follow-your-heart seventies, *location* meant being able to spend part of her year in the Peruvian Andes and part at home in Tonganoxie. Her company, The Peruvian Connection, was an outcome of her desire to be located where she felt happy. In 1971, as a college sophomore majoring in archaeology, she volunteered for a student dig in Peru and developed a passion for the country. Anthropology was to be her life's work; she was not out to make big bucks as a businesswoman. Her dream was to return regularly to a people and place 4,500 miles away. The Peruvian Connection—a mail-order firm featuring alpaca garments designed by Annie, manufactured in Peru, and offered to an upscale American buying audience—turned out to be a profitable way to fulfill her dream.

HAMLETS, HARLEMS, AND HOLLYWOODS

Annie Hurlbut is one of a growing number of women who are successfully turning passion into profits. These women bring in revenues from hundreds of thousands to hundreds of millions annually. They earn six-figure salaries. They don't break the old rules as much as they work around them. The "essentiality of correct business placement" is not necessarily essential to them. They are aware of the drawbacks of locating in out-of-the-way places, but often they set up where they want to and modify their moneymaking plans accordingly.

America has long been dotted with a few female magnates—cosmetic queens, fashion baronettes, culinary capitalists. Today the dots are turning into a coast-to-coast network of enterprising women turning ambition into affluence in dozens of fields. From hamlet to Harlem, from Silicon Valley to the Tennessee Valley, women are seizing a slice of the American Dream, working with everything from chocolate chips to microchips. Though some locations are more promising and popular than others, ladybucks are being made from likely and unlikely locations.

Passions, Profits, and Places

For Annie Hurlbut, a colorful mail-order catalog with a lush alpaca swatch included permits her to be headquartered on a rural Kansas farm and jet periodically to Peru. Elaine Yannuzzi, creator of Expression unltd., a fancy-food emporium in the middle of nowhere, found another way to locate where she pleased and also turned passion to profit. Experts warned Elaine against trying to turn her love for exotic foods and desserts into a gainful business in suburban Warren, New Jersey; but she had a piece of property there, and that's where she wished to work. Refusing to be intimidated by reason, she began her retail venture in 1971 with $5,000 in savings, 1,500 square feet of store space, no employees, and the idea of luring customers with an array of tasty gourmet samples. Today her store gives away over 350 pounds of food samples a week as part of a lucrative try-and-buy marketing plan that Elaine convinced food manufacturers to subsidize. The rustic gourmet enclave is now a regional tourist attraction and favorite shop spot for epicures as far as a hundred miles away, and it permits Elaine the joy of periodically traveling the world in search of new delights to stock her shelves. Expression unltd. currently employs thirty-five full-time and fifty part-time workers, has expanded to 5,000 square feet, brings in annual revenues of close to $2 million, and earned Miss Yannuzzi the title of New Jersey Entrepreneur of the Year for 1983.

Follow-your-heart and against-all-odds approaches to location are not the soundest or safest ways to create moneymaking enterprises. However, for women like Annie Hurlbut and Elaine Yannuzzi, who use innovation to overcome location, the results are often encouraging. One woman, located in a Tennessee town, decided she wanted to open an exercise studio and profit from her passion for fitness. Months of promotion and advertising got her two customers. Undaunted, she invested in a used trailer, turned it into an exercise school on wheels, and took her venture on the road. Women in neighboring towns provided her with driveway space and customers in exchange for free lessons. Today the woman earns over $40,000 annually from her trailer classes and another $10,000 from licensing agreements with women whom she trains to run similar trailer-based operations in other parts of the country.

Another woman, a Texas charmer with a passion for predicting the future, decided her calling was as a fortune teller. She had read several books and articles on the subject and mastered the techniques of tarot card reading, palm reading, and handwriting analysis. Family and friends, on whom she practiced regularly, enjoyed her panache and believed her predictions. But she learned quickly that in her prim, church-dominated town there was little commercial demand for fortune telling. Too poor to escape to a more favorable location, she built a following by volunteering her services at local church fund-raising events. Her entertaining style and the accuracy of many of her predictions gained her a feature story in the local press. Regional papers picked up on her. Within two years she was splitting the take on fund-raiser appearances all over the country, performing at gala society parties, speaking on college campuses, holding private readings, and earning over $50,000 annually.

Tourists, Turmoil, and Opportunity

Just as ladybucks are generated despite disregard for professorial pronouncements of *Location, Location, Location,* they are also the result of women finding themselves in popular places and exploiting those locales commercially. Susan Berk, a thirty-seven-year-old wife and mother, enjoyed living in Boston. She loved its history, art, literature, and quaint shops. Eager for a pleasing form of self-employment, she persuaded a local historian, an artist, a writer, and a shopkeeper to act as guides on an insider's tour of the city and created Uncommon Boston, an offbeat excursion business. A tantalizing four-color brochure describing tours that include art gallery hopping, chocolate binges, strolls through Boston's period architecture, and Beacon Hill dining expeditions, was her promotion vehicle. It was distributed to local hotels and tourist spots recommended by the Boston Convention and Visitors Bureau. Susan now employs twenty freelance guides, five planners, and a secretary and has watched her company's yearly income grow from $1,900 to almost $300,000 in the three years it's been in operation.

Crowded cities such as New York, Washington, D.C., Chicago, Los Angeles, and Miami are big ladybucks cities. Entrepreneurial, executive, and professional women are creating wealth in these places, despite the fact—and because of the fact—that they are the cities that usually rate poorly when surveyed for things such as "nourishing to entrepreneurs," stress, crime, quality of life, education, pollution, teenage pregnancies. Good money in "bad" places? Yes. Turmoil creates opportunity. Though ladybucks are generated by capitalizing on the charm of a city, as in Susan Berk's case, more often they are earned by treating the ills of an area, nurturing the needy, protecting the haves from the have-nots.

Ruth Clark, the forty-three-year-old founder and president of Clark Unlimited Personnel, the largest black-owned temporary personnel agency on the East Coast, has turned pain into gain for herself and for hundreds of Harlem youths. In 1973, with $3,900 in savings, an understanding of the humiliation of unemployment, and a dream of upgrading her Harlem community, she convinced American Express and Avon (in whose data processing departments she'd worked) to let her supply them with qualified minority workers. Thus was born her New York—based personnel agency, which grew larger and larger as she talked up her services all around the city. Today Clark employs twelve full-time workers in two New York City offices and does over $2 million business yearly.

Similarly, in 1980 when Carol Greenwald was appointed president and CEO of the newly opened National Consumer Cooperative Bank, she moved self, spouse, and children from Boston to Washington, D.C. The relocation was a lucrative opportunity to right wrongs—to reap personal gains and enjoy the rewards of supervising a $200 million operation set up to altruistically fund struggling business ventures shunned by the traditional banking establishment.

For Jacqueline McMickens, a $7,000-a-year New York City corrections officer in 1965, big-city crime would pay off. While working full-time in a Greenwich Village jail, Jacqueline ran a sideline dressmaking business to supplement her salary, took night classes, studied the criminal justice system, worked her way up in the city's Department of Corrections, impressed Mayor Koch, and became commissioner of the Department of Corrections. When Jacqueline resigned in 1986 she was earning $94,500, administering a budget in the hundreds of millions of dollars, and overseeing 8,000 employees and 11,000 inmates.

Marital investigations, missing persons, surveillance—they're all in a day's work for Brooklyn-based private detective Alice Byrne, now in her early forties. When she was twenty-seven, Detective Byrne was Nurse Byrne. She left the nursing profession after suffering a heart attack, divorced her husband, and built Ambassador Investigations, an outgrowth of a small burglar alarm and security guard company she purchased from her ex-husband. Today Alice's agency, which services corporations, lawyers, and private parties, employs ten full-time investigators and forty full-time security guards and grosses $2 million annually.

Back to the college classroom. The professor who has underscored the "essentiality" of *Location, Location, Location* is now advising his students to "start off in the right cities—medium-size cities, growing cities, global cities, pro-business cities." Such, he says, are hot spots for moneymaking. Again, there is integrity and intellect in his position. His advice shouldn't be ignored. It's useful to know the advantages and disadvantages of different locations, the odds of success in one place as opposed to another. But such information can't be taken too seriously—and it isn't by ladybucks earners. Advocating specific money-producing locations is like advocating specific husband-producing locations. It sounds good. It makes sense: "Single women, if you want to get married, go to Alaska. The men outnumber the women there; a large percentage of them are single and eager to wed." Logical, honest advice—but it works only for a limited number of women.

A woman in search of a spouse may entertain the idea of relocating to Alaska, and an occasional one will do so, but most women don't want to move away from home, family, and friends to a place that they're indifferent about, to search for a mate whom they might or might not find, despite encouraging odds. Similarly, a woman living contentedly in crime-ridden New York or stress-filled Miami might acknowledge Mesa, Arizona, as a great start-up spot—but up and move there? Not so fast. Not unless she's unhappy where she is or particularly attracted by Mesa, Arizona.

Most ladybucks earners establish a money base where they find themselves and then evaluate whether to branch out to other spots. Carol Greenwald, for example, moved from Boston to Washington, D.C., when she was appointed president of the National Consumer Cooperative Bank; but she came to Washington with a background of service as an officer of the Federal Reserve Bank of Boston and as the Massachusetts Commissioner of Banking. She was already an established success. The Texas fortune teller eventually left the prim, church-dominated town and set up in Las Vegas—a location that she targeted as ideal for her services—but she didn't leave Texas until she'd accumulated enough cash and knowledge to set up splendidly and successfully in Nevada.

When Nina Blanchard, now owner of one of America's largest talent agencies, decided to try her hand at entrepreneurship, she took many risks; but one she didn't take was to move away from a place she loved. Nina had been a student at Hollywood High School, had held several jobs after high school, and had been fired from most of them; she determined that the only way she would make it would be as her own boss. She knew Hollywood well, understood that beauty and talent were its most marketable commodities, and opened a talent agency on her home turf. She cultivated contacts in the advertising, photography, and film industries, booked unknowns, and turned them into celebrities. Today Nina Blanchard Enterprises represents models such as Cheryl Tiegs, Christie Brinkley, and Shari Belafonte-Harper and bills in the millions of dollars monthly.

HOME-BASING

Ladybucks earners don't locate for success as much as they create success where they are located. Even within the towns and cities where they work, they tend to locate themselves more for economy and convenience than for sales or status. Once earnings are solid and growing, offices move to bigger and plusher headquarters. Initially, for entrepreneurs and many professionals, home is often the base of operations. Dreams turn into dollars from spare bedrooms, kitchen tables, and large closets. Overhead is kept to a minimum, cradles are kept near computers, income is used to fuel more income. Inventory, schooling, sales calls, and advertising take priority over elaborate working conditions.

Susan Berk began Uncommon Boston from her home using a $20,000 loan to create a promotional brochure. Working where she lived enabled her both to expand her operation quickly and to be easily accessible to her young children. Now, with her children older, her business growing rapidly, and a good cash flow, she is moving her headquarters outside of her home.

Susan's approach to location and moneymaking is typical for many successful female entrepreneurs: find a neighborhood niche, fill it from home, and home-base until sales volume is heavy, net profits are high, and home is no longer capable of containing the expanding enterprise.

Though the entrepreneurial woman has an advantage where home-basing is concerned (Carol Greenwald would find it difficult to run the National Consumer Cooperative Bank from her apartment, and Corrective Commissioner McMickens could not have overseen 11,000 inmates from her house), many professional women also home-base their way to wealth, particularly in professions where the line between entrepreneurial and professional is fuzzy.

In 1970 interior designer Lynn Wilson had a Master of Fine Arts degree, three young childen, and a desire to cycle two years of interior designing employment into a business of her own. With two hundred dollars of start-up capital, she set up a home office, bid successfully on a restaurant designing job, worked nonstop for eight months to complete it, and collected $9,500. Several months and clients later, she moved to more spacious quarters and hired an architect, a draftsman, and a secretary, and Creative Environs of Coral Gables, Florida, was born. By guaranteeing customers exclusivity, luxury, and personal attention, she was able to build an all-referral business that has grown in sixteen years to employ thirty staffers, contract for major jobs such as the $15 million renovation of Miami's Fontainbleau Hilton Hotel, and bill $38 million annually. Now Lynn, who began by home-basing, is becoming internationallly based, with an office to open soon in Madrid, Spain.

Fast-track executive women seldom home-base. They climb the corporate ladder by being on the corporate premises—early on and later on. Their ladybucks are earned in the executive suite, and they get there by spending few hours at home. To them, *Location, Location, Location* means where and how their offices are located within corporate headquarters. Image and impression are important. Unspoken standards exist. Competence is crucial; but so are things such as office size, window view, bathroom facilities, desk size, carpeting. A lot of time is spent within the confines of a single office. A lot of business is transacted between desk and door.

Jane Evans could probably do well selling jewelry from her luxurious Connecticut home. But she is not a jewelry entrepreneur; she is a jewelry company executive. Like other ladybuck executives, she has a limousine arrive each morning at 5:30 A.M. to take her to her Manhattan office. Jane is president of Monet, a costume jewelry company with estimated annual sales of $125 million. She oversees 1,700 employees, and is expected to spend a good amount of time behind her horseshoe-shaped desk—and does.

The Entrepreneur as Heroine

Female executives like Jane Evans enjoy great prestige and power but have little leverage over location. Unlike entrepreneurial and professional women, they have to be where there's corporate action. Early on, they position themselves as close to their roots as possible.

When the potential for real advancement arises, they are often forced to inconvenience and uproot themselves in order to move up. Sometimes they must inconvenience and uproot families as well—an action generally considered customary for executive men. When banker Carol Greenwald relocated to Washington, D.C., she commuted for six months between her job in Washington and her home in Boston while her children completed their school year at home and her husband searched for work in the capital. Though corporate relocation policies are being greatly modified, executive ladybucks still don't come easy. The perks of mobility are one of many reasons corporate queens pay high in stress for their success—and one of the reasons why female entrepreneurship is looking good.

Not every executive woman is put off by relocation. A good number like moving to new locations, particularly if they consider a new location exciting or an improvement over the old. However, the element of choice can be minimal. Thus, the female entrepreneur emerges as a heroine. She can structure her future and fortunes in a way not possible for her executive counterpart. Debbi Fields can move herself and her cookie corporation from California to Utah; and she has. She can work from home when she wants to; and she does. Her little girls can go with her to work; and they do. Debbi owns Mrs. Fields Cookies. It is her company. As it's grown, she's grown—from entrepreneur, to employer, to executive. But in reality she still enjoys the freedom of location of the entrepreneur.

When an idea like Debbi's—selling cookies warm out of the oven—turns into a $70-million-a-year empire of cookie shops all over the globe, it can't be headquartered at home. However, many entrepreneurial women with companies now in the $200,000-to-$2-million-a-year range began at home and are still located there. They like the convenience of home-basing; they don't need more space for their particular pursuits. They minimize overhead, maximize profits, and manage their operations as professionally as if they were commercially based. Annie Hurlbut intends to keep her Peruvian Connection headquartered in her parents' farmhouse in Kansas. Detective-entrepreneur Alice Byrne sees no reason to work out of a rented office; her Brooklyn home serves fine. Susan Berk plans to continue running Uncommon Boston from her home as well as from her new outside headquarters.

Post Office Box Locations

Millions of women share a single entrepreneurial fantasy—money in a mailbox. The promised land is not a town, city, home office, or corporate suite. It is a post office box, a mailing address, a place where hundreds of people will send thousands of dollars continually to purchase an alpaca sweater, a monogrammed belt, a cheesecake recipe, a do-it-yourself divorce kit. No worrying about "a site where the potential for success is maximized," "right cities," "hot spots," corporate headquarters, relocation. Ladybucks through a mail slot, envelope after envelope stacked up, each containing checks, money orders, dollar bills.

Lillian Hochberg was twenty-four, married, and pregnant in 1951. An extra fifty dollars a week would have provided a needed margin of comfort. She wanted something she could do from home. Her father was a leather goods manufacturer. The idea was a natural. She began by placing a display ad in *Seventeen* magazine offering monogrammed leather belts and purses. The ad cost $495. To her surprise and delight, it brought in $16,000 in orders. So began the Lillian Vernon Mail Order Corporation—*Vernon* derived from Mt. Vernon, the town where Lillian lived. The company today grosses $110 million.

How often does something like this happen? Lillian Hochberg Vernon, queen of the mail-order trade, is the first to admit that there is "a one in a thousand" chance of someone repeating her degree of success. However, impressive sums of ladybucks are traveling to mailing addresses all over America—often sums the mail-order mavens never anticipated and never even tried to earn via the mail.

Annie Hurlbut didn't start The Peruvian Connection as a mail-order operation. She was wholesaling her alpaca imports at a New York trade show where, by chance, a *New York Times* reporter interviewed her. An article about her alpaca styles followed. Syndicated nationally, it brought in 3,000 inquiries from individuals around the country, who assumed she had a catalog and requested it. She had no catalog. But she now had a substantial mailing list. Sheets of information were mailed out, and a customer file begun. With her mother's help (Annie and mom Biddy are fifty-fifty partners), she moved out of wholesaling, obtained a $50,000 Small Business Administration–guaranteed loan, and created a color catalog.

An appealing catalog, a catchy ad, a customer list—such are the seeds of mail-order ladybucks. Women all over the country are attracted to this form of moneymaking largely because location is insignificant in the success formula. Stroll to the mailbox, deposit the checks, ship the goods, wait for the next day's mail, repeat. Each time a newspaper or magazine feature appears about a Lillian Vernon or an Annie Hurlbut, hopes are ignited. Classified ads are placed, mail-order lists are purchased, post office boxes are rented, and dozens of ladybuck hopefuls wait to see if scores of people are interested in their offerings. Dreams turn into disappointment more than dollars, but for some it works—often enough to keep the money-in-a-mailbox fantasy alive.

Trade Show Locations

Trade shows, like mail-order, fall under the home-basing umbrella. Entrepreneurial women, in increasing numbers, are exhibiting their creations or finds to industry buyers who travel regularly to national and regional convention centers in search of items they can mark up and sell to the public. The convention centers serve as wholesale marketplaces where sellers rent booth space for a few days, write up orders, return home, and fill their orders—from Anywhere, USA. (Annie was showing her imports to retail store buyers at the New York Fashion and Boutique Trades Show when the *Times* reporter stopped by her booth and ultimately changed her operation from a wholesale to a direct-mail business.)

Trade shows are competitive, often with several manufacturers and distributors displaying similar goods, each hoping to garner enough orders to keep in the black and finance another booth rental at another show, months and miles down the road. At all trade shows there are the celebrated names who have turned entrepreneurial fantasies into fortunes; but a much larger percentage are strugglers who dream of the day they will have year-round showrooms, spacious commercial headquarters, national sales representatives, and advertising and publicity agents. Sometimes struggle is rewarded with success—an exhibitor appears who will turn labor into ladybucks.

Barbara Macaire was such an exhibitor. Her company, Skyline by Fabric Design, manufactures colorful kites and banners. Barbara began it as a sideline in 1978. Then an elementary school teacher with two young children, she spent nights designing and sewing, and she sold her output to friends, who resold it at flea markets. In 1982 she decided to abandon her grass-roots approach and try her luck selling to the gift trade. A rented booth at the Los Angeles Gift Show provided enough orders for small setups at shows in San Francisco, Dallas, and Seattle and for a move to a factory facility. Teaching became a profession of her past, and Barbara hired help and built a business that in 1985 grossed over $1 million.

Barbara's sales are still on the increase. Company distributors keep gift shops stocked with her goods. Company reps market her fabric designs at the trade shows she is too busy to attend. Most of her time is spent designing new products, supervising her manufacturing plant, maintaining strong relationships with employees and customers, and testing new uses for her kites and banners.

Barbara has an in-demand product line, an impressive color catalog, a loyal staff, and good cash flow. She is where scores of female trade show exhibitors hope they will be "after a few more shows," when their "children are older," when they "can work full-time." One such woman runs an importing company, Lady Victoria, from her Maryland home. Currently, Lady Victoria is a reach for ladybucks—a reach that may well pay off big, but hasn't quite yet. Though an at-home entrepreneur, Lady Victoria's founder is an adventurer who for the past two years has traveled twice yearly to Egypt to buy native crafts that she thinks will delight American retailers and their customers. These items, thus far displayed at a handful of select trade shows, are proving to be profitable. Sales for next year are projected at $250,000—the type of encouragement that produces visions of volume year after year and a determination to endure the work and the wait.

Trade shows are market barometers that permit product peddlers, from young mothers to middle-aged adventurers to inspired inventors, to hawk their wares alongside the pros. For the price of a stall rental, an idea might turn into an industry. Such was the case for twenty-two-year-old Sharon Corr. A fervent health food aficionado, Sharon dreamed of inventing a product that would become a superseller in the health food field. Sensing a growing national interest in natural beverages, and intrigued by ginseng—an herb known to provide stress relief—Sharon and her husband, Bob, formulated a ginseng-based natural soda beverage, Ginseng Rush. They took six cases of it to a National Nutritional Foods Association trade show, distributed one-ounce samples, and came home with orders for 10,000 cases. Today, seven years later, Corr's Natural Beverages is a multimillion-dollar corporation that employs twenty-five workers in its Chicago headquarters, has fourteen bottling plants throughout the United States and Canada, and sells seventeen natural beverages (including the first natural white chocolate soda ever made).

Party Plans

Sharon turned her ginseng into gold via a trade show, but sometimes industry shows don't work at all. Some women pay high booth rentals and set up attractive displays, only to watch buyers crowd into adjacent booths. Such was the experience of Mary Carson, a $9,000-a-year secretary who in 1985 turned a $20 investment in fake acrylic fingernails into $3 million in sales. Working from her garage, she painted hundreds of the fake nails a variety of colors, rented space at a beauty-industry trade show, and encountered a complete lack of buyer interest. Undeterred, she tried another marketing method—the party plan. She would sell her painted nails through home parties in the Tupperware and Mary Kay tradition. The plan worked. Four thousand sales representatives in forty-three states now sell Mary's nails to customers who pay twenty-five dollars for a set of nails in one of twenty colors—a lot of scratch for nails, but customers pay it gladly.

Why do customers pay it gladly? Why no takers at an industry trade show and thousands through demonstrations in people's homes? Because Mary had an item that needed more than rack space in a retail outlet. It needed demonstration in a private, pressure-free location. Mary's representatives teach customers, in living-room locations around suburban America, how to trim the fake nails, apply them, file them, maintain them.

Because living-room locations provide an opportunity for hands-on learning, trying, tasting, and testing, they generate ladybucks that would be difficult to spawn through commercial outlets. Party-plan selling allows women to turn unlikely ideas into major industries. One woman grosses a quarter of a million dollars a year selling sensual undergarments and sex aids to neighborhood women who gather over coffee and cake to examine sex-stimulating scents and negligees with boas. Demonstrations and fashion shows spark jokes, stories, and orders. Another woman, with a pyramid sales force in the thousands, cashes in on America's obsession with diets. Like Mary Carson, she tried to market her powder at an industry trade show and found few takers. Refusing to be discouraged, she adopted a "have blender, will travel" approach, visited living rooms, offices, and community centers, demonstrated her shake-and-slim approach, shook up $300,000 in profits, and recruited representatives to follow her lead and share her revenues.

Carole Jackson, founder of the Color Me Beautiful consultant training company, stumbled accidentally into party-plan selling. A trained color analyst, Carole dreamed of expanding the fashion industry's narrow range of colors and helping women select shades that were right for them. Divorced, with two children to care for, she wrote a book, *Color Me Beautiful,* to advance her dream. Included in the back of that instant best-seller was a coupon for fabric swatches that women could take with them when shopping for clothes. Hundreds of swatch orders poured in, along with requests from people asking to be trained as color consultants. In 1981, with six employees, the thirty-nine-year-old author founded the Color Me Beautiful consultant training company in McLean, Virginia, to train and license individuals to help women choose clothes and makeup in hues suited to their skin, hair, and eyes. The firm now employs forty-five staffers, has four hundred consultants worldwide, sells a line of cosmetics and videocassettes, offers a color program for men, and reaps revenues of $4 million.

Lane Nemeth's company reaps ten times that amount. Lane is founder of Discovery Toys, an educational toy company she began in a California garage in 1977. A former schoolteacher and day-care director, Lane saw an unfilled marketplace niche for sturdy play items that teach motor and cognitive skills. She designed and developed a medium-priced line, hired outstanding schoolteachers to demonstrate it at home parties, and built a 12,000-member pyramid sales force offering an ever-changing line of over a hundred toys.

Flea Market Locations

Fleaing for fortunes? Can it be done? Yes, small fortunes are being amassed by a large handful of vendors who fill the wants, needs, and greeds of the moment. Transporting their offerings to an impulse-buying public, working from cars, tables, pushcarts, and penthouses, dozens of American women are proving that one person's bag lady is another's enterprising entrepreneur. From bagels to baubles, a waiting market is being found and serviced. One woman, operating from her station wagon at an "Every Sunday" flea market in Southern California, nets five hundred dollars for her day's efforts. Known as the "Bagel Lady," she sells nine varieties of bagels for a dollar each to lines of regulars who return weekly to feast on her tasty rings of dough. Another one-day-a-week moneymaker sells monogrammed leather wristbands from a series of proven locations in New York State. An average of four hundred adolescents per flea site whip out two dollars each for a bracelet with their name painted on it in the color of their choice.

Fleaing on a more professional and permanent level is Louise Berenson of Boston. The year was 1981. Louise had a passion for the color purple, found local craftspeople to make up purple paraphernalia, rented a pushcart for two hundred dollars a week, became one of several pushcart peddlers in a heavily trafficked area, and began Purple Panache—a burgeoning quarter-of-a-million-dollar retailer of purple-only products ranging from teddy bears to dice. Louise, now branching out into mail-order sales and licensing, currently spends much of her time tracking down new and novel purple goodies and administering her purple empire, while twelve employees work the cart seven days and six nights a week.

Fleaing on a plusher plane is a Manhattan maven who sells the treasures of the rich and famous at "invitation only" tag sales held in customers' antique and collectable-filled high-rise apartments. If you have gems to unload, and a fleaer you're not, it's Marylyn Malkin to the rescue. From gold to gowns, paintings to pottery, Marylyn evaluates their worth, knows who'll buy them, and arranges a showing. In a win-win situation, buyers are pleased, sellers are pleased, and in-demand Marylyn is pleased—with her hefty commissions.

Repping for Riches

Marylyn is known in Manhattan's inner circles, but the average flea market vendor is a bagel lady, a bracelet lady, a plant lady—a nameless peddler identified with a particular product, a particular location, a particular day of the week. On a per-day basis she reaps ladybucks, but they are ladybucks sans status, without the recognition given other women who turn ideas and interests into income. A prestige step above this type of vendor is the ambitious rep—the saleswoman who travels to a variety of locations and sells manufacturers' goods to retailers. Initially she works from a car, which houses her samples and order books. The more experienced and successful she becomes, the less she travels to customers and the more they come to her—to where she sets up, be it at a series of trade shows or at a permanent showroom.

Mary Storch, thirty-eight, describes herself as "born to shop." Always interested in discovering and talking up new and unusual items, she decided in 1976 to try her hand as an independent manufacturers' rep. After a year of trudging through eight southeastern states with mediocre merchandise and dismal results, she developed a sense of what sells and became the first woman to sign a lease at the Atlanta Merchandise Mart. Her tiny company, Collectables, was set up to represent giftware manufacturers. Working with one employee, she filled her six-hundred-square-foot showroom with colorful, clever impulse items such as the Kitchen Witch (a Scandinavian good-luck symbol that when suspended in a kitchen is supposed to keep the cook from burning food), which was one of America's hottest-selling gift items between 1977 and 1980. Today, Collectables occupies 4,700 square feet in Atlanta and Dallas combined, employs twelve workers, and sells over $2 million annually to thousands of retailers who visit Mary's showrooms regularly.

One grandmother of seven, who describes herself as "an entrepreneur with nothing to sell," decided to become an "entrepreneur's entrepreneur." She knew several craftspeople who created quality boutique items that they retailed locally and sporadically for giveaway prices. Sure that she could do better for them—and herself—she rounded up samples of their work, rented a small stall at a fashion and boutique trade show, and took orders from boutique owners catering to upscale customers. The orders were small and repeats trickled in—an ideal situation for the novice rep and her craftspeople, who weren't yet geared for large-scale production. After two years and eight shows, this energetic grandmother signed exclusive rep agreements with four artisans capable of superior and speedy output, designed an attractive promotional catalog, and built relationships with the retailers who moved her clients' creations. Today she reps for twenty talented artisans, potters, and quilters who love production but hate selling. They appreciate her marketing efforts, and she appreciates the commissions she receives from gross sales of over $600,000 a year.

FRANCHISING

Where a rep sells other people's products for profit, a franchiser permits other people to sell her products, services, name, and know-how for profit—to duplicate her entire business setup in another part of the country. A woman turns an interest into income, gets publicity, admirers. Her company name becomes known. Would-be imitators are aroused. They want a piece of a proven opportunity— an entrepreneurial slice that will enable them to capitalize locally on something that has worked in a distant city or state. For an upfront investment of several thousand dollars and a yearly royalty fee, they are freed from the imagination and risk required to give birth to the American Dream. They adopt it once it is born and booming. Turnkey entrepreneurship cushioned with training, secrets, supplies, and support.

Joan Barnes's turnkey package allows women in twenty-three states and Canada to capitalize on the fitness craze in a unique way—baby body-building. Joan's franchise operation, Gymboree, was created from her desire, as a new mother, to find a situation that integrated productive play and parent networking. In 1976, unable to find such a setup, Joan began a kiddie gym on a tiny budget in her local California community center. Word of mouth created demand, publicity, and ultimately seven other Gymboree locations. Four years later, how-to inquiries began pouring in from women interested in imitating Gymboree's operation. Joan found some investors who believed her idea could work nationwide, packaged her concept, and began selling franchises. To date, Gymboree has sold over three hundred franchises, with revenues for the coming year projected at well over $5 million.

Women who buy and sell the American Dream in franchise form live all over America. Location is incidental to a major draw in the franchise formula—service reproduction. Though some ladybucks come from such things as tried, proven, and cloned brownie shops, most come from service offerings—like Joan's parent-child play classes—that cater to new-age needs and that can be profitably reproduced.

Consider the American service explosion and the dramatic rise in female entrepreneurship. Contrast the 80 percent death rate of new business starts with the 4 percent rate for franchise starts. What do you see? American women eager to purchase turnkey programs with names like Gymboree, Merry Maids, Decorating Den, Jazzercise, Mail Boxes Etc., USA, Diet Center—and American women eager to provide the turnkey opportunities to package their successful operations for duplication in Manytowns, USA.

What Joan Barnes is to bouncy babies, Sara Addis is to ailing seniors—a combination of cause, caring, and cleverness. Sara had a strong affinity for the elderly and had done years of volunteer work with them while tending her family. Always dreaming of ways to upgrade their lives, she saw a double-edged market niche—some of the elderly needed companion sitting; some needed low-stress employment. In 1978, House Sitters af El Paso, Texas, a home-based service, was begun with a tiny advertising budget and six hand-picked workers eager to sit homes, people, pets, and patients with Alzheimer's. In 1983, with 150 First-Aid-trained sitters working for her, fifty-three-year-old Sara sold her $350,000 business and became a franchiser. Today, Sara Care Franchise Corporation trains franchisees to operate quality-care sitting services and receives a 7 percent royalty from its thirty-seven national franchisees' annual earnings of $3.5 million.

Though there is currently more demand for franchised service—rather than product—operations, some clever product vendors are creating franchises that sell seemingly unlikely items to grateful customers. Here the trip from local ladybucks to national franchise often includes a home-basing approach that has proven profitable and readily replicable. Such is the story of Mildred Auskel. Mildred started CI International twelve years ago with a three-month $20,000 loan. Her idea was to bring moderately priced framed, decorative paintings, party-plan style, to people intimidated by art galleries. Neighbors chat and sip wine while a CI International rep shows them ready-to-hang paintings priced from $49 to $169. Mildred's company, based in Tempe, Arizona, had grossed about $3 million in 1985 when it began selling franchises in the Southwest.

LANDS OF A THOUSAND DREAMS

It's too early to say when or whether Mildred's franchises will begin popping up outside the Southwest, but her dreams have turned into dollars, and it appears that the dollars are multiplying nicely. Would Mildred have been successful had she been located in Albany, New York, instead of Tempe, Arizona? Is Tempe an easier place to turn ambition into affluence?

Going back to our professor who advises *Location, Location, Location* and who talks about "medium-sized cities, growing cities, global cities, pro-business cities," the answer is that Mildred had a strong edge because of where she was located. The professor thinks several cities in Arizona are excellent locations for moneymaking. Unfortunately, not everyone eager to turn dreams into dollars finds herself in an Arizona city that is nourishing to entrepreneurs. Many female hopefuls must—and do—play out their dreams in undreamlike locations. But for those fortunate enough to find themselves in the "right cities," there is cause for comfort.

Though ladybucks are created from Manytowns, USA, certain locations spill over with female success stories while others must dig deep for local heroines. Part of this is population-linked. A town of 100,000 has more stories of all sorts to tell than a town of 1,000. But there's something else. Certain places produce many women who work hard and win big for a seemingly foolish reason—they produce many women who work hard and lose big. A nonjudgmental blurring of winning and losing occurs in a fertile and fostering environment, often with yesterday's loser becoming tomorrow's winner, with one woman's dream becoming another's dollar. There emerges an outpouring of possibilities up for grabs in these lands of a thousand dreams.

What are some of these lands of a thousand dreams, these "right cities," places where it's easiest to turn labor into ladybucks? The list grows and changes monthly, and different experts produce different lists, but certain spots look good and are mentioned often. Phoenix, Scottsdale, and Mesa, Arizona, receive high praise. Lots of importing, tourism, technology, and art. Lots of prettiness. Lots of affluence. Lots of hometown pride. Plenty of customers with the money to pay for appealing products and services, such as those supplied by Mildred Auskel's paintings-via-party-plan company.

California, perhaps more than any other state, is filled with "garage-to-gold" tales, with stories about individuals who worked from garages or similarly modest setups in dozens of California towns and turned their work into wealth. Lane Nemeth began her $40-million-a-year Discovery Toys out of a garage in Martinez, California. Mary Carson painted fingernails into fortunes from her Southern California garage. Barbara Macaire's million-dollar kite company began at her home sewing machine in a San Francisco Bay–area town, not far from where Joan Barnes was beginning her Gymboree company in a community center room in San Mateo. Much of California is a land of dreams tried, retried, and realized. Currently, Santa Rosa and Petaluma, in Northern California, and San Diego, in Southern California, are favorite mentions because of the growth there of high-tech companies, the high quality of life, the need for service industries, and the expanding affluent populations (often fleeing from crowded and competitive San Francisco and Los Angeles).

Massachusetts—like much of New England—is getting academic applause for transforming its image from old industrial economy to new business boomtowns of high-tech, low-tech, and no-tech offerings. Professional women are in high demand. Executive women are scaling the corporate mountain in a relatively egalitarian atmosphere. Entrepreneurs such as Louise Berensen and Susan Berk are turning passion for things like the color purple and the back streets of Boston to profits in the hundreds of thousands of dollars a year.

Some Texas towns are receiving high grades. The Austin–San Antonio region, benefitting from the research being conducted at the University of Texas, is becoming a new Silicon Valley in need of dozens of niche-filling enterprises to accommodate a growing, intelligent, affluent population.

Similarly, Gainesville, Florida, also the home of a major university (the University of Florida) looks promising for women interested in medicine, engineering, computer sciences, and industrial development. Tampa, St. Petersburg, Fort Myers, and West Palm Beach are considered hot spots for turning entrepreneurial interests into income.

Experts are looking closely at tiny Spring Hill, Tennessee (a half-hour south of Nashville), now that it might be the site of General Motors's $3.5 billion Saturn automobile plant. It's considered a "might-boom" town, likely to be in need of executives, professionals, and service and product sellers.

Connecticut, because of its affluence, its proximity to New York, and its encouragement of small and large businesses, is a land of a thousand dreams for female executives, entrepreneurs, and professionals. Expanding towns, such as Stamford, that now headquarter several major corporations are providing advancement opportunities for women with sharp eyes for bottom-line profits and executive-suite power. Towns such as Greenwich and Darien, with high family incomes, are rich in opportunity for entrepreneurs with luxury services and products to offer. And because Connecticut is a state of power and plenty, therapists of all sorts are setting up and successfully serving the mental and physical ailments of the rich, the almost-rich, and the jealous-of-the-rich.

In the Midwest, some Minnesota cities look to be future ladybucks lands. For the executive with entrepreneurial proclivities, there's Minneapolis and St. Paul—technology-driven cities with corporations endorsing *intrapreneurship* (entrepreneurship within a corporation). Professionals stand to do well in Rochester, Minnesota, a cosmopolitan city with smalltown charm. Home of the Mayo Clinic, Rochester is now undergoing a renaissance that experts believe will dramatically multiply its medical technology base, its industrial base, and its population, making it the hottest growth city in Middle America. Indianapolis, Indiana, is another "right city," receiving praise for a civic stance very friendly to businesses large and small.

Though they were hot dream-to-dollar cities in the 1970s and early 1980s, economists predict new developments in Raleigh and

Durham, North Carolina, and in Atlanta, Georgia. Formerly research and corporate-growth cities, they are expected to experience a big boom led by small companies and entrepreneurs.

BE IT EVER SO HUMBLE . . .

Hot spots, right cities, and lands of a thousand dreams are places pregnant with possibility, ripe for moneymaking. Opportunities and encouragement abound for native daughters to turn labor into ladybucks. However, when female success stories are compiled and scrutinized, people, not places, tell the story of ladybucks: Annie Hurlbut and her Peruvian importing enterprise headquartered in rural Tonganoxie, Kansas; Elaine Yannuzzi and her try-and-buy gourmet shop in out-of-the-way Warren, New Jersey; Ruth Clark and her minority personnel agency in Harlem; Sharon Corr and her natural beverage business in Chicago; Jacqueline McMickens turning crime into a career in New York City. Are they located for the ladybucks they've earned? Not in a textbook or business-school context. None of these women are headquartered in medium-size cities where corporations, industry, research, and affluence are moving in.

Women who live in ripe-for-moneymaking cities begin with an edge. They can cycle advantage into greater advantage, location into ladybucks. However, entrepreneurial and professional women who make money from not-ripe-for-moneymaking locations turn adversity to advantage. They soar beyond their locations. They find their markets through mail-order, incentives, trade shows, reps, and franchises. They get their merchandise to the masses. They devise marketing methods that they otherwise might not. In the professions, they find opportunity in chaos and squalor, and they capitalize on it. They branch out, educate up. Like women located in more propitious places, they turn sideline, home-based ventures into far-reaching presences. Sometimes it takes a little longer; they may work a little harder; but they build bankrolls from living rooms they like, towns they treasure, cities they choose.

Women with executive aspirations are more limited in location than entrepreneurs or many professionals, but the executive psyche is prepared to locate out and up; that's built into the game plan. Mobility is not misery for the corporate queen en route to the executive suite. Executive women—and some professionals—are trained for moneymaking, for their companies and themselves. They learn early on that location often must be subordinate to advancement. Born entrepreneurs are seldom taught this lesson. They don't know that *Location, Location, Location* is the three big things a business *must* have in order to succeed. They don't know that wealth can't be generated from anywhere. And because they don't, they turn fantasies into fortunes from right places, wrong places, and no places— places not even on most maps.

CHAPTER 2

Aluminum Spoons

Once in a while, ladybucks are created by genteel ladies of silver-spoon backgrounds. Once in a very long while, they are created by paupers raised in spoonless huts. Most often, they are created by women who, while growing up or as young adults, experienced varying degrees of deprivation or disillusionment. Fueled by aluminum spoon circumstances, they turn their deprivation or disillusionment into direction and drive—and ultimately into dollars.

The road from aluminum spoon to ladybucks is sometimes paved with forgetfulness and fabrication. Ms. Ladybucks sits by her pool, gazes at her acreage, and tells the querying reporter that she remembers a childhood spent sleeping in a bathtub, eating scraps, wearing hand-me-downs, never being hugged, always being punished. A practiced and polished squalor-to-success saga. An against-all-odds tale that impresses the reporter, inspires the masses, and elevates the moneymaker's ego. The greater the gold amassed, the greater the grief remembered. From hell to heaven. What difference if one actually slept in a modest bed rather than in a bathtub?

People like rags-to-riches, pain-to-gain tales. Exaggeration doesn't dim their appeal; often it enhances it. However, if truth be told, ladybucks aren't the result of fate's horrible hand avenged as much as of personal anguishes, angers, humiliations, and longings that could have led to stagnation instead of success, or to delinquency instead of dollars, or to self-hate instead of self-pride. Anguishes, angers, humiliations, and longings are the aluminum spoons that many women experience, but that only a few amend into wealth.

POVERTY

Poverty is an aluminum spoon—particularly comparative poverty. Lyndon Johnson once said, "When we were growing up, we were all so poor we didn't know poverty had a name." He was joking about a state of shared privation. Poverty is more poignant for those who don't share it, who know it has a name, who are the have-nots among people who have plenty. For certain females the awareness of this relative poverty is an acute call to action, a wrong that must be righted. It humbles them, it makes them feel unequal, it is intolerable. They long for luxury and forge a strong connection between longing, labor, and ladybucks.

When Mary Kay Ash realized, as a young child, that she was the poor kid on the block, she didn't retreat from the mainstream of her community. The comfortable lives of the other girls her age made her envious; but rather than accepting herself or her family as misfits, she saw a situation that required "some catching up to do." Mary studied hard and became an accomplished student. She became exceptionally responsible, mastering her local public transportation system at seven years old and bargain-shopping for family needs. Like many entrepreneurial winners, she was enterprising early on, always seeking and finding small ways to supplement the family income. Adults admired her abilities and accomplishments and wanted her as friend and influence for their children. To this day Mary maintains friendships from her early years, but now with the inner satisfaction of being a financial equal and more, of knowing she has labored long and far surpassed those little girls on the block who began better and had it easier, of knowing that Mary Kay Cosmetics has made her one of America's richest women.

Similarly, Edna Hennessee "always wanted something better." Child of a poor farm family, she picked cotton, milked cows, and determined to have a nice, clean business of her own. A friend, whose mother worked in a Merle Norman Cosmetics shop, took her into the shop and introduced her to what would become the field of her future. Edna knew immediately that she wanted to own a cosmetics shop. She did neighbors' laundry to accumulate start-up funds. With less than four hundred dollars saved, she opened a tiny cosmetics studio, where she sold commercial preparations and tinkered with new ingredients on the market. Her tinkering led her to come up with a product that cured her acne. She perfected it, hired a chemist, and in 1973 began Cosmetic Specialty Labs (CSL) of Lawton, Oklahoma. Today Edna heads a $5 million operation specializing in incubating new product lines and fledgling companies. CSL has lauched over 1,500 private labels, employs over two hundred full-time workers, and sells to over 4,600 companies. Edna enjoys her wealth and spends many hours sharing the how-to's of it with women's groups around the country.

Far removed from Mary Kay's makeups and Edna's labs is Ruth Clark's $2 million personnel placement business. As a child growing up in Harlem in the 1940s and 1950s, Ruth knew glitter and goodies abounded nearby, but they were not hers to enjoy. She yearned for pretty clothes and quality toys and vowed that one day she would earn enough money to buy anything she wanted. Poor, black, and eager to begin her trip to the top, she skipped college and took a two-week course in keypunch operation. The course led to jobs in data processing, contacts, and the confidence to begin a temporary employment agency that would turn Harlem into hope for minority youths with backgrounds like her own. After her temporary agency proved profitable, she opened a permanent agency outside of Harlem. Clark Unlimited Personnel became the only black-owned employment agency with two locations in the New York metropolitan area. Currently, Ruth is franchising her business in major cities throughout the United States. She has a growing list of *Fortune* 500 clients, sits on the boards of several major corporations, and relaxes regularly and regally in her lavishly decorated offices, where she recalls with pain and pride the years of sacrifice and struggle that brought her there, that permit her a rich collection of expensive clothes and jewels, that have earned her countless professional awards and much public acclaim.

Poverty as Powerlessness

Poverty is sometimes perceived as a state of powerlessness more than inequality. No correcting the boss, for fear of being fired. No telling off the landlord, for fear of being evicted. No disagreeing with the doctor, for fear of being neglected. There is a stressful, negative connection between poverty and power, a connection that can be made positive only by reversing the poverty. For some women this powerlessness hurts more than the poorness. They want ladybucks so they can speak and act with courage and consequence, without fear of reprisal. They yearn not so much for material comforts as for the ease to effect the change that money can bring.

As the oldest of five children, Sharon was the family gofer. Her parents poor, she was expected to assume grown-up responsibilities. When she was eleven, her mother was diagnosed as having cancer. Barely able to function, Sharon's father relied on Sharon to keep in touch with the doctor and to see that her mother was taking her medicine and not exhausting herself. Sharon cooked, cleaned, tended her young siblings, and took care of her mother. Bright and observant, she questioned some of the doctor's treatments and medications. She believed they were hurting, not helping, her mother— weakening her, accelerating her decline. She spoke to her father, who said, "The doctor knows what he's doing." Frightened but determined, she told the doctor how she felt. He smiled, nodded, and kept prescribing the same treatment. She spoke to her minister, who told her to trust and pray. She turned to her teacher, who told her to get her mother to a doctor in a big-city hospital—something her father had no funds to do. Just before her thirteenth birthday, Sharon held her then-eighty-pound mother and watched her die after months of excruciating pain. She was certain that had her mother received better medical teatment, she would have lived longer and suffered less.

Whether Sharon's assessment is accurate is uncertain, but it prompted Sharon to give up most childhood recreational activities, study hard, get a college scholarship, and go on to become a doctor. A serious, sensitive young intern, she resolved to become a rich doctor—a surgeon whose opinion would carry power in a profession filled with egos.

Sharon has lived out her resolve. Her income is over $200,000 a year. She is a formidable force in the field of renal surgery, and she has helped some of her siblings establish themselves in positions where their voices will count, where they will have more power than their parents had.

The powerlessness of poverty is a spur for many women who, like Sharon, aim for the top in professions and careers. For them there is a dual reward—cash for comfort and intellectual clout that commands and corrects. Beneath Sharon's now composed, professional demeanor is a young girl who fervently believes that had she been a doctor when her mother was ill, things would have been done correctly and her mother would have lived longer and painlessly.

Similarly, behind the cool facade of one celebrated public defender is an adolescent who remembers visiting her mother in prison for three years because the family had no funds to fight an unjust larceny charge leveled by one of the town's prominent citizens.

Responsible for initiating and maintaining her company's excellent on-site day-care facilities is a corporate vice-president guided by the memory of a six-year-old latchkey child who wished she could see her mommy after school.

These women, now at the peak of power, remember well childhoods of impotence, defenselessness, and hope without influence— childhoods that would have been different had their families not been meekened by poverty.

APPEARANCE

Appearance is a popular aluminum spoon. Just as common poverty produces a push for profit and power, so too does uncommon appearance—particularly appearance that is perceived to be unpleasant. Most women find fault with their looks without seeking profits in pimples; but for some a poor complexion, an oversized body, or unmanageable hair is a cause for self-correction, curing others, and creating wealth. Today the "corrections business" bristles with women trying to turn imperfections into industries.

Edna Hennessee began her cosmetics business as a path out of poverty; but that was not her only reason. Were she interested solely in building a company selling pleasant products, she might have considered opening a candy or jewelry shop. Why was she so impressed by the Merle Norman store that her friend took her to that she would try nothing else and focused exclusively on establishing herself in the cosmetics field?

Edna liked the Merle Norman shop because it was a lifestyle removed from her family's farm; but her captivation and consequent commitment to the cosmetics industry stemmed from a longtime bout with acne. The condition affected her emotionally and socially as well as physically. She hated the way her face looked, and she dreamed of having a clear complexion. Experimentation with several commercial preparations had proven futile. The day Edna stepped into the Merle Norman shop, she saw not a cure, or even a potential cure, for acne, but a field where she felt she belonged.

Appearance and Belonging

The woman who seeks to capitalize on a defect in her appearance is like the psychiatrist who enters psychiatry in the hope of finding self-help and eventually financial reward. A feeling of entitlement exists: Who, if not I, is qualified to probe and profit? The woman burdened with an unpleasant appearance is familiar with the situation, knows what helps and hinders it, understands the sensitivities of people similarly afflicted. She belongs in the field to better it, better herself, better others, and better her bank account, if possible.

Just as Edna Hennessee felt she belonged in the cosmetics industry, Pat Swift believed she belonged in specialty modeling. Early on, she realized that fat provokes intolerance similar to that provoked by racial differences. The "large one in a family of thin people," she was rejected and ridiculed because she was heavy. Not surprisingly, Pat studied criminal justice in college—a field with even-the-score applications. What surprises, initially, is that she left this field while working as a Bloomingdale's detective to try a profession that was likely to reinforce the rejection she'd experienced growing up—a profession that stated unequivocally, "This is not where you belong!"

While working for Bloomingdale's Pat was offered a one-time, by-chance, photographic modeling assignment for fashions geared to the oversize woman. The resulting advertisement, which appeared in *The New York Times Magazine,* led to other modeling jobs requiring a pretty, plump girl. Pat decided she enjoyed modeling and would change professions. She would model full-figure lines full-time. Large-size clothing was a $6-billion industry; it needed attractive, large-size models. She belonged in the field. Not so, she was told. Despite her success, no agency would sign her. They regarded her appeal as faddish with no long-term potential. Theoretically, she belonged; commercially, she was a misfit. Unfair though it was, the business used size 8 models to advertise size 14 fashions. There was no permanent place for Pat.

Pat created a place for herself. Determined to model, and with no agency to represent her, she began her own agency in 1978. Today. Plus Model Management, which represents petites, older women, and large-size men as well as large-size women, is headquartered in a mid-Manhattan penthouse office, employs twenty-five full-time and fifteen part-time workers, has a client roster of 2,000, and bills $2 million annually.

Pat turned weight into wealth because she felt she belonged in modeling, despite the fact that the prevailing forces disagreed. She called on manufacturers and department stores and convinced them that full-figured women could be appealing, persuasive salespeople for their large-size fashions. She battled and broke many of the psychological and professional barriers erected for stout would-be models. Largeness is not a handicap, she learned, when positive self-image is fought for, fostered, and communicated. Aware of the hefty woman's fragility of self-confidence, she initiated "prep and pep" sessions for her agency models—meetings built around the concept that big is not bad and can be beautiful and profitable. Her sessions provide psychological reinforcement, tips on modeling in stores and at photography shoots, and hard-nosed business advice. Her "love your body" encouragement is now publicly available through her book, *Great Looks: The Full-Figured Woman's Guide to Beauty,* which contains beauty, exercise, and fashion tips designed exclusively for the big woman.

Turning Fat to Fortune

Stoutness, more than any other appearance-linked liability, stimulates the female fiscal psyche. Large-size women with moneymaking impulses feel that they not only belong in obesity-related ventures, but that they are the best equipped to devise and direct them. Pat Swift is one of several women launching heavies on modeling careers. Hefty, beautiful Mary Duffy of the Big Beauties Agency also provides manufacturers with big models for big profits. Currently, at least five other heavy women around America run, or are beginning, agencies to service the large-size fashion industry with attractive models of ample measurements.

Because millions of American women are fat—or believe themselves to be—$10 billion a year is spent on help-the-heavies foods, medications, exercise salons, counseling groups, fashions, and matchmaking services. An impressive slice of this $10 billion goes to professional portlies who counsel other portlies on self-acceptance, to heavies who have found love among their own and are using computerized but compassionate matchmaking services for their stout sisters; to one-time fatties who have found cures in canisters and now sell these powdered cures to others seeking to imitate their weight losses; to stout, stylish women who reap weighty profits from high-style clothing shops catering to the fashion-conscious large woman.

Generally, the fat-to-fortune formula works best for women who acknowledge a negative connection between stoutness and self-esteem and who create an offering that treats both together. Weight Watchers didn't become a gold mine for Jean Nidetch because of its menus alone. Advice, pep rallies, clapping, and congratulations for shedding pounds and sharing details are an integral part of a program that works because as fat fades, self-worth is taught and nurtured.

One popular and profitable exercise and self-esteem program for overweight women, Woman-at-Large, is run by partners Sharlyne Powell and Sharon McConnell, who call themselves and their customers "fluffy" rather than fat, believing it impossible to say "fluffy" with cruelty or "fat" with kindness. They promote the philosophy that fat is fluff and can be feminine and that heavy women can be healthy and happy. Sharlyne and Sharon began Woman-at-Large because they had no place they could go to exercise without embarrassment. They found that just as society at large shuns the overweight, so too do most exercise and fitness groups, considering them health risks, unsightly to look at standing still (let alone jumping around in a sweat), and a turn-off to thinner, more attractive customers.

Sensitive, encouraging, and caring, Sharlyne and Sharon provide a comfortable environment where large women work out to a series of routines designed specifically for them. Their facility is a haven for the woman unable to keep up in the standard aerobics class and for the woman who could be hurt by jumping and running exercises that put heavy stress on knees, ankles, and feet. Unsuccessful at finding a qualified, overweight exercise instructor for the program they planned, Sharlyne and Sharon became instructors themselves. They read whatever they could find that applied to exercise, fitness, stretching, and choreography, studied up on the cardiovascular system and muscles, and adapted their findings to an exercise regimen that would serve the needs of women like themselves. To further the self-esteem of their customers, they developed a large-size, stylish line of leotards, tights, and exercise clothing, so that fitness and fashion could be combined for those who wished it. Currently, Woman-at-Large is franchising into a strong, nationwide operation, carrying private-label cosmetics and customized exercise videotapes as well as exercise clothing. Anybody will be permitted to purchase one of the franchises, but only compassionate, well-trained, "fluffy" instructors will be permitted to teach the classes.

Taking Hair into Hand

What do you do if your complexion is clear, your weight is average, but your hair is horrible? It ruins your looks. Are your earliest memories of limp, lifeless locks; or of stringy hair of a color you hated; or of hair that needed treatment for which there was none? If your name is Paula Meehan, you didn't put up with it for long.

Out of high school and engaged in a part-time acting career, Paula had spare hours to focus on correcting her appearance. She hated not her red hair but rather the fact that it detracted from her looks because there were no products on the market that catered to redheads. There were lots of treatments for blondes, for women with graying hair, for women eager to change their hair color, but the redhead was forgotten. Products that worked on other hair shades did not work on Paula's. They didn't properly protect her hair from the elements, or adequately condition it, or enhance or highlight it, but instead drabbed it. Like Edna Hennessee, who tinkered with various commercial preparations and cured her acne, Paula experimented, created a product that improved the quality of her hair, and set about developing a hair-care line tailored to the needs of the redhead. Today, Paula's Redken Corporation is a multimillion-dollar company providing quality preparations for red hair and other hair colors. Now happy with her tresses—and her entrepreneurial success—Paula is free to enjoy life (in her mansion, which once belonged to Elvis Presley) and pay her husband a couple of hundred thousand dollars annually to make sure Redken never gets in the red.

Renee, the only brunette in a family of blondes, decided she was born with thick, dark hair by mistake. Compare-and-despair sessions punctuated her puberty with pain and longing. Her mother and sisters, admired for their silky golden locks, offered comfort: "Full hair is feminine (unlike a full body); color doesn't matter." Color mattered to Renee. She wanted correction—and sought it in a bleach bottle. Her hair turned an ugly orange; her scalp broke out in sores. Twenty-one and obsessed with becoming a blonde, she worked her way through a series of salons and came up with a beautician who agreed to administer a biweekly, two-step hair color treatment: bleach out the black, shampoo in the blonde. Because the black roots had to be treated so frequently, her head became a chemical wasteland. Within a few months her hair thinned and began falling out. Her femininity, diminished by dark instead of light hair, was now destroyed. Therapy was advised. Wasn't self-acceptance, not hair manipulation, the real answer? Perhaps, but Renee wasn't interested in acquiring a "learn to love yourself as you are" philosophy.

To hide her now-thin, back-to-natural, dull black hair, Renee purchased a big light-blonde wig. Though people chuckled behind her back, maintaining that her skin and eye coloring clashed with the wig, she was happy. She loved herself in the wig and felt beautiful. The only problem was that the wig didn't look like real hair. With all else solved, she was flying high and inspired. She got a Small Business Association—backed loan and began her own wig business, designing and developing a selection of colors, textures, and styles that looked more natural than real hair. A few society matrons learned of her work, tried her wigs, and were pleased. Word of mouth made Renee popular among the ladies-who-lunch crowd. Within a couple of years, she had a society and show business clientele paying high prices for her one-of-a-kind custom designs. Her wig wealth now in the million-dollar range, Renee has nurtured her dark tresses back to thick, shiny health, looks like Cleopatra, and is writing a book on the beauty of black hair.

LONELINESS

Jean was boring, humorless, quiet, and without spark. Other children didn't want her at their birthday parties. In junior high school she began reading how-to-be-popular books. They didn't help. In high school she kept to herself, maintaining average grades and wishing she were on the cheerleading squad. In college she linked up with a few Outies like herself. Before her senior year she left college, moved out West, and joined a cult. The cult financed itself by selling flowers. She discovered she loved flowers, had a knack for creating eye-catching arrangements, and became the cult's biggest fund-raiser. Eventually she disentangled herself from the cult and went to work for a florist with a large party-giving clientele. Today Jean heads a blue-ribbon catering firm, earns a six-figure salary, and reaps continual plaudits from clients who credit her with the success of their functions.

Jean is still boring, humorless, quiet and without spark—or so she believes. Except that now people vie for her attendance at their parties—not just as a caterer, but also as a guest. "Because I make a high salary in a social field, it's assumed I'm interesting," she says. "A few words of well-placed chitchat about a new entrée stretch far on the party circuit." Is thirty-eight-year-old Jean happier than eight-year-old Jean? "Yes, not because I finally have the type of personality I'd like, but because now I'm sought after even more than many people I know with really engaging personalities."

Jean's present popularity softens the memories of a lonely childhood. Like other now-accomplished Outies, she couldn't acquire popularity based on charisma but got it based on career. Had she been a born crowd-pleaser, would she still have become a successful executive? Charm is often cycled into cash by crowd-pleasers who promote products and themselves to privileged positions. A magnetic personality is usually a plus. However, loneliness also produces ladybucks. It's an aluminum spoon that feeds the Outie a drive for acceptance—drive that sometimes produces prosperity, attracts admiration, and lessens loneliness.

Circumstantial Loneliness

Loneliness is not just childhood-linked. It is also circumstantial, situational. It can hit anytime, anyone—and sometimes it hits someone who won't tolerate it. Increasingly, loneliness is being turned into ladybucks by women who weren't unpopular as children but who feel isolated as young adults. Often the isolation is mobility-linked— a wife moves to a new part of the country to accommodate her husband's job, or a couple ups and starts again in another state, hoping to impove their living standards.

Today Joan Barnes, founder of the Gymboree Franchise Corporation, is a self-satisfied wife, mother, and businesswoman. She enjoys her restored Victorian home in California's pricey Marin County, drives a Jaguar, and travels the country teaching others how to duplicate her success. But life wasn't always so pleasant. In the early 1970s, having moved from New York to Califorina, Joan felt isolated and overwhelmed by motherhood. In an effort to alleviate her aloneness and be "the best damned parent around," she set out to learn what makes infants and toddlers happy, sociable, and secure. She found her answers in "purposeful play"—play where competence and confidence are fostered. Thus began some "purposeful play" of her own—the development of a progam of planned exercise, rhythm, and motion classes for toddlers that became the beginning of Gymboree—and the end of her loneliness.

Because Joan felt isolated, she was determined to do something that would not only remedy her loneliness but also prevent her children from feeling lonesome. Today many women-owned businesses begin with similar intent. A mother feels isolated for one of a number of reasons, wants to help herself and ensure social activity for her children. She taps herself for ideas, sees an entrepreneurial solution, and creates an enterprise that both lessens her loneliness and provides her children playmates. America is dotted with home-based play groups, dancing schools, and art classes that were begun to prevent parent/child loneliness and to provide a little pocket money. Usually these ventures do just that. Occasionally they provide a lot more than pocket money, surprising both the entrepreneurial mother and everyone else.

Joan Barnes is one of several entrepreneurs surprised by the astounding financial success of a venture begun primarily to combat loneliness. Another woman, a newly divorced school nurse with two adolescent sons, not only felt alienated from her tongue-wagging community but worried that her boys—now estranged from their father—would have neither a responsible male figure in their lives nor the family summer vacations that they loved and looked forward to. As a transitional solution, she teamed up with the principal of her school and began a teen travel camp: the principal, a kind and caring gentleman, would provide some fatherly influence for her sons (and the other campers), and her boys would have a social and enjoyable summer.

It worked. Everyone had a great time—the nurse, her sons, the principal, the campers. Monetary profits, as had been anticipated, were modest. When the summer was over, everyone went back to school. After Christmas, inquiries begin arriving from the parents of the satisfied campers. What were the nurse and principal planning for the following summer? Nothing really; nurse and sons were now adjusting nicely to life without spouse and father. But why not go it again? Reinforce a good idea. This time, a summer of experience behind them, the duo developed a formal brochure, a price list, a tour talk, a slide presentation, and a testimonial sheet. Four times as many students signed up for their second program. So started one of this country's most highly acclaimed and successful teen travel camps—an unexpected moneymaker that, in its five years under her supervision, allowed the nurse to travel the world, delight her children, move to a new home, and accumulate a bank account not possible on a school nurse's salary alone.

Shyness

Shyness is a close cousin of loneliness. The shy woman is spurned not for her drab personality but because people don't get to know if she has any personality at all. She is persona without presence—unless she starts to become a prospering persona. Then the shell of shyness cracks. People make more of an effort to know her. They want to know how she's doing it. And the meek moneymaker forces herself to reach out to people. She wants them to buy her products—and to like her.

Most shy individuals wish to become extroverts not to make money but to make friends. They try to speak and find themselves speechless. As children, usually with few friends, they retreated into a world of daydreams—daydreams that sometimes led to dollars. When Roberta Williams, now twenty-eight, was a schoolgirl, her teachers commented on her report cards, "Bright, has potential; but daydreams too much." Roberta was painfully shy, feeling most comfortable removed from reality—immersed in fairy tales, storytelling, intrigue. As a teenager, she decided against college or a career, married a computer programmer, and within three years found herself with two babies and an Apple II computer for company. Still fond of fairy tales, storytelling and intrigue, and indifferent to computers, she paid little attention as her husband worked at the computer. Then one day in 1980, while watching her husband fooling around with a commercial computer game she found herself glued to the monitor, fantasizing about inventing a screen game of her own. Meticulously, she plotted out a whodunit, *Mystery House,* which her husband translated into computerese. A two-hundred-dollar amateur advertisement placed in *Micro* magazine brought in $167,000 within a year and led to Sierra On-Line, an Oakhurst, California, software company selling space-age fantasy games devised by Roberta. Roberta's six-year-old company now employs sixty people and sells $10 million annually.

Roberta relishes not only the financial profit her company has brought her but also the personal gain. "I can now talk to people without feeling shy. I've grown. No longer am I floundering in a world where I don't fit in." Because of her flair for storytelling, she worked her shyness into security—monetary and social. Now she considers herself personable, capable of interacting with others, influencing them, and influencing an industry. She feels she can "create a world the way I want it to be—and not just in games." Her shyness, which has given her prosperity as well as pain, will always be part of her, but no longer so big a part.

Shyness doesn't ever fully disappear, but success is its best battler. Lynn Wilson, creater of the $38 million Creative Environs interior design firm in Coral Gables, Florida, was once so shy that when she had to give a speech to her eighth-grade class, she did it in pantomime because she couldn't open her mouth to talk. She remembers herself as an introverted wallflower. Introverted though she was, she had an eye for beauty, a talent for art, and a desire to transform the ordinary into the lush. Realizing she had to transform herself before getting the chance to transform anything else, she forced herself to apply for a scholarship to the University of Miami, where she could study art. She got the scholarship, and once at the university, she forced herself to try out for cheerleading (an activity of extroverts) and got on the squad. From then on she continued to curb her shyness with extrovert pursuits that brought her artistic abilities to the attention of the architectural industry and ultimately led her to create a business that has become one of the interior design industry's giants. Though now exceptionally successful, Lynn admits to still having to work on her shyness. However, today she can do so while riding in her Mercedes Benz 450 SLC or while dining in her $2,500 bleached rhinoceros-skin suit or while jetting off to India on one of her spur-of-the-moment vacations.

DISCRIMINATION

Whereas loneliness is personality-linked, discrimination is heritage-linked. The black, oriental, or Hispanic is an outsider for reasons that can never be changed. Lynn Wilson could force herself to partake of activities that reduced her shyness and led to wealth. Roberta Williams could emerge from her shyness by creating fantasy on a screen and turning it to fortune in the real world. Joan Barnes could work her way out of isolation and into "purposeful (and profitable) play." The minority moneymaker can't work her way out of being black, brown, Hispanic, or oriental. Loneliness can be lessened; appearance can be altered; poverty can be reversed. Heritage stays as is. It's an aluminum spoon that can drive a minority member to escape not her race but the prejudice it provokes.

The best proven antidote for prejudice is prosperity—confirming the "Living well is the best revenge!" philosophy. In the early 1970s, Mary Flatt wasn't living well. Brown-skinned, of Filipino descent, she was far from the fair-haired girl of Des Moines, Iowa. She had no college or business background, no marketable white-collar skills. She tried available jobs such as waitressing and bartending, got bored quickly, and left them within a few months. After a while, she left Des Moines. With her husband, Jim, she ended up in Las Vegas.

Jim got a job as a casino dealer. Mary took whatever jobs she could get—waitressing, working as an Avon lady, selling Liquid Embroidery. During a trip to San Francisco, she went to a party and saw something that would be the turning point of her life—a messenger delivering a singing telegram. It was standard Western Union—straight and serious, not amusing to herself or the other guests. But Mary was struck with an idea: why not create singing telegrams that were wild, witty, sexy, offbeat, and fun? She returned to Las Vegas, worked from home, and created a company that sent costumed singing and dancing show-business hopefuls bursting into parties and places with Macho Man Grams, Harem Grams (a singing messenger and three belly dancers), Happy Divorce Grams, Gorilla Grams. Born in 1976, Eastern Onion is today the largest singing-telegram company in America, with dozens of thriving franchises throughout the United States and Canada. And Mary, once regarded as another struggling ethnic, is now admired as successful, sensuous, and "exotic-looking."

The Immigrant's Dream

Though success diminishes discriminations, American ethnics like Mary Flatt don't initially seek it for racial reasons. They've learned to live with prejudice; they just want to live better. "I wanted to be able to pay the rent," says Mary. The desire for racial equality and acceptance comes later, when the new moneymaker becomes civic-minded, sitting on committees, hosting benefits, performing as role model to her people—thus escalating her image and income. The immigrant is a little different. Early on, she equates success with racial acceptance: "I am a minority, but if I begin my own business and make money, I will be accepted in America." She is driven by the American Dream. There is no Cuban Dream, Korean Dream, Asian Dream. The immigrant wants to be part of America, and because this is so important, sometimes she sees opportunities that native-born Americans miss or are too lazy to pursue—or are not the best qualified to pursue.

The immigrant is ideally qualified simultaneously to capitalize on the unfilled niches in the American marketplace and to have a natural "in" with her countrymen. Korean immigrant Sonia Suk is a real estate mogul. When she arrived in the United States, she spoke little

English. While working as a window-washer, she improved her English and took a real estate course. Soon she got a job selling cemetery plots to fellow Koreans. Sonia earned little but realized that a lot could be made acting as an intermediary between Americans with something to sell and Koreans with desire to buy. From her rented apartment she began Sonia Suk Realty—a Los Angeles company that sells restaurants, shops, buildings, and property to her countrymen and that has created a two-mile-long Korea Town in Southern California. Today, Sonia still works out of her apartment, but now she owns the whole building, another apartment complex, a shopping strip, and some land. California Koreans reaching for their slice of the American Dream know to reach for Sonia's phone number.

Gaining Position from Prejudice

What do you do if you're a black woman with a desire to make it in a white man's field? You're ripe for triple discrimination—as a black, as a woman, and as a trespasser. Such was the situation of Theresa Wilborn, now owner and president of the $2.5-million La Feminique construction corporation of Cleveland, Ohio. Before beginning her company, Theresa worked eight years as a financial counselor for Cleveland's Department of Community Development, Rehabilitation, and Conservation. This was her introduction to the construction trades. While mastering the ins and outs of the construction industry, she earned an associate degree in applied science in architectural and construction-engineering technology. With a background of employment in city government, hands-on contracting experience, technical training, and an emerging entrepreneurial impulse, she was ready to build a construction business. Cleveland's construction industry, although less than thrilled, would have to let her try. It was the early 1980s; laws and programs existed to protect and assist minority business hopefuls, female-owned enterprises, and woman-owned construction companies. Developers of government projects were legally bound to subcontract up to 20 percent of their jobs to minority-owned firms. Theresa could profit from prejudice. She was well qualified to bid under general minority set-aside programs and Women Business Enterprise set-asides.

Today, as she wins bids she never would have won earlier, Theresa is shifting from government-funded building to the more profitable private construction sector. She enjoys her position as a Cleveland business leader, as a role model to disillusioned local youths, and as a black woman thriving in a white man's business. Because she had a friend in the law—legal programs devised to encourage minority business beginners—she could profit from, and rise above, the poison of prejudice.

TRAGEDY

Tragedy is an aluminum spoon that strikes suddenly. It often produces despair and ruin. Sometimes it produces despair and resolve. Occasionally it produces despair, resolve, and riches. A female mourns the loss of someone or something she loved, drowns her sorrow in work, perseveres, determines to create something new and nice— and does. She creates ladybucks. Financial triumph springs from tragedy as it does from poverty, homelessness, loneliness, and discrimination.

Anne Sadovsky's tragedy was the untimely loss of youth. Daughter of an abusive alcoholic father, she ran away from home at fourteen, married, and had two children by nineteen. Just after her second child was born, her husband suffered permanent brain damage in a car accident and had to be institutionalized. With no marketable skills, no money, and a ninth-grade education, Anne became head of the household. Legally responsible for her husband's medical bills, she was forced to divorce him in order to put whatever money she could earn toward the support of her babies. She took a few low-paying clerical jobs and soon left them to work as a sales representative for Mary Kay Cosmetics—a company she credits with teaching her motivational and rhetorical skills that would change her destiny.

Anne came to passionately believe that with a positive attitude one can minimize all obstacles, survive and surmount any tragedy. She developed a love of public speaking, of captivating an audience, of motivating her listeners, and she went on to test her talents in the real estate field. There she rose quickly to a high-level marketing position. In 1981, she borrowed $3,000, enlisted the support of some real estate contacts, and set up shop as a commercial evangelist, teaching others how to succeed in sales, business, and life—as she

had. Today this forty-four-year-old survivor heads Anne Sadovsky &
Co. of Dallas, Texas, which employs thirty-five staffers, gives two
hundred seminars yearly to a quarter of a million people, and produces annual revenues of over $1 million.

Though certain tragedies are more universally acknowledged than
others, tragedy isn't gradable on a relativity scale. Is the death of a
parent less tragic than the death of a child? Is the loss of a spouse
more tragic than the loss of a best friend? Is sudden paralysis more
devastating than sudden blindness? It depends upon the perception
of the victim of the tragedy. One blunt woman speaks for several
silent sisters when she says, "Everyone consoled me when my husband died; I needed consoling when the bastard was alive."

To bright, active eleven-year-old Linda Wachner, most of whose
body was suddenly imprisoned in a plaster cast to correct severe
curvature of the spine, a year of virtual immobility was a terrible
tragedy. She didn't know if she'd ever walk again or how bleak her
physical future might be; but she vowed that no matter what happened, she'd have a glorious financial future. One day she'd be
chauffeured in limousines instead of ambulances. She would head
a company, have a career in fashion, dictate her destiny. Her body
impaired, her mind ran away with resolve.

Now forty, Linda has more than lived out her longings. She rides
in limousines, walks, runs, skis, and plays tennis. She has climbed
the corporate ladder from department store salesgirl, to assistant
buyer, to buyer, to apparel industry whiz kid, to head of Max Factor's
U.S. operation, to president and chief operating officer of Max Factor.
Currently she is stepping in as president of Warnaco. Like many
successful executives, she evokes admiration and animosity. But
even her detractors admit that the determined girl, who once lay
encased in plaster, is today a woman positioned to one day head a
billion-dollar corporation.

Divorce

Because it is now so common, divorce doesn't seem an event of
tragic proportions. But for many women, particularly middle-aged
women spurned by their spouses, it can be devastating. Our sympathies are strained by the similarity of the stories: the philandering
husband leaves the devoted spouse for a younger woman; the bald-

ing husband, facing a midlife crisis, needs "space"; the faithful husband, with children now grown and gone, realized he never loved
his wife to begin with. Commonplace, yes; but similarity of story
doesn't make the pain less poignant. Millions of women contemplate
suicide as an alternative to survival as a divorcée. Usually they work
through their grief and go on with their lives. Sometimes they work
through their grief and go on to create lives grander than they had
had before or imagined themselves having.

After her husband divorced her, Catherine didn't smile for two
years. For this attentive wife, the hardworking mother of five, a religious Catholic, "this was the worst thing that could happen. It in-
validated all my adult life; there was nothing to look forward to."
Catherine turned to her parish priest, who told her she must pull
herself together (for her children's sake, if not her own) and "maybe
think of taking a job." Raising five children was enough of a job for
her, but she needed money. Determined not to leave her children
alone, she tried envelope-stuffing and telephone sales, both of which
brought her pennies in profit and hours of boredom. An article in a
magazine about a woman franchising a sitting-service company
prompted an inquiry into the operation. Catherine liked what she
learned. For a few thousand dollars, she would receive all the training
and supplies necessary to run a business that would match people
who needed help or care with people qualified to provide it. From
a desk at home, she could make $40,000 a year and more supplying
house sitters, invalid sitters, baby-sitters, pet sitters.

Catherine purchased the turnkey program. The training seminars
made her feel "excited for the first time in years." She loved the idea
of selecting and supervising individuals who would provide quality
care to the elderly, to children, and to animals. She called friends,
family, parishioners, parents of her children's friends, local hospitals,
and people her priest recommended. Her enthusiasm was contagious; she generated a large network of "givers and getters." Almost
everyone needed a sitter, needed part-time work, or knew someone
who needed one or the other. Soon Catherine's company not only
offered the standard services but had branched out to fill local needs.
She had an "Irish lore" sitter who companion-sat elderly and infirm
Irish individuals who reveled in hearing stories of their homeland; a
"cake bake" sitter who baby-sat children eager to learn how to make

"fun and fancy" cakes; a dog sitter who specialized in training disobedient and devilish puppies; and a plant sitter capable of rejuvenating the most wilted weeds.

Within three years, Catherine was sitting pretty. Initially incredulous at the thought of earning $40,000 a year from home (or anywhere), she found herself earning three times that—and loving her work and her new life. Today she still finds it difficult to talk about her divorce, but no longer does she consider her life "invalidated" or herself having "nothing to look forward to." At the moment she is very much looking forward to a May wedding with a veterinarian she met through one of her pet sitters.

Death

Like divorce, death is a tragedy that can alter a life dramatically. The loved—or maybe unloved—one is gone. The bereaved is left with grief or relief, with money or with debts, with drive or with the lack of it, with anger, fear, and guilt. Generally the more tragic, untimely, and unexpected the death, the greater its potential for affecting—postively or negatively—the lives of those most immediately touched. A good number of businesses, professions, and careers had graveside origins. Some women launch literary careers after the loss of a family member. Seeking catharsis, they skillfully recount the details of the death of a child, sibling, spouse, or parent. Their stories tap the human heart—and the human pocketbook. Personal loss becomes financial gain. Similarly, other women, inheriting a business without a boss, pick up not pen but self and become boss lady, escalating business and self to positions of prestige and power that the company founder never would have believed possible. Still other women, driven by a need to forget—or a need to eat—or a need to remember—begin and build enterprises or careers that wouldn't have interested them had death not struck.

Death frequently produces "memorial motivation." A woman wants to remember—and wants others to remember—what happened. She wants to give meaning to a son's death in a car crash, to a husband's death from heart failure, to a mother's suicide, to a brother's murder. Her motivation is not monetary, but she makes money nevertheless.

One college coed, an aspiring music major, found herself "jolted into activities" that would bring her a quarter of a million dollars before she was out of her twenties. Notified that her sister had been raped and murdered, the coed emptied her dorm room, returned home, and left college behind. Her interest in music continued. She wrote a song about her sister and sold it for a few hundred dollars. The money financed a martial arts course. The course led to a job as a martial arts instructor. Through the job she met the inventor of a portable electronic alarm that was ideal for single women, travelers, or senior citizens—easy marks (as her sister had been) for criminals. The device was part of an offering structured by an investment firm. The former coed put up $8,000 and came out $30,000 ahead. Continuing a pattern of pursuing ventures related to her sister's tragedy, she became a silent partner in a new martial arts studio begun by her boss. She left her job and worked twelve-hour days for a political aspirant with hard-line views on the treatment of rapists, murderers, criminals. The politico won. And she won, too—a $20,000 job in state government. Today this twenty-six-year-old earns $25,000 yearly from her silent partnership in the martial arts studio, $26,500 from her job, and has just received over $100,000 as her share of the profit of a film she invested in about rape, murder, and retribution. She is taking courses in criminal justice and plans to begin a consulting business specializing in this area.

Related to memorial motivation is "carry-on motivation." Here, the deceased has left something substantial for the bereaved to build on. The opportunity exists to escalate an estate into an empire. The beneficiary, propelled by grief or greed or both, can grasp gold and glory. Whether the motivation is to keep an accomplishment alive, further it, or further herself, she is well-positioned to rise to the role of entrepreneurial celebrity.

Such is the story of Helen Boehm, of Edward Marshall Boehm, Inc., a firm that sells sculptures of birds, flowers, and animals to kings, presidents, and millionaires. Currently, Boehm porcelains are considered priceless works of art. They are found in distinguished private collections throughout the world and in museums from the Metropolitan to the Vatican. Every President since Kennedy has purchased the company's figurines for use as official gifts. New projects are always on the company drawing board, and profits are multiplying. Helen meets and mingles with world figures. Nancy Reagan poses with her, Prince Charles dances with her, Princess Diana compliments her. She loves it all; but eighteen years ago, when her husband Ed died, life was less rosy and royal.

Ed had been a farmer with sculpting talents and some quality pieces to show; Helen had been a Brooklyn-born Italian immigrant with a talent for promoting talent. One day, Helen called the Metropolitan Museum of Art in New York and convinced them to show her husband's work. They did. She then approached *The New York Times* with a story about a "farmer turned artist," making sure to mention the Metropolitan's endorsement of farmer Ed's sculpture. They printed it. Daily sales trips with Ed's work in tow began paying off. Pieces were sold; investors were found; and farmer Ed became a full-time sculptor. Boehm studios soon became a moneymaking enterprise. Ed Boehm, modest and gifted, provided the product; Helen promoted it. After Ed died, Helen could have lived comfortably and unobtrusively. She chose not to. She took over as head of Boehm, initiated timely works, beautiful designs, and customized baubles (such as a solid-gold camel with diamond eyes, which she sold on a jaunt to Saudi Arabia), and pursued the rich and famous. The rich, the famous, and the art-minded rewarded her with commissions for thousands of pieces. New hobbies, such as sponsoring polo teams, followed. Additional showrooms (most recently, one in New York's Trump Tower) were opened. More people were introduced to Boehm collectables. And the Boehm company artists continued to turn out the fashionable figurines.

Today, Boehm is one of the most celebrated names in porcelain sculpture. Helen Boehm remembers her talented husband with great fondness while enjoying a life that she considers the American Dream come true: gorgeous jewels, meetings with Britain's royal family, an apartment at the Hotel Pierre, a house on the Delaware River, a horse farm, a limousine, a Duesenberg, a Mercedes coupe.

NONFULFILLMENT

Nonfulfillment is a very vocal aluminum spoon. Once when women spoke of nonfulfillment they were referring to a lifestyle limited to pleasing a husband and children. Today nonfulfillment is discussed in terms of frustration more with a career than with a lifestyle. "If I had known what teaching was really about, I'd never have entered the profession," says an elementary schoolteacher struggling to exist on a $16,000 salary. "Not only is the money terrible, but the profession has negative prestige."

"If I had known how competitive this computer field would become, I would have gone into architecture, which is what I really wanted," says a disillusioned data processor tinkering with the idea of going back to school.

"Tell me about all the money lawyers make, and I'll tell you about a profession glutted with female attorneys supplementing their incomes with menial jobs," says a law school graduate unable to establish a profitable practice.

Many women deal with career frustration by talking about it. Venting disillusionment to a sympathetic ear can be cathartic. Tips are picked up that make coping easier. But for some individuals talk and tips are but a prelude to correcting inequities by changing careers. Nonfulfillment is a persistent plague that must be treated—sometimes with remarkable results.

Seven years ago Sandy Feldman was earning $11,500 a year as a nurse. She had a strong interest in the nursing profession and a strong complaint against it—the $6.00-an-hour wages that would rise to $6.10 were she to acquire a Bachelor of Science degree. Unmotivated by a ten-cent-an-hour salary increase and armed with critical-care nursing experience and a clever service idea, she began Critical Care Inc., an agency that places nurses in hospital operating rooms and on intensive-care floors for periods of one to three months. But instead of using the traditional salary arrangement of most temp agencies, Sandy initiated a superior setup. Hospitals pay her nurses directly (instead of through her Critical Care agency), thus allowing her to save on bookkeeping time and expenses, charge lower fees, and maintain an in-demand agency with files on more than 1,500 nurses who are placed regularly in over forty states. Sandy's nurses enjoy the opportunity to work in a variety of hospitals, and Sandy enjoys the $80,000 to $100,000 that she now receives annually in placement fees.

Nonfulfillment is commonplace in careers once considered female "safeties" or "transitions"—employment that women would train for in the event they didn't marry or for the purpose of self-support until they did. Nursing, teaching, bookkeeping, secretarial work, and social work fall into this classification. Generally, they don't pay highly. Though these low-paying careers often turn dedication to disgust, they also serve as springboards for supersuccess. Increasingly, women like Sandy Feldman, armed with in-depth knowledge in traditional female fields, are turning experience into real remuneration.

In 1979, schoolteacher Judy Connolly spent vacations doing secretarial work. Her combined teaching and secretarial pay was $14,000 a year—a salary situation she saw as hopeless. A friend convinced her to try Wall Street. Judy took a summer secretarial job at Merrill Lynch, became a registered rep, and never returned to teaching. Today she manages over four hundred accounts and uses her teaching skills to motivate clients and direct new brokers. For her efforts she earns from $85,000 to $250,000 in a good year—fulfillment well beyond her grandest expectations. "I knew I could make it if I was given a chance," says Judy, ". . . but I never dreamed that I could get to where I am today!"

Like other women who go from nonfulfillment to ladybucks, Judy Connolly was "given a chance" because she took a chance. Judy tried the brokerage business, liked it, took a difficult test to qualify for stock sales, and left fourteen years of teaching behind. When nonfulfillment causes an unbearable awareness of gross underpay or underemployment, chance-taking mounts. It's a do-or-die situation—move on, start over, or be forever frustrated.

In 1974, Linda Aylesworth took a chance that would take her from underemployed editor to executive recruiter. When Linda signed on at a large Chicago management consulting firm, it was with the understanding that she would edit consultants' reports, make them clearer. After a year she found she not only wanted to make them clearer, she wanted to write them herself, to contribute more to the company, to become a consultant, herself. Her reports would be more interesting than the ones she'd been editing.

She approached her bosses. It was an old-line firm; they would have none of it. To be a consultant there, she would have to get an MBA and put in time at a smaller company first. They advised her to "be a good girl, go on back and edit." She had had it with editing. If she couldn't become a consultant, she would try out for a public relations position within the firm. She submitted a proposal to the company publicist, outlining her skills and offering to work at low pay to acquire experience. This didn't work out, either. Linda left the firm. A female consultant she knew introduced her to some people beginning an executive recruiting firm. Linda worked for them for a while and then struck out on her own. In 1976 she began her own headhunting firm, with a partner. In 1980 she bought out her partner. Today her thriving company, The People Bank Ltd., specializes in recruiting middle-management employees for growing corporations, filling a critical niche in the headhunting field and providing Linda with a sense of accomplishment and a six-figure salary—unattainable as an underemployed editor.

FROM LONGING TO LADYBUCKS

Poverty, homeliness, shyness, prejudice, death, and disillusionment—are these the roots of riches? Often yes. In certain individuals, reduced circumstances create a "mission mentality"—a deprivation-driven longing to make things better, to make the hurt go away—to make money. In a capitalist society the creation of wealth has a lot to do with the cancellation of pain. Ladybucks don't erase all memories or right all wrongs, but they provide women with a leap of faith between hunger and hope—a chance for tomorrows better than yesterdays.

Ladybucks are not just a deprivation-driven windfall. The labor that leads to ladybucks comes from positive as well as negative circumstances. A loved little girl, told from crib to college how exceptional she is, how success is waiting for her, how everyone is ready to help her achieve it, is also well positioned for financial accomplishment. This is the other side of the genesis of super-achievement. The ladybucks phenomenon is psychologically based, whether prompted by pain or privilege. However, even in the best of all possible societies, reduced circumstances far outnumber privileged ones. The generation of women producing wealth is not one of silver spoons. Ladybucks are primarily an aluminum spoon triumph.

CHAPTER **3**

The Four A's

Three women meet at a party. Each is determined to become rich. The conversation turns to moneymaking. The first says, "I can do anything I want to do." The second nods. "I am determined," she says. "I have goals." The third boasts, "I have guts." The hostess's teenage son, overhearing the conversation, tells the women, "You three should begin a business. Together you have what my football coach calls the three A's of accomplishment—attitude, ambition, and aggressiveness." The women smile and continue talking to each other. The boy leaves. Five years pass. Today the boy is a Heisman Trophy winner and a wealthy football player. The three women, no richer, still meet at parties and chat about becoming rich.

Too bad the women didn't chat more with the boy. He understood the effectiveness of trait fusion. His football coach taught him well. Attitude, ambition, and aggressiveness are a winning trio. Combined with a fourth A—action—they are the raw materials of ladybucks. Alone, any one or two of the four A's is generally insufficient for ladybucks creation. Fused, the four A's are a force of consequence.

ATTITUDE

A woman who believes she can accomplish whatever she wishes has a winning attitude, but it won't make her a winner. Not alone. Though she has the self-confidence to go from wanting to getting, too often—as in the case of the woman at the party—that's all she has: a positive attitude unbolstered by the other three A's. Many low-income women are surprisingly self-assured individuals. They display can-do attitudes with don't-do results.

Everyone was certain Sunny was slated for success. Captain of her high school cheerleading squad, she fired up her classmates with "we can win" spirit. Everything from her name to the personal philosophy blurb in her yearbook—"With self-confidence you soar; without it you sink"—reflected her seeming ability to turn any dream into deed. In college she was a favorite with peers and professors. She projected the image of a winner; it won her popularity. In the business world, that's all it would win her.

Sunny graduated from college as a communications major and took a job as an advertising trainee. In her standard Sunny way, radiating a positive mental attitude, she became a people-magnet. Colleagues were sure she would rise quickly to account executive. She didn't. Fellow trainees maximized opportunities, carved out clout, inched themselves into coveted positions. Sunny's positive mental attitude wasn't paying off. "I was a self-confident loser. I believed I could be whatever I wanted to be, but I didn't know what that was," says Sunny. "I had no specific goals, so I didn't talk up or walk up my skills. I became a glorifed girl Friday. And I wasn't unhappy."

Today, divorced with two children, Sunny is unhappy that she doesn't have the money or position she could have had. Still blessed with a positive mental attitude, now she also has a clear goal—to build a flourishing public relations agency.

Sunny's begun her agency. She adopted an aggressive stance, soliciting loans, expert assistance, and favors. Now she regularly promotes her skills and herself, asks for business, and requests referrals. She moves purposefully. Her company is starting to show good earnings. It's too early to tell how far Sunny will soar or whether she'll ever reap ladybucks; but it's certain she's not counting just on a positive attitude to make her rich.

The Admirable A

The individual who displays a positive mental attitude evokes admiration. Unlike the other three A's (ambition, aggressiveness, and action), a self-confident demeanor is deemed a definite plus. It is a trait that wins friends, influences people, and receives praise from teachers, preachers, and parents. The moneymaker who says "I clawed my way up because I was ambitious" may be truthful; but she's not telling the most touted truth. People like to hear how she made it to the top because she believed in herself, had a can-do approach to success, a positive outlook. The latter sounds virtuous, has an almost religious ring, makes one want to cheer. The moneymaker who enjoys playing to the crowd usually highlights the importance of attitude and downplays traits such as ambition or aggressiveness. It's good for her image; it's good for her business.

A positive mental attitude is a particularly applauded trait for women. It is smart, sensual, nonoffensive, and nonabrasive. Mary Kay became one of America's richest women by possessing and promoting this trait. Thousands of women have brought her philosophy of cycling attitude into advantage. Those who seek to sell her products are taught the power of positive thinking as part of an effective "motivate the seller and the seller will motivate the buyer" plan. The Mary Kay saleswoman learns to believe in herself and in the Mary Kay product. Thus empowered, she convinces buyers that the creams in the pink jars improve appearance and consequently boost self-confidence. Everyone comes out ahead, with either money, a winning attitude, or both.

The Infrequent A

A positive mental attitude is a marketable commodity. It is sold in much the same way as exercise lessons. Just as a fitness guru offers seminars and videocassettes promoting his program, his philosophy, and his regimen, so too do attitude specialists rely on seminars and tapes to get their messages to the masses. A positive mental attitude is hawked as a success-producing characteristic available for a price. Self-improvement aficionados, eager to give themselves a winning edge, pay the price. A demand exists for new and improved attitudes. Most individuals possess, if not defeatist attitudes, realistic ones, which according to the attitude experts are insufficient. There is a belief—and many moneymakers endorse it—that a positive mental attitude carries a mystical power that keeps the success engine chugging. True or not, even doubters of this power of positive thinking admit it doesn't hurt to learn an "I can do it" approach to life. That this approach must be taught, and that people are willing to pay sizable sums for instruction, underscores the fact that a positive mental attitude is generally not inborn or early bred. Studies show that it is particularly not inborn or early bred in most women.

"I was very lucky," says Dr. Paula Moynahan, one of America's most renowned and remunerated plastic, reconstructive, and cosmetic surgeons. "From earliest childhood on, I was taught the power of positive thinking." Paula's father, now a retired policeman, and her mother, a housewife, gifted their daughter with a strong sense of self-belief and a mission: to help others feel good about themselves. "As a very little girl, I showed an interest in science, nature, working with my hands. My father told me often that I should become a doctor, that I had the required interest and intelligence and it would be an excellent way to help others." Paula responded favorably to her father's opinion. From the time she was six years old, whenever she was asked what she would be as an adult, she replied, "A doctor." She never doubted that she would turn desire to deed. Years later she would encounter prejudice in getting into medical school and in entering the field of plastic surgery. In 1964 there was no welcome mat out for women interested in becoming doctors and especially in becoming plastic surgeons. It didn't matter. Paula was well-armed to battle and beat those who would prevent her from living out her childhood dream. Her father had instilled in her an "I can do it" attitude that would get her through difficult examinations and damaging discrimination.

Would Paula have made it without a positive mental attitude? "I don't know," she admits. "Family faith meant everything to me. It made me believe in myself when I might have wavered. It gave me stick-to-it-ive-ness when I was told by colleges, 'Forget about being a doctor.' " Now a nationally acclaimed physician with offices in Waterbury, Connecticut, and on New York's Fifth Avenue and with one soon to open in Palm Beach, she advises those pursuing success in any field to "follow the teachings of Dr. Norman Vincent Peale, try to develop self-faith, learn to think positively."

Sadly, Paula's situation is rare. How many fathers, particularly fathers of modest means who have not lived out the American Dream themselves, are able to imbue their daughters with the kind of positive mental attitude that can be channeled into professional supersuccess? Even the most well-intended ongoing pep talks generally fail to produce success on any grand scale. However, a young girl filled with faith in self and future is fortunate. She may not have other things necessary for superachievement; she may be shot down by peers and powers that her parents cannot counter; but she's far more fortified against failure than the average female.

Godmothers and Grandmothers

The average female doesn't have parents like Paula's. Nor does the average ladybucks earner. For many reasons parents can't or don't gift their daughters with abundant doses of self-confidence. However, ladybucks are usually earned by women who had someone—a godmother, a grandmother, an aunt, a teacher—who prompted their winning attitudes. New York–based psychotherapist Arlene Schofield speaks for many female achievers when she says, "It's amazing how far a small amount of encouragement can go, and how handicapped one can be without it." Arlene, sho credits her grandmother with giving her the doses of approval that cushioned her professional climb, maintains that a parent isn't the only one equipped to impart self-confidence. "That it be gotten is more important than who gives it," she says. Because too often it is not gotten—no one is around to give it or interested in giving it or understands how to give it—a psychological niche exists that is being filled by therapists like Arlene, who counsel individuals and families in need of attitude build-up.

Carol Jenna, founder of the $5 million Jenna & Co, Ltd., a San Francisco Bay–area sports marketing agency that matches athletic events in need of financing with corporate sponsors, is positive mental attitude (PMA) incarnate. "I believe a woman can do anything she sets her mind to," says this mother of two who in 1978 singlehandedly turned a love of sports into a popular, prospering, fully staffed agency that simultaneously serves corporations such as B. F. Goodrich, Levi-Strauss, and Del Monte and promotes underfinanced sports such as boardsailing and running events.

Carol tells the story of how, in her desire to have attractive legs, she hung a picture of beautiful legs on her bedroom wall. "Every day I would look at that picture," recalls Carol, "and tell myself, 'You can have legs like that, too.' " Now possessing shapely legs, Carol credits the photograph with stimulating her to exercise several hours daily until she acquired the limbs she longed for. She also credits something besides the photo—an aunt who made her believe she could accomplish anything she put her mind to. Like Arlene and several other female superachievers, Carol makes little mention of parental input in the development of a positive mental attitude but talks of another individual whom she considers a significant factor in her success. The feeling comes across that it would be lovely if all parents dusted their daughters with loving dabs of self-confidence but such is not a common reality—one must often seek dusting and dabs elsewhere.

Many a ladybucks earner is like an Oscar-winning star, thanking producer, director, co-star, and agent for the award. The ladybucks earner, today often a media celebrity, routinely credits so-and-so and so-and-so "for showing me how to believe in myself, for teaching me the power of positive thinking." Often the so-and-so is a godmother figure who, during a critical period in the moneymaker's life, entered the scene with not a wand but words. The words, unexceptional when recalled and recounted, were sufficient to inspire the self-confidence that combined with other traits to turn wishing into winning.

One high-level executive for a *Fortune* 500 firm smiles as she tells her godmother story. "Elsa wasn't really my godmother," says Claire. "Actually, she was an older cousin whom I loved and my mother disliked. Mother disliked Elsa because she believed that Elsa spoiled me. I was one of six children, and Elsa made me feel I was the most important one. She bought me pretty clothes as gifts, told me I was beautiful, called me Princess. Elsa was an uneducated, kind woman with no great psychological insights to pass along. She could probably be called ordinary, but she made me feel extraordinary, and I will always be grateful to her."

Elsa told Claire she was beautiful, called her Princess, bought her pretty clothes. She didn't say or do anything that would send the psychiatric community cheering in the streets, but "she made me feel special and that was everything," says Claire. "Perhaps had I been badly abused Elsa's attention wouldn't have been so consequential. I don't know. But it made me feel I could be someone important."

Claire is correct. A godmotherlike figure can do wonders for the self-esteem of the average child. A girl like Claire, fortunate enough to have such a person around or venturesome enough to search one out, is blessed. However, though a few kind words and deeds can go a long way, usually they can't go far enough for seriously mishandled children. Such is the plight of many women who are eager to carve out profitable financial futures but afraid to try. They ask the collective question, "Why won't I try someting new, different, exciting?" The psychologically inclined know why: lack of faith in themselves or their abilities; fear of failure—a fear frequently learned in childhood, reinforced in adolescence, and ingrained by adulthood. Rightly or wrongly, these women often blame parents for their stagnation. They hear the advice, "Put your past behind you; forget what was, you can't change it; change what is!" But such advice seldom rouses women who perceive themselves as psychologically damaged by early parental mistreatment, even women who've had godmothers and grandmothers to ease the harm.

Attitude Unlearning

"I had so much unlearning to do," says Patricia, now a $200,000-a-year giftware importer. "I didn't even have the courage to place a display ad until I stopped seeing myself as a born loser." Patricia, who now maintains profitable relationships with exporters from around the world, regularly places dozens of display ads, initiates clever direct-mail campaigns, and moves thousands of pieces of merchandise monthly from distant shores to suburban doors, insists she could not have put her past behind her until she confronted it and conquered it. "I was paralyzed by parents too poor, burdened, and disillusioned to instill self-confidence in me. They couldn't instill it in themselves or each other. Because I considered poverty such an embarrassment, I became a sucker for every get-rich-quick book our local library had. Eventually I ended up in a seminar given by the authors of one of these books; that was the beginning of a process which would change my life."

The seminar Patricia attended stressed the role of positive thinking in the success formula. Patricia realized that she was a negative thinker and that she had a pessimistic mental attitude, an inhibiting self-image. The seminar didn't change her self-image from loser to winner, but it spurred her into three years of psychotherapy and two years of concurrent career struggle that would. "I had to move backward before I could move forward," says Patricia. "I had to examine a response pattern instigated by my parents, understand it, understand them, mourn for what might have been; and then—and only then—could I begin to unlearn that pattern and reconstruct a productive one."

Not every woman needs years of therapy to unlearn a negative mental attitude and develop a positive one. People enter this world with different degrees of genetic resiliency. Sometimes seminars alone provide sufficient impetus for change. Hypnosis has helped several women improve their self-perception. Loving and patient friends and spouses often do much to end self-doubt and increase self-assurance. Whatever works is fine, as long as it produces a healthy mental attitude.

AMBITION

Unlike PMA (Positive Mental Attitude), which is always admired, ambition is both an admired and an abhorred trait. Filmmakers love to depict it. It is the stuff of greed and glory, a quality of the evil and the righteous—and of women who reap ladybucks, be they evil or righteous or a little of both. Like attitude, ambition does not work alone. The woman at the party who said, "I am determined; I have goals," personifies ambition without aftermath. Nothing comes of her ambition. It could lead her in a dozen different directions, highlight her talent, heal her heartache, or change lives. But it doesn't. It is worthless.

Women who create ladybucks are ambitious and get mileage out of their ambition. They are cravers of consequence. They don't necessarily crave the money they ultimately earn, but they are ambitious for something they consider worth striving for and align their ambition with the other A's (attitude, aggressiveness, and action) and go after what whey want.

Kathy Kolbe, a crusader at heart, had a mammoth ambition, given the mediocrity of most school systems. Kathy envisioned a utopian educational system where superior students were challenged into creative and critical thinking. She knew her two children weren't the only gifted youngsters who were bored in their Arizona grade school, so in 1975 she began a summer school in Phoenix to teach bright students to maximize their intelligence. The school quickly grew from forty to two hundred children, each paying sixty dollars a week. Kathy soon discovered that there was a scarcity of publications directed toward the superior student. She called New York publishers and asked them to publish education material for the gifted. They declined, claiming the market was too small to be profitable. Kathy disagreed. She took five hundred dollars in savings and founded Resources for the Gifted, a publisher of innovative learning materials. A catalog sent to 3,500 parents and educators brought in orders in increasing numbers. Today, Resources for the Gifted employs twenty full-time workers, publishes over one hundred educational aids, and grosses close to $4 million annually.

In 1985, *Time* magazine named Kathy Kolbe one of seven Americans to share its Man of the Year Award. Said *Time* in describing Kathy and the six other recipients, "These are men and women who have seen a problem or a public need and figured out a solution." The statement went on to discuss the significance of "iron determination" in the seven achievers' struggles for solution. Kathy, like most ladybucks winners, has all the A's of accomplishment, but it is her "iron determination," her ambition (more than her positive attitude, or good-natured aggressiveness, or tendency to action), that keeps her plotting a revolution in the educational process. Currently, she is driven to enrich not only school systems but corporations as well. She believes that corporations, like schoolteachers, can maximize productivity by understanding the four "conations," or learning styles, that constitute mental behavior (the basis of the Kolbe Concepts program). Employees, like students, fall into one of four categories: Quick Starts, Implementers, Fact-Finders, Follow-Throughs. Through a test Kathy has devised—the Impact Factors Profile (IFP)—bosses can assess workers' thinking styles and place them in positions best for their particular talents and motivation—to the advantage of both employer and employee. Judging from the corporate response to the IF test, Kathy's newest ambition is destined to increase the profits of Kolbe Concepts and Resources for the Gifted.

Tasting Change

Women like Kathy are fired up by possibilities for profit (social and/or financial) that others either overlook or underestimate. The publishers who ignored Kathy's request for materials for the gifted under-estimated the market for such offerings. They shrugged off her suggestion. It didn't excite them. But it did excite Kathy. Before her first learning aid rolled off the presses and into the hands and minds of thousands of eager buyers, Kathy could taste the change such material would bring. *Tasting* change is the nucleus of ambition. Change isn't simply envisioned; it is superenvisioned, to the point where one focuses on it constantly. It is seen, touched, played with. A hounding hunger exists. There *must* be a feast of fulfillment.

"For thirty-four years I walked around as though my feet were stuck in cement buckets," says Colleen Goodman. "I worked at a few part-time jobs, raised my children, helped my husband get ahead. I dreamed of owning a little business of my own, but the right idea never hit me—until this." The "this" is a cheerful, busy printing shop that nets Colleen $50,000 a year—a figure her accountant predicts will double within three years. Colleen, admittedly not "a courageous type," chose to cash in on someone else's "right idea." She had read an article about the money that could be made by franchisees and was intrigued. An investigation into different types of franchises eliminated "taco huts, rug cleaning services, exercise studios, and several other businesses that didn't interest me or were too expen-sive." Printing interested Colleen, and the price was affordable. She liked the thought of making invitations, booklets, flyers. "The fran-chise was well presented. It seemed easy to learn, neat, a nice way to serve the needs of a growing community."

Today, Colleen is happily serving the needs of her growing com-munity—and her own needs. Her "little business of my own" is not so little; and if Colleen's new ambition is realized, it will be the first of a chain. She is determined to "own five printing franchises within a hundred-mile radius so I can oversee them properly." She laughs when she talks about her plan. "I was never so ambitious for success until I started to taste it; now I don't want just a little business, or a single business, but a little printing empire by the time I'm forty. I can't believe how much I fixate on this goal. I see myself driving to each of my shops, meeting with the managers, praising good work, correcting mistakes."

Increasingly, ladybucks are being earned by women like Colleen who, via a turnkey (franchise) package, cash in on someone else's idea, enjoy their new successes, and become uncharacteristically ambitious, driven beyond old selves and dreams to scale the Midas Mountain. Whether it's one's own idea or someone else's is less important than how much ambition flows through the veins. When one begins to taste change, degree of hunger, not origin of idea, turns vision to victory.

Moneylove

For women like Kathy Kolbe, improving an established system is a primary vision. The money consequently derived is secondary. For women like Colleen, empire-building and the money that flows from it are primary. But she too provides a needed service. Need, greed, a combination of the two, and other factors drive women to pursue activities that serve consumers and themselves. Women who create wealth are often propelled by visions vaster than bankrolls. They see better school systems, better working conditions, better health care, better a lot of things. But they also see better earnings for themselves. They may funnel their incomes back into their businesses, live modestly, and accumulate few material possessions, but their earnings are the major yardstick by which they gauge their accomplishments, evaluate their worth, measure their influence, determine their power. They are not consumed with lust for ladybucks, but they have a healthy case of moneylove—something that many societies consider crude but that enterprising American women feel little need to defend.

"I am truly motivated by money," says Janice Jones, president of Chartwell & Co., a $15 million investment and financial consulting firm that she founded in 1980. When Janice graduated from college in 1973, she got a job in finance, tasted the money and power of Wall Street, and was hooked. Her keen fiscal instincts led her to trade employment hours for stock in a dollar-a-share electronics company that she sized up as a potential winner. The stock soared to eighty-eight dollars a share and many Wall Street insiders sized up Janice as a potential winner. She went on to serve four years as vice president of a private banking and investor relations firm. There she observed that many men who were becoming rich in the equity market weren't any brighter—and were often less bright—than she was. It moved her to begin her own company. She unabashedly admits that she wanted to become wealthy, not because she covets furs or cars or jewels, but because she loves making money, for herself and others. "I'm a builder, not a spender," she says, talking about the pleasure she gets from building equity in the small, growing companies that she considers to be in the forefront of technology. Her long-range goal is to set up an institute to help others get business training. In the meantime she builds equity by taking shares (more than fees) for the financial services she renders. Currently, she holds equity positions in over fifty public and private companies that she's targeted as future moneymakers.

Figurephobia

In years past women didn't talk much about building equity, stock shares, or technology. This is partly, but not only, because they were less ambitious or more interested in creating families than in creating capital. Women used to want to raise families, and still do; but today they are learning and talking a new language—mathspeak—an idiom that empowers them to turn fantasies into fortunes. Words such as *equity* are part of the working vocabularies of female moneymakers. They understand equity, balance sheets, formulas, cash flow, and interest rates not because they are necessarily interested in these things, as are Janice Jones and a few other women who carve out fortunes in financial fields, but because they've discovered that familiarity with the arithmetic of moneymaking is the foundation of success in all fields.

Less and less often is female ambition being squelched by figurephobia. Today enterprising women force themselves to mathspeak. They learn how money multiplies exponentially, how to communicate with bankers, how to finance expansion, how to diversify. The women who reap ladybucks don't entrust all to accountants or financial advisers. They seek advice and use it to maintain control of their finances. They understand what's happening in their ledgers and bank books and invest income with the belief that it must be cycled up geometrically and painlessly. They know that ambition to earn money in a particular area—be it finance, fashion, printing shops, educational publishing—must be tempered by the truth that real money is made by those who try to be as comfortable with numbers as with the products or services they sell.

AGGRESSIVENESS

Ambition is the drive behind accomplishment. Aggressiveness is the spunk, the guts to initiate offbeat strategies that bring ladybucks within reaching range. Too often, women filled with fine attitudes and ambitions don't earn anything near what they could because they don't talk up or act up beyond the boundaries of polite or conventional behavior. They have strong self-images and strong goals that are canceled by weak or meek or forceless approaches to problem solving. They don't outline and initiate plans of action that will make their companies or careers soar. They feel worthy; they envision themselves building big businesses, heading major companies, earning large fees, but they don't envision the forceful, insistent behavior that is often necessary to achieve this.

Aggressiveness alone is like attitude or ambition alone—not enough. Many women are fearless but accomplish nothing. Like the third woman at the party, they "have guts" but reap neither gold nor glory. They have guts without goals or guts without the genuine self-confidence that keeps aggressiveness from becoming obnoxiousness. However, when aggressiveness combines with ambition and a positive mental attitude, a formidable trio exists. Here emerges the woman with can-do spirit, specific focus, and the spunk to tread where others fear to tiptoe.

In an emotion-packed White House ceremony, Vice President George Bush presented Jolyn Robichaux with a plaque that honored her as Minority Entrepreneur of 1985—a title bestowed by the U.S. Department of Commerce. Jolyn, who heads a Chicago-based ice cream manufacturing company with sales in excess of $5 million, is the first black woman to receive this prestigious national award. Her journey from Chicago's South Side to the White House ceremony was influenced by death, discrimination, and negatives that afflict many new companies. It was also influenced by Jolyn's aggressiveness—a force that enabled her to turn restrictions into riches.

Jolyn and her husband bought the financially troubled Baldwin Ice Cream Company in 1967 for $25,000. Jolyn worked there in a secretarial capacity. She had no formal business training or education and knew nothing about employee management, marketing, or the company's day-to-day operations. In 1971, her husband died suddenly. At the time Baldwin's gross sales were $300,000. Jolyn decided to take command of the company. She would learn what she had to learn and do what had to be done to bolster and build the struggling enterprise.

Jolyn enlisted the aid and support of Baldwin's manager, company workers, and a Department of Commerce program designed to help minority-owned businesses. She devised new operating strategies and office procedures and worked tirelessly to learn every tactic that could result in bottom-line profits and increased sales. She also aggressively pursued government-regulated operations. Jolyn made appointments with major bank presidents, and acting in a manner that would initially bring sneers but would ultimately earn her the respect of Chicago's banking community, she brought along a questionnaire she'd developed and interrogated the presidents about their banks. She wanted to know what services their banks could provide Baldwin. The bank presidents were amused—a black woman with an ice cream business, questioning them about their operations. What kind of a loan was she seeking? they asked hesitantly. After all, there were restrictions to be observed. No loan, she told them. All she wanted was to send them Baldwin's quarterly financial statements for review. Relieved, they agreed. Two and a half years later, when Jolyn was looking for expansion capital, four banks were fighting each other to loan her money.

Jolyn made it clear to hospitals, schools, military bases, and any and all government-regulated operations that she wanted in. She approached Chicago's O'Hare International airport, and once again well-planned aggressiveness paid off. She was told that under the existing contract all concessions in any field were restricted to one company. Ice cream was spoken for at O'Hare. Invoking the Freedom of Information Act, Jolyn requested a copy of the contract. She read it carefully. Interestingly, ice cream and popcorn were specifically exempt. Jolyn wasn't asking for something that was technically restricted, just something that had been assumed restricted by other ice cream companies who were reluctant to push beyond initial resistance, obtain the contract, read it, and question it. Baldwin became the first minority-owned concessionaire to gain access to O'Hare. Today it maintains three thriving concessions there, to the wonderment of several local ice cream manufacturers.

An Ugly Trait

Although a positive mental attitude—and sometimes ambition—are considered admirable, aggressiveness is often considered an ugly trait. Jolyn got what she wanted from the bank presidents and from O'Hare. After the fact her aggressiveness was applauded. It had worked. It had enabled her company to expand. Baldwin, the bank Jolyn chose, and O'Hare all gained. No one lost. However, had Jolyn been unsuccessful in her approach to the banks and O'Hare, she might well have been criticized. "The woman was pushy." "Her demands annoyed people." Such is the story of aggressiveness. It is an unheralded characteristic. It offends. It angers—unless it works, at which point it's called chutzpah, guts, spunk.

Jolyn makes no apologies for her aggressive posture. She believes that women, particularly minority women, must be forceful in order to succeed. Like many who create ladybucks, she sees herself as a survivor. Aggressiveness is neither admirable nor ugly but is necessary at times—at times when it can make the difference between sinking and soaring. Those who know Jolyn well consider her warm, generous, and giving. Many women who've made it on their own are warm, generous, and giving—beneath their brash exteriors. Aggressiveness is a quality cultivated to counter potential oppression.

Muriel Siebert, fifty-three, the first woman member of the New York Stock Exchange, the first female superintendent of banks, and a multimillionaire for many years now, was not born brash. She was born a midwestern Goldilocks, daughter of a dentist, and was taught niceness, hopefulness, and civility. She arrived in New York in 1954 with five hundred dollars, a can-do attitude, and the ambition to succeed in the financial world. The financial world wasn't waiting for her or any woman. She learned early on that men earned more than women and were treated better. She developed a steely independence that "I would not have had to develop if I had not been a woman." With it came a hard, businesslike exterior, a don't-mess-with-me manner, and an ease with profanity. Muriel talks not of recognizing opportunity or of maximizing it in textbook terms but rather of "grabbing it." She claims no particular strategy for success. "I tumbled along," she says. "I saw this, and I grabbed it. I saw that, and I grabbed it."

Muriel's grab approach to success worked. She "tumbled" from a sixty-five-dollar-a-week research analyst position in 1954 to a partnership at Stearns & Co. in 1960 to a $445,000 seat on the New York Stock Exchange in 1967. She grabbed opportunities others wouldn't touch—and in doing so grabbed the headlines and revolutionized the brokerage business. After a federal ruling ended fixed commissions on brokerage trades, Muriel defied Wall Street tradition, slashed fees, became one of the first discount brokers, and redefined the world of finance and her place in it. Many hated her; many feared her and considered her a rabid feminist, a brawling broad.

The years have not softened her aggressiveness but have exposed the soft heart that beats behind it. Muriel gives generously of self and fortune to individuals interested in entrepreneurship and other pursuits she favors. Though there were no female mentors when she came to Wall Street, Muriel acts as such to many younger women starting their own enterprise. She sponsors women in the arts, foots tuition bills for people of potential, and shares her experiences and knowhow with women's groups around America. Her aggressiveness, only slightly tempered by recognition and riches, encourages women to put punch in their personalities, to tread without timidity to get the gold seldom rewarded to the refined.

Aggressiveness vs. Assertiveness

Aggressiveness is a punch above assertiveness. It is more offensive. It is often more effective, too. Meredith, a forty-eight-year-old corporate executive with an excellent twenty-four-year employment record at a major corporation, was called into her boss's office one day and told she was "being terminated as of tomorrow." "I felt as though I'd been socked in the stomach," she says. "I thought I was being called in for congratulations. . . . I had recently developed a profitable marketing plan for one of our clients." Dazed and incredulous, Meredith returned to her office "to recover." An hour later, she drafted a letter to the vice president in charge of personnel outlining her years of service, contributions to the company, awards received, promotions earned, salary increases, and her unexpected and unexplained dismissal.

"It was an assertive letter," says Meredith. "I made it clear that I felt violated as an individual and an employee. I had been loyal to the company; the company had been disloyal to me." The vice president telephoned Meredith. He'd "reviewed" her letter. She "should not have been terminated with only a day's notice"; she "would be given three weeks to leave." No explanation was offered for the sudden firing. Meredith stepped up her assertiveness, requesting a face-to-face meeting with the vice president. "He met with me and talked about division reshuffling, the company's need to cut expenses, decreased sales . . . even the drop in the price of oil. The truth was, I was getting too old and expensive to keep, especially since I was two months away from being eligible for benefits given after twenty-five years of service."

Still hopeful of reversing her firing, Meredith put the truth on the table. The vice president looked at his watch, told her he was late for a meeting, stood up, and escorted her to the door. "So much for assertiveness," says Meredith. "I'd always recoiled from aggressive women, believing more could be accomplished by being firm and soft-spoken. It took this to make me forceful and outspoken."

Meredith took legal action, charging the corporation with age discrimination. The corporation talked around the charge in court, saying they'd offered Meredith "the opportunity to resign," and had given her six months' severance pay and promised excellent recommendations. Meredith spoke up "more pugnaciously than I'd ever believed myself capable of." She'd done her homework, and uncovered cases of similar company dismissals. She named guilty parties and discussed in detail how, once learning of her lawsuit, corporate officers tried to "bribe me with chickenshit offers" and "threaten that I'd never be hired by any corporation if I continued to pursue the issue." She spoke loudly, clearly, and boldly, undermining the claims of the polished corporate defenders with accurate, incisive, focused attacks. She won her lawsuit, the admiration of former colleagues, and, most significantly, the plaudits of many of the corporation's clients.

Meredith would turn these plaudits to profit. The money awarded in the lawsuit financed her own public relations and marketing firm. Now, experienced in the art of aggressiveness, she began to build her company partly by pursuing the corporations' clients, particularly those who had cheered her victory, whom she had brought in, whom she had worked with. She networked, established personal relationships with former business contacts, "goodmouthed" her interest in small firms, and indirectly badmouthed the corporation's neglect of lesser accounts in favor of the biggies. A master at marketing and special events planning, she bid on and won away projects that would have gone to her former employer. As an independent, she could "comfortably underbid, offer guarantees of exclusivity, turn on a dime, provide incentives a large company can't compete with." Today, after five years on her own, Meredith earns almost double her corporate pay and is happily self-employed. Her bitterness is modified by her success; but, she reflects, "yes, I turned adversity to advantage, but I had to turn myself into a different person, someone I don't always like."

Aggressive and Self-Like

Meredith echoes the sentiment of many ladybucks ladies pushed into aggressive behavior. The aggressiveness is reaction more than action—reaction to iniquities, inequities, people, and situations that would cause underemployment and unemployment and thwart ambition. In their rise to riches, many career climbers and entrepreneurial hopefuls find themselves adopting brash mannerisms, practices, and patterns. Often the higher they rise, the less they like the self they see emerging. "I heard myself on a tape recorder, and I ashened," says a high-salaried New York sportswear designer. "My son was playing a joke on Mommy. He tape-recorded me talking on the telephone. I sounded like a brassy bitch; it wasn't me!" It wasn't the "me" she once was but the person she had had to become to deal with slick manufacturers, temperamental customers, off-price retailers, ad agencies, and salespeople, "all the leaners and leeches whose income and status depend on a designer's imagination and risk-taking, who have the loyalty of snakes and the ethics of pimps."

What's a woman to do if she's self-assured and ambitious but can't act aggressively, no matter how trampled on, no matter how clear the call for immediate, forceful behavior? "Hire people to act aggressive for you," says the sportswear designer. "Agents, reps, union leaders, partners with big mouths—you see it all the time on Seventh Avenue." She's correct. Intermediaries with "big mouths" are used often and not just on Seventh Avenue. All over America, wherever ladybucks are earned, there are female moneymakers who don't want to act aggressively, who believe that aggressivenes is a hideous trait in women, who can't be aggressive even if they want to. Regardless of how critical the end, the words won't come out, the tone is wrong, the acts don't work. Respondents who should be moved or intimidated are unaffected or amused. Bully power is thus summoned forth. Aggressiveness isn't abandoned as a moneymaking trait, but like a tedious management chore, it's delegated to someone more capable and comfortable with it. The "bully" enjoys his or her role, customers respond better to the bully, and the female moneymaker is spared.

Unlike positive mental attitude or ambition, aggressiveness is a trait that is possible to delegate. It's important in the four A's formula, but it's not essential that it be included in the moneymaker's trait pool. A surrogate can jump in with the fists, foul words, forcefulness—the muscle that can move mountains and make millions. However, the woman who is aggression-capable and comfortable, who knows when to exhibit it and how to focus it, is in a superior position. Not dependent upon the words and ways of a surrogate, she controls who is approached and what is said, demanded, negotiated, and threatened.

Most ladybucks earners don't completely delegate aggressive behavior. Like the sportswear designer, they don't like the hard shell they find forming around themselves, but they see it as part and price of the success formula. Aggressiveness, they believe, is something others can help with but not a trait to be assigned away to a deputy. Those most comfortable—and effective—with aggressiveness learn it as children, as a defensive mechanism, an athletic skill, a taught maneuver. The woman who has to cultivate it as an adult is at a disadvantage. First she must unlearn nonaggressiveness. This can be harder than unlearning a negative mental attitude. The individual working to reverse the latter sees herself acquiring a quality everyone loves. The woman trying to reverse nonaggressiveness knows she's pursuing a trait people not only don't love but often hate, particularly in women.

Aggressiveness and Street Smarts

The latecomer to aggressiveness often treats it like a concealed, protective weapon. Fearful of appearing arrogant or making enemies, she uses it sparingly and cautiously, when there is clear need. It is pulled out only when other avenues of approach or defense are closed. The early learner of aggressiveness uses it more freely and naturally. Lynette Spano Vives, president of Software Contol International (SCI), a three-year-old, multimillion-dollar distributor of microcomputer software and services to over four hundred corporate and government clients, is seldom gentle or understated. She never was. Never had the chance to be. She is a fast-talking, super sales executive who knows little about academics and everything about aggressiveness. Growing up in a tough Brooklyn neighborhood, she learned young about self-protection and shrewdness. Formally uneducated, she knows little about computers (her executive team is computer-savvy) and everything about getting what she wants. She views herself as brash and "colorful" but not arrogant or abusive. Her struggle for survival on big-city pavements made her street smart, strong, fearless, and sure of her capabilities.

On her path to prosperity, Lynette took a job as a salesperson for a New York software distributor. Displeased with her $150 weekly salary, she asked her manager to put her on commission. He refused. She went over his head to the president of the company and promised him she would increase sales by 20 percent if she were put on commission. The president gave her the go-ahead. Lynette hit the streets of New York, talking to anyone and everyone who might be in need of computer software. Within eighteen months she brought in $2.5 million in orders. Her annual income jumped to $52,000. In 1983, with two co-workers and the idea of a one-stop shop, she began her own software company. By offering advice and training, along with a full software line, she believed she could tap markets that her boss wasn't reaching. She tapped them, triumphed big, and worked up to a thirty-member staff and an annual salary of $100,000 to $200,000. Lynette's main ambition is to become independently wealthy. With an attitude of believing she can get anything she wants and the aggressiveness to get to those who can help her and to tear into untapped territories, it's likely she'll succeed.

ACTION

Action is the A that must always be present. Without it there are no ladybucks. Attitude without action is an untested blessing—can-do-it-ness without proof. Ambition without action is untested hope. Aggressiveness without action is untested guts—spunk without follow-through. Action is the cement that turns the A's into giant companies and six-figure salaries. Millions of women toy with ideas. They toy but don't try, or they don't try long enough for any project to pay off. There is no real action, no long-range follow-through. Like the three ladies at the parties, they talk and talk and talk about becoming rich but don't turn words into work, education, career steps, business plans, management teams, marketing schemes—or money. They talk about the cars they'll buy, the homes they'll decorate, the trips they'll take. Sometimes they attend seminars where they commiserate with others over the struggle to come up with good products or services to sell, or the capital to get started, or the difficulty of going it alone. They talk; they commiserate; they believe that one day they'll really act. But they seldom do. And in those instances where they work up the momentum to move themselves, they don't move themselves far enough.

Mary Ann makes exquisite porcelain dolls. She dreams of one day selling them to private collectors, specialty shops, and upscale department stores, affording herself a better workshop, helpers, and a quality kiln. She's taken three courses and read dozens of books and articles about turning a hobby into a business. She talks about signing and dating the heads, torsos, and limbs of her dolls so that future generations of collectors will be able to determine their authenticity. Mary Ann knows her work is excellent; she knows that somewhere out there there is a market for it. She's outspoken about the quality of her creations, and is quick to explain their superiority over similar porcelain dolls, to discuss an eye or a finger or to highlight the virtues of her production techniques. She's even exhibited her dolls at an exclusive juried crafts fair, where three sold for over three hundred dollars apiece.

Mary Ann is thirty-eight. Thus far, she's made $1,000 from her dolls, an amount she claims she could "make weekly if I really wanted to." Mary Ann *does* "really want to." She loves making dolls. She's fast, skilled, and happy to work ten hours a day at her craft. Why no ladybucks? Because Mary Ann is a committed hobbyist, not a committed moneymaker. She loves the act of creating dolls, but not the act of creating an ongoing business, requiring employees, salespeople, management teams, tax forms, market targeting, advertising, contracts, and bookkeeping. She is product-oriented, not business-oriented.

Mary Ann is an artist, not an entrepreneur. She wants the money her dolls could bring, but she won't act to create an enterprise that will get her dolls from her studio to shops and stores around America. Every now and then, she makes a small move, like exhibiting at a crafts fair or, more recently, talking up her work to a market rep with showrooms in Atlanta and Dallas. But she never follows through. There is no continual action to move her dolls into the commercial arena. Unlike Lynette Spano Vives, Mary Ann will not hit the pavement with her product day after day until she writes up thousands of orders. She cops out with "I have to be in my studio to make the dolls." Currently, there are over a thousand dolls decorating the shelves of her workshop, waiting for buyers she's not reaching—a fact she chooses to ignore.

The women who create ladybucks don't ignore crucial facts. They understand that passion for the product, no matter how exquisite, is just a tiny element in the elaborate process that produces fortunes. These women act not only to create quality products (often, as in Lynette's case, someone else creates them) but to create customers. Mary Kay Ash built one of America's most successful cosmetic corporations not because of her passion for her skin creams (which she did feel) but because she got millions of others to feel her passion and pay for her products. She went out and talked to groups of women about the virtues of her products. She sold them on her creams and on the money they could make by selling them to others. She fired her audiences up with energy, enthusiasm, and sales techniques. She devised awards incentives for top sales performances, formulated payment plans, and hired supervisors with sales records and hands-on experience with her product. She acted and acted and acted, primarily to create cash, not creams. Had she had dolls or doughnuts or computer software, she also would have created ladybucks. Her actions would have turned any reasonable product into profits.

Women of action frequently make fortunes selling very ordinary products and services. Lynette's one-stop shop computer stores are a useful product/service combination—but are only slightly related to Lynette's success. Her idea was tried before and after Lynette with unremarkable results. Lynette is successful because she combines attitude, ambition, and aggressiveness and brings them to life with *action*. Her offerings are good. She continually comes up with new products and services. But she outdistances her competition mainly because she is a constant doer, always going after new customers, government contracts, hardware firms, growing companies—markets that she either creates or takes from others. Each new sale motivates her to go after another and another.

THE "A" WAY

Attitude, ambition, aggressiveness, action—the raw materials of ladybucks, much more important than the "right" product or service. The three ladies at the party often talk about the difficulty of coming up with a good product or service or employment opportunity. Were one handed them, they would do nothing with it. Many technical geniuses and inventors of wonderful widgets are disillusioned to discover that venture capitalists back people, not products. Sure that the cleverness of their ideas or inventions will attract investors, they learn quickly that product or service accounts for less then 10 percent of a backer's investment decision—because an offering, no matter how innovative, seldom amounts to more than 10 percent of a company's potential to grow.

Moneylenders and employers look primarily for the four A's. Once it's established that they exist, the problem is to determine whether they exist in productive proportions. PMA (Positive Mental Attitude), but not conceit. Ambition, but not greed. Aggressiveness, but not arrogance. Action, but not wildness. One venture capitalist puts it in chemical terms: "Hydrogen and oxygen combined can produce water or an explosion, depending how much of each you mix in." One woman, certain investors would fall all over each other to lend her money, was surprised to learn that the four investors she approached all turned her down for the same reason. They admired her can-do spirit, ambition, and proven willingness to work hard. But they were dissuaded by her aggressiveness. It bordered too strongly on the arrogant, the offensive. They were afraid potential customers would recoil from her and thus they rejected her company.

There is one way—the "A" way—to turn ideas into income and dreams into dollars. Accomplishment can be motivated by dozens of things, ranging from fantasies to fear, but it is culminated by the four A's combining in correct proportions. It's a magic mix. There exists no precise "one part attitude, two parts ambition" formula. It's a fragile mix, ignited by luck, controlled by timing, and rewarded by ladybucks.

CHAPTER 4

The Three I's

Imagination, intelligence, and intuition are the fairy dust of ladybucks. Sprinkled on the four A's, they accelerate success. Careers are launched, businesses are born, fortunes flow, and industries grow. But large doses are unnecessary and often harmful: Too much imagination, too little reality. Too much intelligence, too little routine. Too much intuition, too little reason. Reality, routine, and reason are the necessary tedium of triumph. The three I's, sparingly sprinkled, are the catalysts of triumph—rare, fleeting, fragile endowments that modify the four A's to transform potential into profit.

When Louise Berenson began Purple Panache, she was bored with her office job, in love with the color purple, and unable to find attractive items in that color. That was enough to build a business around. She went to Faneuil Hall, headquarters of Boston's upscale Quincy Market (a tourist mall famous for turning ordinary street vendors into affluent pushcart peddlers) and convinced the market managers to rent her a pushcart on a two-week trial basis. That done, she went to craft cooperatives and found people willing to make her purple products in small quantities. So began what would mushroom into a rapidly expanding business. Louise, amply equipped with all the four A's, demonstrates what a dash of imagination, intelligence, and intuition can do. It took a bit of imagination to dream up the idea of peddling purple-only paraphernalia; some intelligence to use local craftspeople as independent contractors; and good intuition to know that thousands of individuals would share her passion for purple. Huge doses of these qualities weren't required. Such is the nature of the three I's—a small amount, added to the four A's, acts as a catalyst in ladybucks production.

IMAGINATION

Imagination, abundant in childhood, is attacked early on in the aging process. Its enemy is "common sense." A solid virtue, common sense helps one survive in the real world. It prevents injuries, illness, and death. The admonition "Where's your common sense?" is spoken daily in thousands of homes peopled with parents and children. "Where's your imagination?" is heard much less frequently—parents know it's there. It's part of young dreams and schemes—the dreaming and scheming often shelved by adolescence and abandoned by adulthood. A chubby little girl imagines herself a glamorous model. By adulthood, if the chubbly little girl sprouts into a chubby big girl, reality reigns. Fantasies of modeling are erased—unless the girl keeps her imagination active and, like Pat Swift of Plus Model Management in New York City, modifies the dictates of common sense to create a modeling agency to market herself and other big beauties. Because she refused to let common sense kill her fantasy, Pat turned largeness to ladybucks in modeling—a triumph of imagination over common sense.

Controlling Common Sense

Common sense is crucial in order to survive in the real world and to thrive in the financial world. However, it must work with imagination to prevent mental constipation and dream-death. If imagination says, "Why not start a purple-only business?" common sense should say, "It's a bit wacky; it's a limited market; try it, but move slowly—work from a pushcart; don't sign a storefront lease." If imagination says, "Why can't a plump person model; there are lots of plump clothing buyers around?" common sense should say, "It's chancy; people like seeing clothes on thin models; but the large-size clothing industry is growing; some women might prefer seeing offerings on women their own size; maybe some manufacturers and retailers can be convinced to try larger models." Common sense can be a positive, as well as a negative, in the genesis of ladybucks, as long as it qualifies, but doesn't cancel, a fantasy.

Helga, raised in a rigid, puritanical family, always wanted to be an artist. She dreamed of living in a cottage by a lake, painting all day and selling her pictures to people who would hang them on their walls. Helga confided her dreams to her parents and was told, "Artists can't support themselves; most people can't afford paintings; become a teacher and you can teach your pupils to paint." Helga obeyed. She taught school for thirty years. Her students loved her art lessons. The school and town benefited from numerous art programs and projects she initiated. She brought beauty and color to a community of laborers and small merchants. When Helga retired, her childhood dream was reborn. Her savings and pension enabled her to purchase a small lakeside home and spend her days painting. When she had accumulated a few dozen works, she hired a professional art photographer to make up a portfolio and visited art galleries and gift shops in tourist towns of the region where she was raised. They loved her work. It was a colorful, quaint slice of American life— a world Helga knew and portrayed well. She consigned several paintings to three different galleries. In her first year of exhibiting, forty were sold for a total of almost $25,000—twice what she'd earned in her last year as a schoolteacher—and interest in her work was spreading to other parts of the country.

Helga died recently, just before her second year as a freelance artist. At her funeral the preacher, who had known her all her life, eulogized her as a wonderful daughter, teacher, citizen, friend, and artist, and near the end of his eulogy, he said, "Helga always imagined living the life of an artist. She delayed her dream for thirty years. One can only guess how great her impact on the American art world would have been had she lived longer."

One wouldn't have had to guess had Helga not just lived longer but begun earlier. She put her dream on hold for thirty years. She imagined her life as a full-time artist. She imagined the scenes she would paint. She imagined her work hanging on patrons' walls. But she couldn't imagine modifying her parents' advice and trying out her dream while she was still a young woman. She was choked by common sense. She allowed it to cancel her fantasy for three decades. Whether she had an addiction to financial security, or a fear of poverty, or a reluctance to upset her parents, why didn't she at least compromise? Why didn't she try her hand as an artist during her annual two months' summer vacation?

Helga is like many women who "almost it" with ladybucks. They start too late, or don't start at all, or start and give up too easily. They are hardworking women who work hard for the wrong ends. They are common sense slaves, paralyzed into inaction, waiting for ideal conditions. When their imaginations begin to stir, they douse them, delaying a fantasy, killing it, not nurturing it properly. Instead of acting like Louise Berensen or Pat Swift and keeping common sense in its place, they permit it to wash away their imaginings.

Ideas

Ladybuck earners don't have to struggle to keep common sense in its place. They know how to control it when it endangers their imagination. Their dreams don't die easily. They don't wait for ideal conditions. If anything, they have to struggle to keep seductive ideas in their place, to control the temptation to move too quickly or too far from reality.

Ideas are the seeds of ladybucks. Fortunes sprout from a thought like "large can be lovely" or "purple can be profitable." Behind every female fortune is an idea that made it to the finish line. Also, behind every female failure is an idea that didn't work out. Often it is the same idea behind both fortune and failure, proving that ideas alone are nothing. Thousands of women permit common sense to crush good ideas out of existence, but today more and more women are testing out ideas—similar ideas. They'll come up with a thought such as Pat Swift's "large can be lovely" and go to market with it in one form or another. Largeness can be turned to ladybucks in modeling, counseling, food supplements, diet programs, exercise clubs, clothing shops—and they're going to try to do it. Usually the trying pays off for a few, but for most it leads nowhere near ladybucks—not in the obesity field or in any other.

The statistics are not encouraging. In the entrepreneurial world less than 20 percent of all business starts are still around after five years. In the corporate world, for every twenty middle-management positions there is only one senior management job available. In the professional world women are gaining entry and recognition but 35

percent less remuneration for their services than their male counterparts. However, there is very good news. Many more women than
ever before are starting their own businesses, making the corporate
climb, entering professions—and making it big.

Ideas alone have little to do with success and failure. An idea
dawns, a woman takes it and runs it into the winners' circle. Envious
onlookers wait for the dawning of a new idea, believing that when
it happens to them they'll run with it, too. Generally the women who
win do so because of the way they've run with their ideas, not because
of the ideas themselves. If Louise Berenson had had a passion for
the color aqua, not purple, she'd probably own a booming business
called Aqua Action instead of Purple Panache. Had Pat Swift decided
that old, rather than large, was marketable, she'd likely head a million-
dollar modeling agency representing grandmothers.

Ideas are necessary. Nothing happens without them. However,
their significance in the overall moneymaking process is exagger-
ated. One elderly Greek lady who built a popular three-million dollar
restaurant put it well when questioned about her success by a local
reporter. The young man asked where she got the idea for her
restaurant. The woman looked at him incredulously. "Idea? What
you talk about idea? A restaurant not idea; it's a business; you cook
good, you make money!"

Innovation

Innovation is the ingenuity of imagination. A good idea is a good
idea; but a good novel idea is better. Money is made by women like
the Greek restaurateur who sell ordinary but high-quality products
and services in a traditional manner to a ready market. However,
with scores of women now vying for the same slice of consumer
income or the same upscale career slots, all other things being equal,
innovation can provide a winning edge. Selling purple crafts is more
innovative than selling crafts in every color. Representing heavy models
is more innovative than representing thin models. In a competitive
marketplace a clever angle draws media attention, publicity, and
customers. Couple a clever angle with a clever marketing method,
such as running Purple Panache from a pushcart, and the gods
smile.

The gods don't smile for long, though, unless they're fed a steady diet of innovation. One clever idea or marketing method isn't enough. Currently, Louise Berenson is branching into mail order with a catchy purple catalog that will offer a growing assortment of purple goodies. Pat Swift has extended her modeling agency to represent petites and large-size men.

Barbara Macaire, whose prosperous San Francisco–based company, Skyline by Fabric Design, manufactures kites and banners, says, "In this business you don't think about innovation; it's understood; it's what accounts for the continual popularity of our products."

In a business, whether it is thought about or not, innovation is a vitamin shot. A new product or a new slant on an old one, a new service or a new way of offering an old one, a new advertising method, a new office look—novel ideas, closely watched, regulated, and judged, lead to increased profits. A good initial idea is maintained, enhanced, added to, kept current, and modified when necessary. Even companies and cultures that have placed a high premium on tradition are now looking at the marketplace with an innovative eye.

In Japan, where female executives are rare, Lady Systems Engineering (Lady SE) is run by a woman, for women professionals. The Tokyo-based software engineering company provides Japanese women with part-time consulting work that is difficult to find in Japan's male-oriented society. The company's female programmers work in some of Japan's largest companies, including Fujitsu, Toshiba, and Timeshare, bringing Lady SE over half a million dollars in sales in 1985, its first year of operation. The company expects to experience 50 percent growth in 1986, says Kazuko Yamada, founder of the all-woman temp firm. Kazuko, who studied economics at Japan's prestigious Keio University, taught flower design before founding Lady SE under the corporate umbrella of the $34 million Japan Systems Engineering conglomerate. Now the managing director and president of Lady SE, Kazuko says she formed the company because she and Japan Systems Engineering were convinced that the marketplace needed it. Women were interested in career opportunities, and Japan's software industry was coming of age—intrapreneurship and innovation, Japanese style.

Sometimes innovation is offbeat, amusing, witty, timely, or controversial. Purple-only products, hefty models, trendy kites, a Japanese flower arranger turned intrapreneur to provide employment to female programmers in a male-dominated culture. But frequently it's cleverness without color, too—a new employee profit-sharing plan, a new mailing method, a new telephone number or answering service—innovation without dazzle. One woman, a high school chemistry teacher, devised a skin blusher with rejuvenating qualities. She marketed it via direct mail with excellent results. As her business grew, she invented and offered new preparations and developed a loyal and large mail-order following. Her annual gross sales were over half a million dollars and multiplying, but then she noticed a decrease in profits. Cost analysis indicated that one of the culprits was the postal service. Mailing costs had risen sharply. To keep her sideline business prospering, the chemistry teacher determined that she had to find a cheaper way to mail her preparations. The cardboard containers she was using were not only costly but weighty. A bagging firm manufactured a solution: padded cosmetic bags in three different sizes instead of the standard cardboard boxes stuffed with Styrofoam that she'd been using. Her mailing costs fell; her net profits rose.

Changing a telephone number from 942-7841 to 942-8833 is not a wow!-producing bit of innovation; however, a financial consultant who so simplified her phone number found that by doing so she got 20 percent more calls and consequently new clients that she otherwise wouldn't have. Customers like easy-to-remember, easy-to-dial phone numbers, and 8833 is less demanding than 7841. Similarly, switching from a telephone answering machine to a live answering service is not likely to impress a business analyst as a piece of notable innovation, but one three-hundred-dollar-an-hour commercial photographer insisted, when queried about her success, that her business began to mushroom when she "got rid of that damned answering machine that everyone hates." The photographer didn't feed the jaded business analyst the dramatic innovation he'd hoped for—perhaps the use of a new lens or a new developing technique—but a meat-and-potatoes kind of ingenuity that also leads to increased sales.

Visualization

Visualization is the "fast forward" of imagination. A mind whirls into the future and envisions what will be. Among the most beautiful words in English poetry are Tennyson's: "For I dipt into the future, far as human eye could see, / Saw the Vision of the world, and all the wonder that would be; / Saw the heavens fill with commerce, argosies of magic sails, / Pilots of the purple twilight, dropping down with costly bales; / . . . Till the war-drum throbb'd no longer, and the battle-flags were furl'd; / In the Parliament of man, the Federation of the world."* These words were published in 1842, long before the invention of the airplane or the establishment of the United Nations, but Tennyson saw it all happening. He saw mental pictures of what would happen at another time—in this case, in a future century.

The women who earn ladybucks also "dip into the future," but not as "far as human eye could see." They visualize days, weeks, months, years into the future, but not, like Tennyson, a century. They see mental pictures of themselves pitching products to potential customers, reviewing progress reports with employers, inspiring workers, talking to the press, enjoying corporate clout. They close their eyes and see themselves partaking in activities that will bring them closer to their goals. They are poets of imminent profit, not distant progress.

Sometimes they even preach what they practice—for pay. Kay Porter and Judy Foster, founders of Porter Foster, a thriving consulting firm that conducts a comprehensive program, "Mental Training For Peak Performance," are the personal and professional embodiments of the power of creative visualization. Both successful runners and sports psychologists, they met at an athletic event, agreed that their victories were related to their abilities to visualize themselves in the process of winning specific events, and teamed up to spread the word. The same visualization techniques that enhanced their athletic performances enriched their business success. Today, after less than three years in business, the pair run clinics, workshops, and seminars all over America. Prominent individual athletes and athletic teams swear they owe their victories to Porter

---

*From "Locksley Hall" by Alfred, Lord Tennyson.

Foster's training programs. So strong is their support from the American athletic community—providing training to the Olympic Scientific Congress, the Women's Olympic Marathon Trials, the National TAC Master's Track and Field Championships, and dozens of other top athletic organizations—that the women have no time or need to try to expand beyond their golden market.

Today dozens of hopefuls in every area from sports to sex flock to seminars, workshops, and clinics to learn how to visualize their way to success. They spend millions annually on books and videocassettes that purport to teach the "see your dream; be your dream" philosophy. For many, it's all one "impossible dream" that never comes true. But an amazing number of ladybucks earners credit their persistence not to natural visualization abilities but to taught visualization skills. "It's too bad we have to be taught how to imagine," says a $200,000-a-year banking executive who worked her way through college, business school, and the corporate maze to a position of executive power, "but by the time you get anywhere near where you want to be, you're lucky you can see what is, let alone what could be."

INTELLIGENCE

Intelligence is overrated in ladybucks production. The smartest women do not make the most money any more than they make the happiest children, or the best marriages, or the most fulfilling lives for themselves. Nor do the most-educated women make the most money. Today most ladybucks earners are women who have earned bachelor's degrees, followed by those who have incomplete college educations. Professionals are the most formally educated of the ladybucks earners, followed by corporate MBA's. Entrepreneurial women are the least formally educated, eager to explore their ideas in the real, more than in the academic, world. They are also the biggest moneymakers. These women value hands-on experience more than textbook theories. Many of the older ones did not attend college at all. Like Mary Kay and Lillian Vernon, they learned by trial and error and made fortunes without having professors show them how to write business plans, or raise venture capital, or maintain cash flow. For them, a college education was not affordable or, like today, something that many women have. When they were young, when college was attended, it was for teaching or nursing training.

Today some younger entrepreneurial queens also have made it without college degrees. Debbi Fields didn't need a sheepskin to create a multimillion-dollar cookie empire. Roberta Williams, head of the $10 million Sierra On-Line software company, devised space-age fantasy games that thrill a generation of children without ever setting foot into a four-year institution. Anne Sadovsky didn't need college to build a million-dollar seminar business that has taught thousands of college graduates how to succeed in sales, business, and life. However, most entrepreneurial ladybucks earners today are college graduates. They acquired their degrees for reasons ranging from "I didn't know what else to do with myself at the time" to "I felt there was so much I wanted to learn." Whatever their reason, whatever they got out of college, most believe that college enhanced them as individuals. To that extent education influenced their subsequent success. But the real nuts and bolts of moneymaking can't be learned in a classroom. The intelligence that relates to moneymaking is a particular kind of intelligence. It is street smarts; it is the ability to size up people; it is the ability to influence and impress customers and clients. Even in the professional world, where advanced degrees are mandatory, the biggest moneymakers are not the women with the highest IQ's or those who hold degrees from the most prestigious universities; they are the women who are "people smart."

Judgment

Knowledge of one's field is important. Customers don't want inferior products or services. But except in the most highly technical fields, one need not be brilliant to offer quality. Sound judgment is much more consequential. Jill Yolen, president of Modern Tobacco, a multimillion-dollar tobacco distributor, speaks for many corporate leaders when she says, "The real winners in business are not the superbrains, or even the individuals who do the most things right, but the managers and supervisors who make the least mistakes in dealing with customers and everyday problems." A company, a career, or a professional practice profits to the degree that the woman in charge exerts good judgment in handling employees, employers, customers, clients, snafus, and the complaints that inevitably arise. The occasional bold strokes of genius make headlines, but it is always the behind-the-headlines judgments that turn genius to income. Judgment is intelligence tempered by practicality: Will this work? Will the employees be satisfied? Will the customers be pleased?

One woman who built a successful chain of beauty salons was distressed to learn that her company's profits had begun declining soon after she'd relinquished management control to her daughter. The daughter had been thoroughly trained in every technical aspect of the business. She knew a lot about maintaining equipment, ordering supplies, and keeping records. But she knew little about dealing with employees and customers. A bright, well-intentioned young woman, her sins were more of omission than of commission. She was aloof to the employees and customers with whom her mother had established warm relationships. She neglected the touches of caring and courtesy that came naturally to her mother, believing that fairness, good prices, and quality service were sufficient. They were important, but not sufficient. Employees who had worked beyond the call of their jobs to please her mother stopped doing so. Customers who'd been loyal to her mother began trying other beauty shops. The daughter had a formal education that her mother hadn't had the opportunity to acquire. She had a business waiting for her when she completed graduate school. She was far more sophisticated than her mother in her understanding of the world of finance. But she lacked her mother's good judgment in dealing with people, and it was reflected in the company's earnings.

Doesn't even the simplest soul know that employees work harder and better when given an extra touch of kindness from their employers, or that customers enjoy special treatment? Yes. And the simplest souls usually do. They exert the best judgment in dealing with employees and customers. Women like Mary Kay Ash, Lillian Vernon, and Debbi Fields who are not padded with layers of formal business training are liked by their employees and customers. Ironically, women who spend long years and large sums in advanced business programs sometimes have the most difficulty dealing with employees and customers. In a sense they're too bright. They've studied everything about employee motivation and management, maintaining good customer relations, offering incentive plans. They know what to do, but too often they get caught up in large issues and suspend judgment in dealing on "little levels," or they delegate judgment authority unwisely.

Generally the largest ladybucks are earned by women who exert good judgment on all levels. Some cynical business analysts poke fun at Debbi Fields for her insistence that her extraordinary success is closely related to her stress on employee and customer "feel good" feelings as part of company policy. They look for more commercial explanations—shop locations, distribution procedures, financing from Mrs. Fields's husband. One competitor calls her an "airhead," claiming she couldn't have built the business without her husband. The fact that she promotes a "feel good" response in people and deems this significant is totally undervalued.

In addition to good "people judgment," sound product and marketing judgment leads to ladybucks. Debbi Fields offers several customer-tested, popular varieties of her warm cookies. Customers are not limited to chocolate chip cookies, or even to any one kind of chocolate chip. Also, her offerings are sold through company stores rather than franchises, which she believes would decrease her company's earnings. Similarly, Lillian Vernon's $110 million mail-order business flourishes because Lillian displays good judgment in selecting her catalog offerings, adding new delights to proven favorites and eliminating goods that prove lacking in customer appeal. Recently she added retail outlets to her mail-order company, believing this marketing move will maximize profits.

In the getting and keeping of ladybucks, decisions must be made daily. Often they are tiny decisions of seeming insignificance. Collectively they become critical. The woman who displays wise judgment in her handling of small issues sets in motion a "success chain." An employee is appeased; a customer is indulged; a community is consulted. Together such isolated acts create positive, productive energy. Conversely, a single unwise judgment can generate negative energy.

Joann Crawford, owner and manager of Tigerlilies, a popular million-dollar restaurant in Boston's elite Beacon Hill section, remembers back a few years when she and her restaurant were very unpopular. Like many women who display unwise judgment on the managerial level, her sins were of omission more than commission. She neglected to confer with prospective neighbors before beginning her business. The site she had chosen for Tigerlilies was in an historic district. Joann misjudged community response to her plan. Many would-be neighbors didn't want a commercial enterprise in their midst. Technically, Joann was within her rights. Though zoning had recently been changed to permit only residential structures, a grandfather clause in her lease permitted her to open her restaurant, since one had previously existed on the site. The neighbors didn't care. They were determined to prevent Tigerlilies from opening. They fought Joann every step of the way.

Anger escalated into legal warfare. The fights were expensive. Joann paid $10,000 for a beer and wine license that usually costs $800; most of the $10,000 went for lawyers' fees. In addition to the financial loss, Joann was emotionally spent. The negative energy between herself and the Beacon Hill community was costly and could have been defused had she acted at the outset of her project rather than reacted after it became a major community issue. Joann knows this in hindsight and has subsequently proceeded very cautiously to create an accepted, charming, quality establishment. It now grosses twenty times as much as the average woman-owned restaurant. But hindsight is expensive. Good judgment demands foresight—a commodity that seldom comes early in the moneymaking process.

Memory

Disgruntled students often complain that test scores reflect little more than the ability to memorize facts and details. Examinations test memory, not intelligence, they say, failing to acknowledge that memory is a big part of intelligence. It is a very big part, and it has its place in the commercial world as well as in academia.

People are surprised to learn of the large number of dyslectics and dysgraphics who succeed splendidly in the corporate and entrepreneurial worlds, despite extreme difficulty in reading and writing. Though dyslexia and dysgraphia are not conditions to be envied, these problems frequently prompt those afflicted to develop excellent memories early on so that they don't have to read or write more than necessary. They become walking encyclopedias of information, impressing teachers, employers, colleagues, and customers with their ability to quickly call forth names, numbers, dates, places, and facts that their colleagues must commit to paper. One such woman, Kathy Kolbe, president and owner of Resources for the Gifted, the world's largest publisher of educational materials for gifted children, is dyslexic from birth; she says, "When it was my turn to read a sentence in school, I had already memorized the sentence to fool the teacher. I couldn't learn to tie my shoes by watching someone else doing it. I had to break the task down into increments and memorize the increments."

The less a moneymaker relies on printed information, notes, and lists, and the less her need for repeated research of the same facts, the freer she is, the more commanding her presence. Many things can't—and shouldn't—be entrusted solely to memory, but there is a destructive tendency to brain-drain the minute a fact is put to paper—a tendency that weakens power and profits. One corporate vice president likes to claim, "My whole life is on lists and pieces of paper. I never clutter my mind with trivia." But ten minutes with this woman, and you know that the "trivia" may be on lists and that paper notes may be used as back-ups, but that a lot of important information is also in her head. On the tip of her tongue are dozens of facts about major company transactions, who's dealing with whom, who's reporting to whom, who said what at the last executive meeting, what's selling, what's not, what industry analysts predict. Her memory intimidates and impresses. She uses it to put adversaries in their place and to assist allies.

Many ladybucks earners work their way to riches by becoming masters of the podium, speechmakers, supersaleswomen. Required here are public speaking skills, based to a significant extent on memory. Though these women often repeat the same information, arguments, and anecdotes and have learned to anticipate and answer specific questions, they also continually absorb and incorporate new facts.

"It's brain overload sometimes," says Jessica, a twenty-six-year-old export executive who recently climbed her way out of middle management, much to the surprise and envy of dozens of co-workers. "Everyone talks about how young I am. I don't think my mind could handle it all if I were too much older. The company sends me on presentations all over the world. In addition to remembering ten different sales approaches, I must remember dozens of customs of different countries, names and terms I can barely pronounce, all sorts of currency and metric conversions."

Jessica credits her rapid career climb to exceptional memory. She impressed her bosses and customers as being on top of everything going on in several different countries. "Memory is a great advantage in business, particularly in a business where you're always dealing with people; however, there's a stress factor here," she says. "You begin to feel you have to remember everything, and that's tension-producing. You can't remember everything; you have to let go; and you hope you let the right things go and hold the crucial information in your head."

The memory stress Jessica alludes to is commonplace. Today information is not just the top-selling product/service in the United States, it is also a premium sales tool. Consumers make purchases based on information presented to them by sellers—entrepreneurs, executives, and professionals. Money is made in the marketplace, not in the factory. The woman whose memory dazzles prospects with its richness of pertinent data is fortunate. Prospects are impressed into reaching for their checkbooks. However, there is a downside to dazzle: strain. Strain leads to fatigue. "You can get stressed out trying to remember too much," says Jessica. "You've got to prioritize what you remember. I hate the word because it sounds phony; but that's what you have to do."

Prioritizing what's kept in memory and what's discarded or relinquished to paper is essential. "I know currency exchange rates, freight forwarding fees, customs regulations—that's in my head," says Jessica. "But I don't know what I'm going to buy when I walk into the supermarket—that's on a slip of paper in my pocketbook." Jessica doesn't bother trying to remember the groceries she needs. It's a waste of memory space. Alone in the supermarket, with no one to impress, she reaches for her list and fills her cart. But in meetings and face-to-face contact with clients, where time, speed, and fluency with facts are highly valued, she reaches into her memory, not her pocketbook.

A prosperous fashion designer with a terrible memory says, "Everyone teases me that I have five appendages—two arms, two legs, and a telephone. I almost always do business and give interviews by phone, because I can use notes with no one knowing. My memory is awful, but few people realize it because I'm great with pieces of paper. Over the phone I sound sharp as a tack. I don't sound as though I'm reading much of what I say. I sound like it's all in my head, but alas, it's not."

Conceptual Understanding

The above fashion designer manages to work around a poor memory. Though poor recall puts any career climber at a serious disadvantage, it can be worked around in some fields and by certain individuals. This is not so for conceptual understanding. All ladybucks earners possess this component of intelligence. Conceptual understanding is critical thinking, a capacity to figure out how things work, to solve problems, and to see relationships. When students complain that test scores reflect little more than the ability to memorize facts and details, they are in effect saying that they don't want to be tested on rote learning but on conceptual understanding.

Conceptual understanding is the *haute monde* of intelligence—the stuff of gifted children, of geniuses, and of ladybucks earners (who are often neither gifted nor geniuses but who always have enough conceptual understanding to see the connection between ideas and income). Kathy Kolbe considers her dyslexia "one of the greatest advantages I have" because "it helped me become a student of the thinking process before I was even in kindergarten." Kathy was forced to devise unconventional methods of dealing with information. Though she believes "rote learning is important because it forms our intellectul data base," she feels it is too much emphasized in schools. "Our children should be learning not only how to memorize facts but also how to solve problems, how to recognize trends."

Because Kathy had to teach herself this, and because she had two very bright children with learning deficiencies who weren't being sufficiently challenged by the teaching techniques of their local school system, she rebelled against conventional approaches to learning. She began her successful summer school, developed Resources for the Gifted publishing company and soon after, other prosperous companies also built around the theme of conceptual understanding.

Kathy learned as a child how conceptual thinking works. She embraced it as a survival skill because conventional avenues of learning were closed to her. Most females drift more casually into creative and critical thought processes. Unlike Kathy, they're not thrust into them so as to appear normal in intelligence. However, the women who reap ladybucks often were the children who early on favored problem solving over rote learning. They mastered rote and routine assignments when they had to and reached beyond for bigger challenges. Though not then thinking about turning ideas into income, they were eager to turn their ideas to projects, experiments, games, or lemonade stands. They were active, rather than passive, information handlers. They wanted to make things happen, change things, and create things that never existed before. They didn't necessarily struggle to turn agony into accomplishment like Kathy Kolbe, but they sought problem-solving situations that demanded clever solutions.

Dr. Paula Moynahan, now a high-earning plastic surgeon, remembers well "always wanting to fix things, improve things, make things with my hands." Street-educated Lynette Spano Vives, founder of SCI, the $8.5 million computer software firm, recalls building a shoeshine business at nine years old. Carol Jenna, owner of the $5 million sports marketing agency, tells how as a child she "drew a connection between real money and play money, loved playing Monopoly, thinking up ways to beat my sister." Mary Kay Ash proudly recounts how as a seven-year-old she figured out how to use her local public transportation system so she could do the family shopping while her mother worked to support the family during her father's illness. As youngsters, these women all enjoyed challenges, thought in terms of cause and effect, and exercised the thought processes that would later turn their work to wealth.

INTUITION

Intuition is a plane beyond the bounds of calculated, conscious intelligence. Unconscious judgment, memory, and conceptual understanding combine to tell an inventor, "This deal will spawn an industry," to tell an executive, "Your secretary is an embezzler," to tell a professional, "This procedure will fail." Intuition is a disembodied alogical voice that knows because it knows.

When Joan Barnes first decided to sell franchises for Gymboree, logic told her to advertise for buyers. Something else told her not to, that the best people to purchase Gymboree franchises wouldn't come from advertisements. She followed the "something else" and realized that the best Gymboree owners weren't looking to buy businesses. They were individuals who couldn't be reached through a conventional approach. The "something else" that guided Joan's decision was intuition. It led her to understand that to succeed, her program needed motivated mothers like herself. Such women weren't reading ads for franchises. They were individuals like the mothers of the toddlers taking Gymboree classes—women who would slowly discover that they'd like to own a business built around parenting, socialization, and exercise. Joan "knew" these were the people who should run her franchise. She "felt" it. Later on, she could use commercial means to reach potential buyers; but to begin her franchise program that way would be a mistake.

Joan's intuition was right. After she opened her first few centers, inquiries began coming in from her Gymboree babies' moms who were excited about the program and wanted to duplicate it in other locations. Though they saw it as a moneymaking opportunity, they were committed more to the idea of toddler body-building than to the income it would bring. Consequently, true devotees got in at the start of the franchise expansion, positive publicity was engendered, and Gymboree, after ten years, is a firmly established multimillion-dollar kiddie-lifestyle regimen.

The Fermentation Factor

Intuitive solutions to problems seem to arrive all at once, quickly, out of the blue. Unlike calculated solutions deduced over a period of time, they appear as "orphan knowledge," springing from unknown sources. However, appearance deceives. Intuition, which seems to come from nowhere, actually comes from a fermentation process that is days, weeks, or years long. Joan Barnes's intuition didn't tell her the right way to expand Mary Kay Ash's cosmetics business. It told her the right way to market her kiddie gym because years of subconscious assimilation, based on actual experience working with toddlers and their parents, came first. Joan lived, breathed, and obsessed over Gymboree for four years before she knew "suddenly" that she shouldn't advertise for franchisees.

The fermentation factor may detract from the magic and mystery of intuition, but it should put to rest some of the mistrust. Ladybucks earners who make decisions based on intuition don't tread on unfamiliar turf. Just as Joan Barnes didn't dream her schemes from nowhere, Louise Berenson's Purple Panache idea didn't come out of the blue. Actually, it came out of the purple—the purple products she'd spent a lifetime looking for, examining, and wanting; out of a long-time acquaintance with how purple lovers think; out of a passion for the color purple that she consciously indulged on a personal level long before intuition told her she could turn purple into gold. Similarly, Kathy Kolbe's intuition told her she could make money marketing creative learning aids after she'd spent years and years developing successful learning techniques for her private use. Resources for the Gifted was the commercial outgrowth of a lifetime of conscious and unconscious personal experience and problem solving in the educational arena.

Ladybucks are the commercial outgrowth of personal experience. A business or career that seems to surface out of nowhere is the end stage of a gradual tap deep into past places and times, pleasures and pains, victories and defeats. Sometimes the deep tap is direct—Kathy Kolbe's publishing company deriving from her intimate knowledge of dyslexia; Louise Berenson's Purple Panache arising from her long love affair with the color purple; Joan Barnes's Gymboree francise marketing plan the result of observations made during years of teaching toddlers and their mothers.

Sometimes the deep tap is indirect. Lynette Spano Vives's $8.5 million software company was not the result of years of tinkering with software. She knew nothing about software. But she knew a lot about selling. A street kid, she learned about salesmanship and survival at an early age. When presented with an opportunity to sell software for a New York software distributor, she turned a salaried job as an order-taker into commission work. Drawing from her experiences selling other products and services, she became a top software saleswoman and began her own software company. Had Lynette tried selling another useful product on a commission basis, chances are she also would have done well, as she would have tapped into the same wheeling-dealing background. Similarly, Anne Sadovsky's lucrative seminar business sprung from a love of public speaking and an ability to captivate an audience and motivate listeners. Anne didn't have seminar selling experience to draw on. But her enjoyment of and facility for public speaking enabled her to rise to a high-level marketing positon in the real estate field. The leap from real estate sales to seminar sales was logical. Both endeavors require the ability to excite customers into making decisions. When Anne launched her seminar business, she drew from a memory store of past performances.

The Flash

The fermentation factor gives credibility to intuition. However, when intuition hits, it comes as a flash of illumination that doesn't appear connected to past experiences. It's a flash that appears and reappears—a nagging flash. It's a gut instinct that feels as though it's coming not from a fermentation process but from a vague, inexplicable source. The first flash comes as a sudden strike. There is no warning; it can happen anywhere. When Edna Hennessee stepped into a Merle Norman Cosmetics shop, she saw her future immediately. After that, she envisioned herself working with cosmetic preparations, selling them, and developing new ones. Flashes of herself working in that field kept returning. Edna had suffered from acne for years. She had tried various "cures" and they didn't work. When she entered the Merle Norman shop, the fermentation process had long since begun. But the flashing was then to start. This is where she belonged—not in her parents' world of farming, not in another field, but in cosmetics.

Intuition is not a flaky flash based on an impulse or emotion. It is a type of knowledge that, unlike an impulse or emotion, does not fade or change but becomes stronger as time passes. However, it is not always correct knowledge. Women have lost as well as made money acting on intuition. One woman, Sadie, whose intuition led her to turn her love of chocolate into a lucrative chocolate factory trusted her intuition to lead her into an offshoot business—a dial-a-chocolate-cookie retail business. Sadie had a recurrent vision of a section of her chocolate factory converted into a cookie send-out service. She saw dozens of customers daily calling in orders for giant one-pound gift-wrapped chocolate cookies. "The whole idea came to me in a flash," says Sadie, "and it wouldn't go away. I saw my cookies as clever, all-occasion gifts." She was certain she'd hit upon a plan that would dramatically increase her company's profits. Her cookies would make ideal presents for birthday celebrants, office co-workers, thank-you's, and want-to-get-to-know-you's. Blissfully, she began her new venture based on gut instinct "and only a flimsy analysis of what it would take to make my plan work." She liked her idea. It was likable. It was cute, novel, and fun. The local press liked it and gave her some good local publicity. Her friends and family were enthusiastic. Employees were eager to put in a few hours daily at the cookie section of the factory. Everyone hopped on Sadie's hunch—except customers. In order for her plan to pay off, the cookies had to be priced at an amount above what the local market would bear. Sadie invested a few thousand dollars in an idea that fizzled quickly.

"I became unrealistically committed to a venture that delighted me," says Sadie, who stuck with her crumbling cookie business for a year. "Unlike when I began my chocolate factory, I failed to examine all the details. I felt so strongly that my instinct was right that the business had to work eventually." It didn't *have* to work—eventually or at all—and it didn't. Sadie had ignored several little clues that signaled potential failure. "Had I based my decision on cold logic as well as on instinct, I would have scrapped it after a month. By the time I could see and admit my mistake, a lot of time and money had been wasted."

There is a tendency to become unrealistically committed to an action based on intuition. Hunch players know this. If burned once, they tend, as Sadie now puts it, "to go with the no, not the yes"— to follow flashes that say stop instead of go; to respond to premonition more than intuition. "It's always safer to decide not to act than to act; and after your flash of illumination turns out to be a flash of misjudgment, you examine your intuition more carefully," says Sadie.

Hunch Safety

Sadie has temporarily "put the reins" on her intuition, but like most ladybucks earners she'll act on hunches—and not just premonitions—again. However, she'll be more inclined toward hunch safety, toward tempering intuition with reason, toward asking herself if her flashes are consistent with the facts on hand.

"I get hunches all the time," says Louise Berenson. "I try to look at new products in terms of old ones. If purple night shirts sell well, there's a good possibility that purple sweatshirts or running suits will too. But you never know for sure." This spunky purple maven, who twinkles while she talks, says, "You visit the [trade] shows, check what your competitors are offering, calculate profit margins, and pray."

Louise's prayers are answered not because she has a special line to heaven but because she avoids "analysis paralysis." She examines her hunches to make sure they confirm, and don't contradict, what experience has proven. If she likes what she sees, she feels her hunch is safe enough to proceed on. She trusts her intuition and acts. She doesn't analyze her hunch away and become paralyzed into inaction. "Unless you believe in your hunches, you never realize how much you've learned and how far you can go," says Louise. "However, there will be times you'll go with lemons; and what do you do? Make lemonade!"

Louise is a good lemonade maker. She knows that if a hunch doesn't work out, it doesn't necessarily have to be scrapped. There needn't be a financial loss. A product can be repackaged, repriced, resold, "re-anything that might keep it alive," says Louise. Sometimes nothing works, and she has to write off a hunch as a mistake. "I got some fabulously packaged purple worry stones that I was sure would take off like the pet rock"—she laughs—"but they died without a funeral." However, whether profitable or not, Louise's hunches aren't dangerous.

Louise, like many successful vendors of trendy items, follows her hunches in tiny numbers. She purchases small amounts of new offerings and monitors sales closely. When ladybucks stories are spun, there's much talk about the woman who knew in the pit of her stomach that she had a product the public was waiting for, packaged it, took it to market, and gave birth to a business. Generally, the woman didn't charge up Midas Mountain with thousands of way-out widgets. She saw the path to the top, saw the fall she might take, and moved slowly.

The stronger a hunch, the easier it is to disregard safety. A hunch generates a throbbing life of its own. Much humor is poked at women's intuition. Sayings such as "A woman's intuition is an instinct that helps her jump at once to the wrong conclusion" abound. However, in reality female intuition, cushioned with caution, is remarkably productive. Essayist G. K. Chesterton put it well when he said, "A woman uses her intelligence to find reasons to support her intuition." Such is the practice of ladybucks earners.

I IS FOR ICING

Imagination, intelligence, intuition—the fairy dust of ladybucks—are the three I's that ice the four A's (attitude, ambition, aggressiveness, and action). They are the sugar of success, the quick starts, the adrenaline that stimulates the four A's to transform ideas into industries, fantasies to fortunes, grit to gold.

Seven traits combine correctly in psyche, body, and soul, and a business booms, a career skyrockets. Proportions are unknown. How much imagination? How much ambition? How much intuition? How are traits measured? That is the mystery of moneymaking. Moneymaking is an art, not a science. However, the women who possess the four A's sprinkled with the three I's are the finalists in the ladybucks sweepstakes.

CHAPTER 5

Twenty Golden Methods

Ashley, an excellent computer programmer/entrepreneur, can't understand why at forty she's "still struggling when I should be rich." The woman possesses all four A's and all three I's—the seven traits that can turn longing to ladybucks. "What am I doing wrong?" she asks rhetorically. "Jerks are making fortunes in this field! I'm working hard, but it's not paying off!"

Ashley is working hard, but she's not working smart. The "jerks" who are making fortunes in her field have much less computer savvy than she but much more business savvy. Ashley asks what she's doing wrong, but she doesn't really want to know. She's not prepared to change. Though she possesses winning traits, she's not a winner.

Ashley has winning traits in a losing combination. This affects her operating methods so that she doesn't try techniques that will get her what she wants. Ashley is imaginative, intelligent, and intuitive— the three I's of ladybucks—but she's *too* intelligent. She's a theorist, annoyed by the routines required to capitalize on braininess. She recoils from activities such as self-marketing. "I'm not going to plot a media campaign and kiss ass with the press; my work speaks for itself," maintains Ashley. Her work doesn't speak loudly enough to earn her the wealth she's after, but she refuses to accept the connection between publicity and profits, let alone engage in promotional ventures. She's too bright to be bothered. Consequently, she's too bright to be rich.

Similarly, Ashley is blessed with the four A's of ladybucks—attitude, ambition, aggressiveness, and action—but in poor proportions.

She has too little ambition and productive action and too much aggressiveness. She wants to run a thriving programming/consulting firm, but she doesn't want it badly enough to try procedures that displease her. She's not driven by the fierce kind of ambition that would spur her to partake of moneymaking methods. Ashley is a person of action in that she works hard at her computer, and works hard to please the customers she has, but that's it. If she were an employee, that might be sufficient. But she aspires to entrepreneurial ladybucks while rejecting entrepreneurial methods and executive management style. When her accountant suggested she delegate certain tasks to subordinates, she snorted, "I can't; those jerks would screw everything up!" Everyone's a jerk to Ashley, who can't admit that she's "screwing up" herself. When her lawyer talked to her about bartering her services in order to increase her cash flow, she dismissed the idea as "too time consuming. I want to be paid in cash. I don't want to keep an inventory of who owes whom hours or products." Thus, she's neither keeping an inventory nor being paid in cash.

To top it off, Ashley is aggressive to the point of being unnecessarily offensive, even obnoxious. She's not spunky, courageous, or gutsy to a focused end, but nasty in her approach to people—nasty for no reason. Forceful to no purpose. "If I were a man, I'd have a lot less problems," insists Ashley, who has adopted masculine mannerisms that she believes enhance her presence but that have the opposite effect. She speaks, moves, gestures, and bullies like a blue-collar tycoon who commands an audience and demands and receives respect. But it doesn't work for her; she looks and sounds ridiculous. Employees wince. Potential customers back away. Women and men equally are unimpressed by her masculine toughness, her sweeping aggressiveness. "You really need a front man to make it in this business," she contends. "I've walked into places with tree stumps [her term for most men], and it's assumed they, not me, own the company! People address the tree stump and assume I work for him."

Because Ashley despises the fact that "tree stumps" often receive more respect than women in business, she uses a masculine demeanor to attract attention and customers. Her facts are not wrong. Men often do receive more respect than women. However, Ashley's method of dealing with this situation produces negative results. Ashley's methods—her lack of methods in general—account for her failure to reap ladybucks, despite the fact that she sells needed and superior programming and consulting services at reasonable prices.

Just as ladybucks earners possess certain traits in a winning combination, they use a combination of methods that turn work to wealth. Like Ashley, they work hard, but unlike her, they also work smart. They use specific techniques that boost all careers and businesses, plus income-producing techniques tailored to their particular fields of endeavor.

1. Hard Work

It's the dullest but truest of all the moneymaking methods. All hard workers don't reap ladybucks, but all ladybucks earners are hard workers. They put in the hours, tolerate the tedium, plug along, and persist. The world sees the glamour, the gold, the glory. They see the grit and the grief, the grueling days, weeks, and years it takes to get—and keep—the glamour, gold, and glory. But they don't see it as awful. They don't subscribe to the popular misconception that their work is their play; they know the difference between work and play. However, they prefer to devote most of their time to work, living out the James Barrie belief that "nothing is really work unless you would rather be doing something else." They wouldn't rather be doing something else.

"I work while I sleep," says Louise Berenson, "but I love what I'm doing."

Dr. Paula Moynahan beams as she talks about the joy she gets from her three horses, three cats, six dogs, and one goat. An animal lover who delights in the recreational hours she spends with her pets, she says, "I worked hard, faced a lot of discrimination leveled at women seeking to enter the medical profession, put in many learning years to get here, but now my life is a dream come true. I enjoy educating people about their appearance, helping them to look the way they want to look, teaching the benefits of skin care. I have all the blessings of success, but the greatest blessing, after the close relationship I share with my family, is that I truly love my work and hope my future is filled with more of what I'm doing now."

"I'm happiest when I'm motivating people to live out their dreams," says Anne Sadovsky. "I love teaching people how to succeed in sales, business, life—everything."

"There's a lot of detail work, a lot of long-distance relationships that have to be maintained; regulations; legalities; but it's worth it," says Annie Hurlbut, whose million-dollar mail-order business keeps her traveling regularly between her Kansas headquarters and the Peruvian countryside that she loves.

Much ink is given to the "magic" of moneymaking, to the mystique of the women who make it to the top. There *is* some magic and mystique. A lot of things have to fall in place for fantasy to become fortune. And certain women appear to know how to make it happen, to get what they want. However, behind what seems to be magic and mystique is very ordinary daily drudgery—paperwork, legwork, phone work, home work, meetings, and negotiations. It's work-your-way-to-wealth stuff—the traditional American Dream tale coated today with tech-age terms, know-how, analysis, degrees, devices, and procedures. The tech-age input can make the difference between working smart and working stupid, but the toil still takes place.

2. The Art of the Perfect Phone Call

Much of the labor that generates ladybucks is phone labor. Females are frequently derided for spending long hours with a phone to their ear. However, this ability serves women in business well. Because working women are often more phone-comfortable and phone-competent then their male counterparts, they get a lot accomplished on the telephone. (When photos are shot of executive women in their offices, it is common to see them in the midst of a phone call; seldom are executive men photographed in this pose.) Unlike the stereotypical housewife who spends mornings calling friends with idle gossip, ladybucks earners are phone pros. They master the art of the brief, productive phone call, often making dozens of business-related, income-increasing calls daily. They have questions and comments ready and know how to word requests, make points, and answer complaints. They know to call long-winded clients moments before lunch (it's easy to end the call with a "lunch date" excuse), to call dreaded "must returns" when the people are likely to be out, to avoid time-consuming social chitchat by using conversation abbreviators ("One quick question, John"; "I'll keep you just a second, Mary"; "This is a two-minute call, Dave.")

Debrah Lee Charatan, working with little more than a telephone, turned a $2,000 loan into Bach Realty, an expanding $150 million New York City–based commercial real estate firm, in just five years. Debrah, now twenty-eight, had no inside advantages, no backers, no special contacts. She had a small amount of experience in the real estate field, an awareness to sense the enormous opportunities for profit in New York commercial real estate, a dream to become rich, and the willingness to hole up in a tiny, borrowed basement office for sixty hours a week making over a hundred phone calls a day.

Debrah called her way through lists of commercial property owners, searching for landlords willing to sell their buildings or sites. When she found owners interested in selling, she ran three-line classified ads in *The New York Times*. When calls came in, instead of pitching only a single listing, she asked the callers to specify exactly what they were looking to buy and assured them she'd find it for them. It took a while to find marketable properties and unite sellers and buyers, but within six months she had several listings and interested buyers—and a growing number of profitable deals. Today, Debrah has twenty-two sales reps working for her, some of them earning in the hundreds of thousands annually. She hires individuals with no real estate backgrounds and trains them to begin as she did—on the telephone, getting the listings, asking questions, learning about the properties, talking to potential buyers, and collecting all sorts of information over the phone that will ultimately lead to moneymaking closings.

3. Home-Basing

Stories like Debrah Lee Charatan's don't begin in plush $5,000-a-month commercial rentals. They begin in tiny basement rooms, garages, converted bedrooms, and kitchen corners. Ladybucks frequently grow from makeshift, make-do, modest surroundings. Women who turn their fantasies into fortunes sometimes envision themselves working from lavish setups, but the visions are put on hold. Start-up cash isn't spent on location and decoration. That comes later.

Funds are put into immediate cash-generators: good phone-answering systems, quality equipment, impressive samples, and important supplies.

Home-basing is part of American economic history. Our forefathers were farmers and artisans who worked from barns and cellars, until the Industrial Revolution brought them—or their offspring—to factories. However, home-basing is also a twentieth-century business-building technique often used by women. Most home-based endeavors do not reap ladybucks; most commercial-based ones don't either. But a high precentage of female fortunes are founded from home. Eager to simultaneously nurture children and career, to avoid tedious travel hours, to keep overhead low, hundreds of thousands of women a year set up shop at home.

The women who turn their home-based efforts into fabulous financial triumphs take their ventures seriously. They see the potential for ladybucks three, four, ten years down the road. Often they "sideline" while their children are young or while they're working at outside jobs, but their ventures are nourished from home—moving to commercial headquarters only when home can no longer house them.

In 1972, while raising her two small children, Sandra Kurtzig began a part-time venture from a spare bedroom in her apartment. In an attempt to cash in on her mathematics and engineering background, she wrote software packages for small local manufacturers with management problems that could be corrected by computer assistance. Sensing a market need for improved productivity in manufacturing environments, she hired top technical people to assist her and started designing easy-to-use MIS (Management Information Systems) software to automate manufacturing facilities. Today her company, ASK Computer Systems of Los Altos, California, which originated as a $2,000 home-based operation, is a commercially based multinational corporation with eight hundred companies using ASK systems, thirty sales offices, 425 employees, and annual revenues nearing $80 million. Sandra, now thirty-nine, is chairman of the board.

Working from her farm in Elverson, Pennsylvania, Jean Flaxenburg has turned what began as a tiny cottage industry into a huge barn-based business. Her firm, the French Creek Sheep and Wool Company, a multimillion-dollar manufacturer of sheepskin jackets and natural wool sweaters, is still headquartered on her domestic property. Rather than locating in a commercial manufacturing plant, Jean continues to run her now-flourishing enterprise from the same barn where she began with $2,000 and a single sewing machine. Her wool comes from the sheep that graze on the forty acres of farmland that surround her home and barn. Her employees are neighbors who work as independent contractors in their own homes or in work stalls in the Flaxenburg barn. Although most home-based moneymakers eventually move from cottage to commercial headquarters, this back-to-basics work style is currently being adopted by more and more ladybucks earners who believe that for financial and emotional profit, if at all possible, home is the place to begin and stay.

4. Union Avoidance

Were Jean Flaxenburg to use union workers to produce her garments, her company would cease to enjoy good net profits. Like many American manufacturers, unable to endure high labor costs, she would be forced out of business. Like Jean, most ladybucks earners do not employ union labor. Only occasionally do women set up operations. Generally, union labor is shunned.

"If I had to use union labor, I couldn't have built this company to what it is," says Lane Nemeth, talking about the educational toy company she began in a California garage in 1977. Lane benefits from low foreign labor, buying many of Discovery Toys' products from small European and Japanese companies willing to adapt their designs to Discovery's high standards or to produce large amounts of a particular toy in order to sell into the American market. Imported toys and American-made ones are packaged in largely robotized factories. The company's 12,000 full- and part-time salespeople work on a contract basis, as consultants who sell the Discovery Toys via Tupperware-style demonstration parties. Currently, Lane is licensing her company in England and test marketing joint ventures in the Orient. Her production, packaging, and sales methods generate profits that would be unobtainable were union labor costs included.

Importing, automating, contracting, licensing, and franchising are not only techniques that enable a business to garner high profits and branch out all over the country (and world), but they are also production and sales boosters independent of union input. The lady-bucks earners who avoid union labor see themselves not as hurting the American worker but rather as providing other women (and men) with unlimited earnings opportunities, chances to play out their own capitalistic impulses in low-risk ways. Jean Flaxenburg's workers can take on as much or as little piecework as they wish. Lane Nemeth's salespeople can hold as many or as few home-demonstration parties as they can handle. Debrah Lee Charatan's real estate sales reps are encouraged to phone their way to listings and fortunes just as she did.

5. Cloning

Ladybucks earners believe in cloning. They're pleased with their own accomplishments, and they teach others to duplicate their suc-cesses—thus enhancing both self and followers. Techniques such as contracting, licensing, and franchising are much more than just ways to avoid union labor costs. They are ways to turn clever ideas into multimillion-dollar industries.

Party-plan selling enables thousands of recruits to become min-iature Lane Nemeths. Or miniature Mary Kays. Or miniature any woman who creates popular product lines that sell well through home demonstration by enthusiastic protégés.

Licensing is another form of cloning that permits a successful businesswoman to cash in further on a clever idea. An entrepreneur such as Louise Berenson escalated her Purple Panache pushcart business into a national offering by training admirers in other parts of the country to duplicate her success with pushcarts of their own. She sells her idea and her knowhow (but not her company name) for a few thousand dollars a shot, increasing her company's earnings and enabling other purple lovers to flex their entrepreneurial muscles. Similarly, Carole Jackson's Color Me Beautiful firm trains (for a fee) individuals to capitalize, as Carole did, on a widespread interest in color analysis and coordination. Color Me Beautiful consultants are taught and licensed to teach others how to choose wardrobes and cosmetics in hues suited to their skin, hair, and eyes.

Franchising is a firmer—and more profitable—form of cloning. Here a successful businesswoman such as Joan Barnes of Gym-boree sells not just her idea and know-how but her company's name as well—in this case to over three hundred franchisees who buy her products, imitate her setup, and pay her royalties. (There are lots of legalities, as well as ladybucks, in franchising.)

Like Joan Barnes, when Sara Addis began her house-sitting service she knew she was filling a local need but learned that there was also a national market for her idea. By offering sitters to care for home, children, and pets she provided a service that her neighborhood was hungry for. Within five years her service company had grown from six to one hundred and fifty sitters, and Sara was receiving inquiries from women seeking to imitate her operation in other locations. She sold House Sitters of El Paso and began the Sara Care Franchise Corporation, a corporation that trains franchisees to open and operate quality-care sitting services.

6. Self-Marketing

The women who head companies made up of admiring and imitating protégés rise to their positions of prominence through self-marketing. People like Ashley, the computer programmer/entrepreneur who wonders why she's "still struggling when I should be rich," reject many of the methods that might make them rich. Ashley recoils from self-marketing, equating it with "kissing ass with the press," insisting that her work "speaks for itself." Her work doesn't speak for itself; work doesn't speak. She doesn't speak to promote it, and she doesn't use publicists who might accomplish what she's so opposed to doing.

The women who reap ladybucks are effective and willing self-marketers, whether they personally enjoy the process or not, whether they employ many or few or none at all. The more popular and prosperous they become, the more they use public relations people to help keep their names, images, and offerings alive. But initially they alone impress customers, clients, employees, and the media as being competent, clever, take-charge individuals. The products and services they sell are assumed to have merit because these women present themselves as meritorious. Whether they employ ten or ten thousand individuals to sell their products or services, they also do it by selling themselves. They're visible and vocal self-promoters. They give talks, address seminars, exhibit at trade shows, speak to the print media, appear on radio and television talk shows, and chat with customers at their shops. They get out there and let the public meet the person behind the product.

People who buy a franchise such as Sara Care or Gymboree are buying more than a turnkey operation. They are buying the enthusiasm, the optimism, and the effective self-marketing of Sara Addis and Joan Barnes. Similarly, the women who align themselves with the party-plan selling of Mary Kay Ash or Lane Nemeth are impressed not just by Mary Kay Ash's skin creams or Lane Nemeth's toys but by Mary Kay Ash and Lane Nemeth as individuals. Many of Debbi Fields's employees come across as clones, not because they buy her franchises (hers is a multioutlet corporation) or act as independent contractors, but because they are taken with her charm, her vitality, and her bubbly belief in the good feelings produced by her warm cookies. They keep her company's profits glowing and growing because they like her, her attitude, and her belief in her product. Her effective self-marketing is contagious.

Many ladybucks earners are neither franchisers nor employers of thousands but are individuals who work alone or with small staffs. Their incomes are exceptional because they are exceptional at marketing themselves. Linda Perlmutter is a talented artist specializing in watercolors. If she marketed herself and her work as most artists do, she would be like most artists—poor. But Linda is not only a good artist, she is an excellent self-marketer. She is a frequent seminar speaker, a consultant to local cultural clubs, and a judge at community art contests. Linda makes herself professionally accessible to organizations that wish to benefit from her talent. She is not an artist in hiding. Scores of people know her as well as her work. From a studio in her home she teaches art to children and adults. She holds exhibits of their work, promotes the exhibits in the local press, talks to the print media about new art techniques, attends gallery presentations of her own work, and chats with the art buyers. With each self-marketing activity, Linda becomes more and more of an authority figure and a celebrity. Today this personable forty-three-year-old wife and mother has a leading note-card publisher reproducing her work, is producing a videotape for art educators, receives a hundred dollars an hour for her demonstrations, sixty-five dollars an hour for her six-hour-a-week classes, up to fifty dollars apiece for poster reproductions of her watercolors, and between

$1,300 and $5,000 for each of her originals, which are purchased regularly by hotels, corporations, and national and international private collectors.

Similarly, Dr. Paula Moynahan is earning much more than most female physicians—and more than many other plastic surgeons—because she is an excellent self-marketer. Paula gives interviews and information to women's magazines, publishes a newsletter that discusses happenings in the field of cosmetic surgery and in her own career, speaks at seminars and to groups, appears on television talk shows and even on a commercial plugging the college she attended as an undergraduate. She has recently completed a book on cosmetic surgery and will be making the rounds of several television and radio talk shows to promote it and, indirectly, herself. She's not a doctor in hiding, an unapproachable medical person glued to her practice and remote from the public. Paula is an accomplished, acclaimed specialist who has a terrific sense of humor, an ability to communicate with all kinds of people, and a caring, pleasant manner. Were she aloof like many of her colleagues, her professional capabilities wouldn't be reduced, but fewer people would be calling for her services.

Unlike Ashley, who is gruff and manlike, Paula Moynahan, Linda Perlmutter, Debbi Fields, Lane Nemeth, Mary Kay Ash, Joan Barnes, Sara Addis, and hundreds of other ladybucks earners are very feminine women. They aggressively partake of activities that further their moneymaking endeavors, but they have not adopted masculine mannerisms in the belief that such behavior increases effectiveness. They do not look or sound tough or rough. Quite the contrary—they market themselves and their products or services with softness and strength, with femininity and firmness—combinations that take a while to cultivate but that are remarkably successful.

7. *Barter*

When Ashley's lawyer suggested that she occasionally barter her computer services as a means of increasing her cash flow, she scoffed at the idea. She considers barter "too time consuming," wants "to be paid in cash," doesn't want "to keep an inventory of who owes whom hours or products." Ashley's distaste for the bartering process is understandable. Barter does have negative aspects.

However, it also has advantages, and women much more prosperous than Ashley have used it to help boost their companies and careers and continue to use it as a method of getting needed products and services without expending precious capital to do so.

"Yes, I barter . . . sometimes, but I don't like to discuss barter transactions," says a jewelry manufacturer whose pieces are sold in upscale department stores and shops all over America and whose company enjoys net profits of over a quarter of a million dollars annually. This woman expresses the sentiments of many ladybucks earners who know that barter is smarter than warehousing unsold inventory but who keep their barter dealings quiet.

"If everyone thinks that I'm amenable to barter, I'll be flooded with offers of payment in everything but cash," says a successful female attorney who occasionally barters her services "when receiving cash seems impossible."

"I use barter as a supplemental form of income," says an interior designer specializing in celebrity mansions. "Even though my clients are wealthy, their cash is sometimes tied up, so about 10 percent of my income is in antiques and art works instead of money. I take these things as payment, but beautiful though they are, cash is still king."

The "cash is king" philosophy is expressed again and again by ladybucks earners who prefer to receive cash rather than products or services for their work. They prefer to receive cash—and do—most of the time, but occasionally they trade their offerings for things of comparable worth, admitting, like Lois Dale, founder of Barter Advantage in New York City, that "to refuse to barter is self-defeating."

Lois Dale understands the "cash is king" philosophy—America is a cash-based economy. But she is queen of the barter system, an enthusiastic advocate who used barter to boost a tiny carpet-cleaning venture into Dale Carpet Center, Inc., a six-figure operation, and went on to begin a prospering exchange that enables other product and service sellers to similarly benefit from barter.

Lois, a fervent spokesperson for a local barter group where she traded her carpet-cleaning services for the services and products of other members, began her own barter club to capitalize on what she observed to be a cash-poor business economy. To get her first clients, she approached commercial customers whom she dealt with in the carpet-cleaning operation (which she ran from her mother's house and the back seat of her car) and businesswomen she knew from women's groups she belonged to. She convinced them of the value of barter as a sales builder and as a cash-flow preserver and rounded up a good mix of product and service suppliers. Soon word of mouth took over, and Barter Advantage, which was founded in 1981 with $20,000 funneled from Lois's carpet-cleaning profits, one employee, and the fantasy of having hundreds of businesspeople generating thousands of trade dollars every month, began to take off. Known in the industry today as the "First Lady of Barter," thirty-nine-year-old Lois now heads a $1-million-plus computerized clearinghouse where $270,000 of goods and services are exchanged monthly by over 1,200 clients who view barter as a good way to gain new business, clear surplus, save cash, and try expensive goods and services on a trade basis.

8. Seizing Opportunities

Lois first saw barter as an opportunity to build her carpet-cleaning business and later as a potentially profitable business in itself. But like most ladybucks earners, she did more than just see an opportunity—she seized it and turned it into income. Many women see opportunities that can be capitalized on, but they don't turn these opportunities into income. They watch someone else do it and then think, "She stole my idea," or they hate themselves for not acting on their hunches.

A commonly offered definition of an entrepreneur or moneymaker is "an individual who sees opportunities where most people see nothing." This is something of an exaggeration. Most good opportunities are not invisible to the common eye. Millions of women see them all the time. But they don't seize them, embrace them with zeal, or cash in on them.

At the age of twenty-two, Betsey Johnson jolted the fashion industry with zany outfits that sported shower curtain rings, metal discs, and other materials not found on normal clothing. Her wild, wearable, fun creations captured the spirit of the Sixties. Celebrities such as Jackie Onassis, Twiggy, and Brigitte Bardot bought her fashions and helped gain her industry recognition. In 1971, Betsey Johnson became the youngest designer ever to win the coveted Coty Award. More celebrity customers and more awards followed. Her daring designs made her famous and the idol of millions of fashion lovers with sketch pads and professional hopes. But her path to super-success was no more predestined than any other fashion aspirant's. She seized an opportunity and literally made her own path to profits.

While a student at Syracuse University, Betsey won a *Mademoiselle* magazine fashion-design award that offered her a chance to work in New York City. She seized the chance, beat a fast path from Syracuse to New York, and immediately tested her talent. Her ability to tune in to the times was rewarded—which would not have happened as quickly had she stayed in Syracuse. Though ladybucks can be—and are—earned from everywhere, in certain fields relocating accelerates the process. New York loved Betsey Johnson's wackiness. An opportunity to appear in a television commercial came along. She took it, took the $20,000 she eventually reaped from it, took a loan from her father, and began her own company, Betsey Johnson, Inc., one of Seventh Avenue's liveliest rags-to-riches triumphs.

In all fields, but particularly in glamour fields, money is made by women who grasp singular opportunities and the opportunities they spawn as "must-do's" and move forcefully. Opportunities are not casually acknowledged as good possibilities. They are welcomed, held to heart, and taken to harvest.

Jan Dutton has earned millions from an idea as different from zany clothes as lace is from shower curtain rings. However, like Betsey Johnson, Jan Dutton embraced an opportunity others had or saw and ignored. Jan capitalized on a location she found herself in and on a fantasy inspired by white lace and linen. Her company, Paper White, begun in 1981, designs, manufactures, and distributes hand-embroidered white linen dresses, aprons, bed coverings, handkerchiefs, hand towels, pillow shams, and lacy legwear. Jan was living in California and had no thought of starting her own lace and linen goods business. She was managing a flower shop when her husband, a toy manufacturer, was transferred to Hong Kong. She didn't want to go, but once uprooted, she decided to make the best of it. She set about discovering what she liked about the place. She found she liked the opportunity to get quality linen and lace objects made to order at bargain prices. She saw a project to be undertaken— and undertook it.

A dressy, romantic, linen-and-lace-embroidered apron sample was put together and brought back to California. There Jan got apron orders from a local retailer. Encouraged by her California response, she flew to New York and sold more aprons. Then she flew back to Hong Kong, rented a factory, and hired workers to fill her orders. Her apron success led her to see and seize other opportunities. She created sample lace and linen collars, handkerchiefs, pillows, and dresses that she took to American department store buyers and exhibited at trade shows. Her project was turning to profits. Within four years, Paper White was grossing $4 million.

Jan is still coming up with new designs, new products, and new markets. Her customer roster reads like a *Who's Who* in upscale department stores, boutiques, and gift shops. Paper White creations are sold out before they're shipped, proving that in a world filled with shock and rock, glitter and gloss, there is a need for the relief and fantasy provided by the quiet beauty reminiscent of another day and way. Also proven is that those who spot and seize opportunities that others pass up can create wealth far beyond their expectations. Jan saw an opportunity for financial gain, but she didn't expect to make big money. She regarded manufacturing and exporting nostalgia as a project or opportunity too good to ignore, not as a dynamic business idea that would turn into a fruitful industry.

9. Nurturing Niches

A look at ladybucks earners is a look at niche nurturers, at women who sense small but significant wants and needs in the marketplace, develop businesses and careers around them, and nourish these niches into riches. Jan Dutton's Paper White met the desire for lacy luxury and reflection in a hurried, high-tech world. Betsey Johnson's designs filled the need for wildness in a fashion industry that hadn't yet captured the excesses of the Sixties. Sara Addis saw and satisfied a national need for sitting services. Joan Barnes's Gymboree capitalized on the exercise craze by adapting it to toddlers. Sandra Kurtzig recognized a need for computer software to increase productivity in manufacturing plants and developed a line of management information—system packages to fill it. In every field female moneymakers are individuals who see niches, seize them, and, most important, go on to nourish them into profitable businesses and careers.

Many women carve out potentially profitable niches, begin to earn money, but end up out of business or career within a year or two. Nurturing a business or career, like nurturing a child, is difficult. The infancy stages are new and exciting. As the process progresses, there is tedium and trouble along with triumphs. A business or career, unlike a child, can be abandoned when pressures mount, when problems appear at every turn, when good help is unavailable. Ladybucks earners, however, are maternal about their moneymaking ventures. They don't cave in easily. Even when there is little glimmer of hope or reward, they follow through, nursing ideas out of infancy and into healthy young companies and careers.

Lane Nemeth guided Discovery Toys through a torturous beginning that seemed to be ending at every turn. Committed to her quality toy line, she persisted in breathing hope into her failing dream. She pleaded with lenders for life-sustaining financial help (at one point paying 27.5 percent interest), wheedled credit extensions from suppliers, and persuaded her sales force to stick with her. She continually ran short of operating capital and continually had to devise means to get more. In 1981, when her bank denied her financial assistance even after she'd demonstrated her ability to pay back loans and keep her company afloat, she refused to leave the premises, threatening to call in the local media. A quarter-of-a-million-dollar loan was granted. Once Lane finally achieved an adequate financial cushion, her computer system broke down during a rush period. Thousands of Christmas orders were not delivered on time. The commission-dependent sales force was angry. Lane apologized and purchased a new, more reliable computer, along with an automated packing system. It was 1983; Discovery Toys had grown out of its infancy. Today, Lane Nemeth foresees her $40 million nurtured niche growing into a billion-dollar international business within the next fifteen years.

Lane's story is that of many ladybucks earners who nurture niches, despite difficulties, into formidable businesses and careers. These women—often, like Lane, housewives and mothers beginning in small ways with big dreams—nurse their endeavors until they feel they have created either companies that can survive independent of their inputs or careers that have adequately rewarded their efforts.

10. Delegation

A niche cannot be nurtured far as a one-woman operation. Ladybucks come when a woman in charge delegates tasks she does not excel at or can no longer handle alone. Unlike Ashley, who doesn't delegate because she considers her employees "jerks who would screw everything up," ladybucks earners find employees and assistants who don't screw up. When they hire unwisely or heed the words of incompetent "experts," they then fire wisely and find real experts. Rarely are they "born delegators." They learn to delegate because, as one restaurant chain owner puts it, "to not delegate is to work yourself out of business."

Entrepreneurial history contains stories of entrepreneurs like Estée Lauder, Mary Kay Ash, and Lillian Vernon who delegated management responsibilities (in these cases, to their sons and others) and watched their companies skyrocket; and of entrepreneurs who similarly delegated and still saw their businesses plummet. But there are no stories of highly successful businesswomen who made it, or are making it, without help.

Delegating is part intuitive art and part management science. The art is in selecting and keeping loyal, committed, capable key assistants. The science is in delegating correct amounts of authority to these individuals (heaven help the woman who turns over all major financial or marketing control!) and making sure they delegate down the line to similarly qualified help. It's not easy, which is why many entrepreneurial women turn to licensing and franchising rather than try to cultivate their companies into mighty, multi-employee corporations. Unlike ladybucks hopefuls who come up with clever ideas, touch the golden ring for a brief, shining moment, and then watch the grandeur crumble, entrepreneurial winners understand that fortunes grow not from good ideas but from skillful management of the ideas—which cannot be accomplished alone.

A woman comes up with an idea, takes it to market, and makes money. Then something happens—the idea develops a life of its own. It demands more attention than its creator alone can supply. Qualified management is necessary to keep it alive and flourishing.

The woman who created something out of nothing now must turn to others to keep her something from returning to nothing. She must move from entrepreneur to executive—a difficult step.

Difficult, but done, particularly by entrepreneurs who are becoming more and more aware that timely and cautious delegation can turn a good idea into a million-dollar idea. Sometimes a "hot" little company turns to ashes because its founder is reluctant to delegate, or delegates too quickly, or relinquishes control to the wrong people. Delegation requires correct decision making. When do you delegate? To whom? How much control? Do you franchise? License? Work with independent contractors? Or, once a successful entrepreneur, do you establish a traditional corporation and become president?

What works for one entrepreneur doesn't work for another. Debbi Fields, unlike many snack-food vendors, runs her $70-million-a-year cookie empire corporate-style. Her hundreds of cookie outlets are all company-owned and operated. A COO (chief operating officer) handles overall marketing responsibilities. Two vice presidents for operations oversee six regional operations managers, each of whom oversees several stores, with the assistance of team leaders chosen from among the hourly employees. This "down-the-line" management works well for Debbi, president and CEO, who believes she is running a company full of happy employees motivated by performance incentives and supportive company-trained bosses. There are no licensees or franchisees, nor any employee ownership of the company. All cookies are sold by salaried store employees who combine prepackaged ingredients on the premises and bake them in standard store ovens. There is opportunity to work and rise in a well-run organization.

Dalia Ratner, called by some "the Mrs. Fields of muffins," shares Debbi Fields's enthusiasm for warm, freshly baked goods. But she doesn't delegate, Debbi-style. She's a franchiser. Owner of the fast-growing franchise of All My Muffins shops, Dalia parlayed a tasty, original muffin recipe into oven-to-customer shops that offer two hundred (rotated) flavors of four-ounce muffins made with morning glory bran and loaded with fresh fruit, nuts, vegetables, and chocolate chunks. Muffin lovers can bite into warm zucchini walnut muffins, white chocolate chip muffins, piña colada muffins, butterscotch pecan muffins, and other luscious varieties baked fresh in each store every day. Cookie aficionados can savor the "muffies," a cross between a muffin and a cookie (like the top of a muffin), also offered in several flavors.

Dalia's California anchor shop grew into a profitable and imitation-worthy enterprise because she hired top-notch store managers and delegated responsibility wisely while she went about inventing new culinary creations and providing for her husband and three children. Then, sensing a national and international potential for profits, she delegated via the franchising process in order to make ladybucks along with her muffins. "It is a very simplified organizational structure," believes Ratner. "My store and the baking formula for the muffins are idiot-proof."

Proud of her products, Dalia claims, "I am successful because you can't find muffins as good as mine anywhere else in the world." She genuinely believes that no one can bake muffins tastier than hers; but muffin-marketing zeal aside, somewhere in the world there are other talented bakers who could successfully challenge her claim. However, they could not challenge her profits unless they were willing to hand over control to franchisees as she does, or to run a traditional-style corporation like Mrs. Fields Cookies, or to devise some delegation scheme that permitted them to increase sales, keep customers happy, and reach new markets and money.

11. Risk Taking

Ladybucks earners are risk takers—but they take calculated risks. They don't gamble everything in 100-to-1-odds schemes. They're daring but not dumb. Entrepreneurs usually take the biggest risks, particularly risks of a financial nature, but professional and corporate executives who achieve ladybucks often do so because they run their practices like entrepreneurs, or intrapreneurs under the corporate umbrella.

There is a saying that appeals to entrepreneurs: "There are lots of ways to become a failure; never taking a chance is the most successful one." Entrepreneurial success and chance taking must go together. The women who take entrepreneurial risks hope to capitalize on opportunities. They're after challenge, not security. They want to create wealth and build companies, not earn weekly paychecks working for someone else. They learn fast that risk taking is essential for a kitchen-table operation to become a prosperous firm. And they learn fast that the difference between soaring and sinking is the difference between a good risk and a bad one.

There is no way to predict with certainty the outcome of a risk-taking venture. Lack of safety or guarantees is what risk taking is about. To women who don't have an entrepreneurial vein running though their bodies, any financial risk is bad—and their outlook for ladybucks is slim. The questions most commonly asked by lady-bucks seekers are: "Will I lose everything I've saved?" "Will I be able to pay back the loans?" "Will I be out of business if this doesn't work out?" They don't fear risk—often it excites them—but they want 2-to-1, or 3-to-1, or even 4-to-1 odds. Ridiculous 100-to-1 odds are shunned. They gamble, but not on long shots. There must be solid evidence to support the possibility of success.

Though not all risk taking is of a financial win-or-lose nature, the risks that escalate tiny, local enterprises, practices, or careers into ladybucks are. A variety of small risks are taken daily by ladybucks hopefuls, but the risks that lead to riches or ruin usually contain the possibility of losing large sums of money and consequently credi-bility, status, and respect—the clout that goes with the gold.

The story of the supersuccess of Discovery Toys—and of many other longing-to-ladybucks triumphs—is the story of borrowing and paying back loans, knowing that often everything hinges on the ability to meet a loan payment or satisfy a creditor. So desperate was Lane Nemeth to keep Discovery Toys alive that, in order to pay back debts to the Small Business Administration and to manufacturers who had extended her credit, she borrowed $100,000 at an outrageous 27.5 percent interest rate from a factoring agent. Right here it could have all ended. She could have gone bankrupt. The risk, like the interest rate, was too big. Hope was turning to hell. Luck interceded in the form of a venture capitalist who happened to accompany his wife to a Discovery Toys demonstration and was impressed by what he saw. His firm invested $90,000 in Discovery Toys in exchange for an 18 percent share of the company and helped Lane acquire an-other Small Business Administration loan. Lane was able to repay the factoring agent and keep her company afloat. But soon she was out of operating capital again. More "soar-or-sink" loans followed, each one testing Lane's risk-taking tolerance. Today, Discovery Toys is a growing $40 million operation with banks competing to provide expansion capital at reasonable rates. Lane could stop at this point, take her company public, and walk away very rich. If she leaves Discovery Toys—and if she's like many ladybucks earners, she will try something else—she'll take new risks, perhaps be rescued again if risk hovers on ruin, and quite possibly create more ladybucks.

Of all the golden methods that lead to ladybucks, risk taking is most talked about. It is the part of the success equation that excites, delights, and frightens both participant and observer. It is a throw of the dice, a turn of the wheel, a chance to forever change one's own life and often the lives of many. A feeling of tremendous pleasure and power comes from taking an entrepreneurial risk and winning. The women who win don't want to relinquish it. And when they don't have to, it is largely because they've taken the right risks.

12. Connecting and Using

Ladybucks earners connect with and use dozens of individuals who directly or indirectly advance their companies or careers. In his book *How to Make Your Own Luck* (Warner Books, 1981), Bernard Gittelson, megaentrepreneur, industry consultant, and syndicated columnist, states that many would-be entrepreneurs sink because they fail to "connect" on a large scale with a variety of people. Gittelson talks about the importance of asking for what you want and need, of writing letters, of making phone calls. He believes that those who soar in the entrepreneurial world do so because they continually multiply their contacts, expand their social bases, compound their power sources, and reach new people who can boost their companies. Few would disagree with him. The entrepreneurial, professional, and executive women who achieve ladybucks are not your everyday nebulous networkers who occasionally mingle here and there but don't make aggressive moves toward specific people who can promote their success. They are polished users who take— and who give.

Patti McVay dreamed of establishing herself "in a big way" in the Indianapolis, Indiana, business community. Attentive to the plight of two friends who were running a money-losing travel agency, Patti entered the operation in 1977 as an unpaid sales rep. She wooed corporate travelers by offering volume discounts and guaranteeing them the best prices available, quickly landed a hundred business accounts, boldly eliminated all individual accounts, restructured the agency to service only the business traveler, and bought into it. Until recently, this forty-year-old divorced mother held 51 percent of Fifth Season Travel Agency, which under her direction as CEO grew to ninety employees, 5,000 commercial accounts, and annual revenues of $100 million. Did Patti use her friends' agency as a channel to establish herself in Indiana's business community? Yes. She also connected with corporate travelers who were in a position to bring the agency major business accounts. Patti benefited, and so did the people she used and connected with.

Connecting and using requires a sturdy ego. It's opportunistic and rejection-provoking. It's also success-producing. The prospect of pursuing people and being rebuffed paralyzes many idea people into inaction and a lifetime of dull jobs. Career and business therapists talk about developing a "feeling of entitlement" that affirms "I am worthy of help," "My ideas are good," "Everyone benefits from helping me." Emphasis is placed on the need for practice in developing a thick veneer and on the importance of thinking in terms of reciprocity and phrasing requests properly. Countless seminars and books are currently available that purport to teach the ladybucks hopeful how to enlist colleague support, community support, media support, financial support, and customer support.

Today, connecting and using (a.k.a., euphemistically, "networking") are considered an excellent way to boost a business or career onto a ladybucks level. In the past it was considered unfeminine, brazen, and pushy. Not any longer. The woman who learns the names of people who can be useful, contacts them, enlists their aid, or lures their business is now considered pragmatic, not pushy. The question is not whether to connect or not to connect, to use or not to use, but how to connect and use properly and effectively. When a woman has accomplished this, she enters a new league. No longer a novice networker, a supplicant seeking support for a fledgling venture or career, she is "invited" to connect and use. Abundant opportunities are presented to meet and mingle in richer circles.

"After I'd landed a few big accounts and received some print publicity," says one thirty-two-year-old MBA financial consultant, "I found myself receiving invitations for membership in chief executive officers' clubs, women in business organizations, exclusive groups whose membership is determined by sales, salary, or professional status." This consultant, who appears in paragraphs here and there under captions such as "People to Watch," "Women on the Move," and "Making It," says, "In the beginning, when you really need good contacts and connections, not a whole lot of people are there for you; but once you start to make it, you receive endless chances to attend functions, dinners, awards ceremonies peopled by prominent and powerful individuals pleased to talk to you, try your services, introduce you to others, invest in your projects."

In a public relations news release, Dalia Ratner's All My Muffins franchise is described as having "gained international notoriety from its celebrity clientele which includes Suzanne Pleshette, Lionel Richie, and Warren Beatty." The publicity surrounding Estée Lauder's cosmetics company and Helen Boehm's porcelain firm has always mentioned a clientele composed of presidents, royalty, and celebrities of one sort or another. Similarly, the press releases for Carol Jenna's successful sports marketing agency lists famous corporations, such as Del Monte, Levi-Strauss, and Stroh's Brewery, who use Jenna & Co. services. The intention in all these cases is the same—glamour and ultimately profit via association with the rich and famous. A celebrity name is used—name-dropped—to attract potential business. An association is drawn between Dalia's muffins and Lionel Richie's enjoyment of them. Richie isn't formally endorsing the product. He is not a spokesperson for it or the company; but by periodically buying Dalia's muffins, he gives them his stamp of approval—an acceptance that can be—and is—capitalized upon. Similarly, some potential customers take notice of Boehm porcelains because they are said to grace the homes of world figures. And companies impressed by Jenna's mention of her big-name corporate clients take a second look at her sports marketing agency to see if they might want to underwrite one of the sports events she handles. Big-name customers and clients attract new customers and clients. Sales are increased. The ladybucks hopeful profits from the alignment, and the famous names are kept in the public eye. Connecting and using—for everyone's benefit.

13. Intrapreneurship

A more subtle—and currently popular—form of connecting and using is intrapreneurship. *Intrapreneurship* is a word coined by entrepreneur Gifford Pinchot III a few years ago to describe a management philosophy that permits employees entrepreneurial freedom. Major corporations, fearful of losing their more creative workers to upstart businesses of their own, now provide them support, staff, and financing to try their entrepreneurial ideas under the corporate umbrella.

Before the word was coined and before large corporations embraced intrapreneurship as a management concept, clever businesswomen used this technique to build their tiny enterprises into prosperous companies. In 1979, Laura Henderson began Prospect Associates, a Maryland-based biomedical consulting firm that provides technical information, advice, and support to organizations attempting to educate Americans about health-related issues. In order to expand her company and substantially profit from the boom in the health-care market, Laura created an organization of intrapreneurs. Her company is staffed by experts in specific areas of health care such as worksite health programs, smoking prevention, and minority health issues. These specialists run their singular divisions as self-governing units within Prospect Associates. In return for autonomy they bring Prospect contracts in their special sectors of the health-care field. Laura benefits from the new business the intrapreneurs bring in, and her employees simultaneously enjoy the security of corporate sponsorship and the freedom of entrepreneurship. Prospect Associates now has eighty-five employees and annual sales of $3.5 million. It is a thriving intrapreneurial corporation that pays generous merit bonuses, offers an attractive employee savings plan, and provides Laura, who owns 100 percent of the company stock, a growing slice of the $400 billion health-care market.

Not every business lends itself to Laura's kind of intrapreneurial approach. Not every ladybucks aspirant is comfortable granting operating freedom to a collection of experts functioning as little companies within her big company. Intrapreneurship is a combination of delegation, risk taking, and connecting and using. (Large amounts of operating control are delegated, which can be risky, to specialists who are used to attract and contract new business.) This business-building technique often works well for women reaching for lady-bucks in multipart megamarkets such as health care, investment banking, importing and exporting, and education—women who realize that real corporate expansion depends upon employing experts capable of bringing in new customers.

"I don't give it a formal name like intrapreneurship," says a government professor who three years ago left the academic world to begin a firm that consults to American companies seeking to establish trade relationships overseas. Her company, which last year billed $2 million, is composed largely of former professors of political science, economics, and foreign languages who specialize in particular countries. They court companies that would profit from international contracts with their countries of specialization, explain the how-to's, problems, profits, pitfalls, put their clients in touch with experienced export-management agents and freight forwarders, and set up piggybacking arrangements (where a small company exports its products as part of a larger company's export division)—do everything necessary to take a product from a manufacturing facility in Smalltown, USA, to a distribution outlet in Africa, South America, Asia, Europe, or Australia. Each of the professors operates as an independent with an allocated budget, offices, and secretarial help. The firm finances all the professors' operations, and all revenues accrue to the firm, which pays weekly salaries and large incentive bonuses. The government professor who began this now-flourishing enterprise views her company as "a family of happy specialists each doing what they do best." She doesn't label it an intrapreneurial organization, but in effect that's what it is, and that's much of the reason why her employees are happy—they're enjoying the paycheck security that they had in the academic world while exercising their talents in the business world.

14. Capitalizing on Background

Once in a very long while ladybucks are made by a woman who is struck with an idea that emerges from out of nowhere. It is unrelated to anything in her educational, employment, recreational, or family background. She launches a successful business or increases her employer's profits, earns a lot of money or lands a major promotion, and impresses everyone. It is the stuff of dreams and of what happens when dreams come true. However, this is seldom the way ladybucks are earned. Generally, they are created by women who capitalize on their background experiences. Usually the women have studied, worked, tinkered, or grown up around a field that provides them the seed of success.

The government professor who began the above international trade consulting firm did not have a business background in exporting, but she had a solid background in international geography, history, and politics. She was a widely traveled expert researcher who had spent many vacations exploring the profitability of her idea, making overseas inquiries, and laying the groundwork for the consulting firm she hoped to begin. Similarly, her employees didn't luck into $70,000 consulting salaries, suddenly doubling their pay as pedagogues. They were educated academic experts who adapted their knowledge and training to the commercial world.

An examination of the backgrounds of ladybucks earners in all fields reveals tangential experiences that aided their accomplishments. Before Mary Kay Ash began her own party-plan company, she worked for Stanley Products, a direct-sales operation, where she became an expert in the nuts and bolts of selling party-plan style, of recruiting a pyramid sales force of people whose income would increase her own. Decades before Lillian Vernon's mail-order business achieved annual revenues of over $110 million selling an assortment of items from all over the world, Lillian capitalized on the fact that her father was a leather goods manufacturer. The first items she sold were leather purses and belts. Sandra Kurtzig's multinational, ASK Computer Systems, began as an attempt to cash in on her mathematics and engineering background. Lane Nemeth's Discovery Toys company sprang from observations she made and information she gained while working as a day-care center director.

Yesterday and today, the stories of ladybucks were and are the stories of women who use pieces of their pasts to create profits for their futures. Because we are currently a service-needy society, ladybucks hopefuls are now cashing in on acquired skills. Increasingly, women are making impressive sums from organizing information, supervising relocations, chauffeuring, and providing image-building assistance, home-repair help, and matchmaking services. The women who sell these skills and services have usually acquired them un-intentionally or while working as salaried employees, and they decide to modify them into moneymaking opportunities.

Karen Fisher, owner of the one-woman, New York–based Dec-orator Previews, first worked as an executive editor at *American Home* magazine and authored several decorating books. She was repeatedly besieged with requests for decorator referrals. New York Yuppies, short of time and eager to have their living quarters flat-teringly reflect their style and status, trusted Karen to recommend to them the right decorator. Karen trusted her instincts and decided to capitalize on her background in the home decorating field. A year ago, she began a service operation that for a hundred-dollar fee matches clients with one of sixty decorators, who pay her 10 percent of their resultant commissions. So far, after one year in the business, Karen has matched over three hundred clients with compatible dec-orators, for commissions of over $300,000—half of which is profit.

One young woman, a member of a family of small business own-ers, disenchanted with entrepreneurship, decided to cash in on her background by working for someone else. Fluent in a few foreign languages and possessing a good knowledge of the geography, history, and people of a troubled part of the world, she worked her way up in the U.S. intelligence service, becoming an agent and gathering information for the purpose of preventing political prob-lems. Then, after a few years of loyal employment, she decided to leave American intelligence and its mediocre civil service pay for the less dangerous, much-better-remunerated world of corporate es-pionage. She took a $100,000-a-year (plus bonuses) job with an American multinational, capitalizing again on her linguistic ability and Middle East knowledge, and applied her sleuthing experience as a federal intelligence agent to the corporate world.

15. Combining Product and Service Selling

Combining the sale of products with a service business, or the sale of services with a product business, is a popular and effective method used by many female entrepreneurs to multiply their companies' profits. Certain fields such as cosmetics, fitness, image consulting, money management, and high-tech, particularly lend themselves to this approach.

Betty Jo Toccoli of Los Angeles started out as a cosmetics manufacturer. She marketed her company, Laura Lynn Cosmetics, and its products by giving "how to package yourself" talks at cosmetology schools and beauty salons. So great was the interest in her talks that she began Total One Development Centers, a company designed to offer programs for executive packaging via instruction by specialists in fields ranging from nutrition to business etiquette. Today, Betty Jo has a million-dollar-plus dual venture going, with Laura Lynn Cosmetics producing products such as vitamins that are sold through Total One's nutrition service seminars. Betty Jo, who expects to triple sales this year, is certain that if a company can sell its services, product sales will automatically follow—and the wise entrepreneur has products packaged and ready to go.

Judi Sheppard Missett, founder of Jazzercise, a nonstrenuous, simple jazz dance and exercise body conditioning program, substantiates Betty Jo's conviction. In addition to overseeing 3,000 franchises in fifty states and fifteen foreign countries, Jazzercise sells Jazzertogs (a complete line of dance-fitness and leisure clothing), the Jazzercise Shoe, and Jazzercise albums. A professional jazz dancer, Judi wanted to spread the gospel of fitness and fun. Beginning in the early Seventies with a record player, a few records, and space provided by local YMCAs and community centers, she worked as a nonstop one-woman show. Good word-of-mouth recommendations from satisfied students helped expand her business, first into a franchise operation, then into a multimillion-dollar franchise corporation, stocking over 60,000 items and giving Judi, who saw her father work two jobs just to keep food on the table, a net worth of $4 million.

16. Creative Financing

The fact that many fathers are still working two or more jobs to keep food on the table is part of the reason why enterprising women find it hard to escalate their careers or businesses. There is a belief that working women—to say nothing of those reaching for ladybucks status—are "killing" the male provider. "One family, one provider" is a common cry. Though the cry is largely ignored as unenforceable, the American corporate and financial community still does not make it easy for ambitious women. It is much harder for females to move into the executive suite than for men, and it is much more difficult for women to get start-up funds for new ventures. The reasons are sociological and psychological.

Though there are now over fifty million working women, there still exists a lurking sentiment that women should be home, married, raising children, perhaps working part-time when things are tight, but not competing with men in the marketplace. The American ideal of the male breadwinner and the attentive, stay-at-home wife and mother persists, despite divorce statistics, poverty statistics, marriage statistics, birth statistics, and happiness statistics.

There is ample evidence that women must work—yet ample evidence that many people are nevertheless uncomfortable with the concept of the successful female executive, entrepreneur, or professional. She's considered emasculating, threatening, antifamily. Readers of "new woman"–type magazines come away feeling that things are changing, that there's a new spirit in the air, growing equality between the sexes, and new cooperation from the Establishment. They feel this—until they start to reach for real money. Then they learn how the world of real money works, how it takes real money to achieve ladybucks, and how this financing doesn't come easily.

Unquestionably, the female baby-boomers who are now turning forty have made it easier for their daughters to achieve executive and entrepreneurial success. They fought big battles, and women in their twenties are reaping some of the rewards. However, when these "reapers" want to reap ladybucks, they find that it is rarely accomplished by working for someone else. Often they decide to become self-employed. They set up, and then one of three things happens: they go in and out of business within a few years (the fate of most ambitious start-ups); they stay in business, preferring it to working for a boss but earning only modest incomes (a growing situation); or they strike gold (an event that happens infrequently but often enough to inspire hundreds of thousands of women a year to try out, and stick with, their fantasies).

Entrepreneurs who strike gold, who reap ladybucks, begin with the same hopes as those who don't and often with the same amount of money—very little. They struggle along, reaching for new customers, good publicity, better help, bigger profits, and greater cash flow, always hoping for more earnings and less struggle. Then, somewhere along the way, something happens. An opportunity to crack the big time seems within reach, if only some solid financing can be obtained. The women who achieve ladybucks create this financing. They have to. Banks generally won't help them—not until they've proven themselves—but without financing they won't get the chance to. Catch-22 stuff.

The creative part of financing emerges as funds appear to be less obtainable. It starts simply, with personal savings accounts and/or help from family members with good hearts and full pockets, and works up to things such as SBA-guaranteed loans or bids on minority set-aside programs, with all sorts of gradations, successes, and mistakes in between.

Debbi Fields's husband lent her $50,000 to make sure her cookie dream wouldn't crumble. Betsey Johnson's father lent her $100,000 (augmenting several thousand she'd saved herself) to make the move from employee to entrepreneur in the fashion field. Mary Storch, a giftware rep, the first woman to sign a lease at the twenty-two-story Atlanta Merchandise Mart, knew her tiny company, Collectables, could grow into a multimillion-dollar firm, but to make it happen she had to borrow $20,000 against her mother's certificate of deposit—a fact that displeased her father when he found out about it. Other female entrepreneurs received decisive funding from aunts, uncles, friends, or grandparents who hoped to be repaid—and usually were—but who were generous with terms and interest rates. One widow, after working three jobs to put her two sons through college and professional training, received a $10,000 thank-you gift from each of the young men after mentioning that she had a chance to buy into an expanding apparel chain that she was managing.

Most entrepreneurial hopefuls with good ideas and abilities aren't as fortunate as this widow or Betsey Johnson or Debbi Fields. Family and friends either don't have the money to lend or won't lend it if they do have it. Saddened but not defeated, they sell their homes, cars, or jewelry, wheedle financing from private investors, or try for grant money—do everything possible to gather enough capital to keep their dream afloat.

Carol Jenna began her sports marketing agency with $10,000 obtained by selling the only piece of real estate she owned. Mary Storch, in addition to the $20,000 she borrowed against her mother's certificate of deposit, sold her car. One eager divorcée called in a tag sale specialist, opened her closets, drawers, and jewelry boxes, and said, "I need $15,000 to open a marriage consulting agency." Janice Jones began her now $15 million investment firm, Chartwell & Co., with money she had saved from a Wall Street investment and $50,000 put up by a private backer impressed with her financial insight. Annie Hurlbut was able to move her fledgling Peruvian Connection out of wholesaling and into direct-mail sales of $1 million a year with a $50,000 SBA-guaranteed loan that enabled her to produce an enticing color catalog. Lynette Spano Vives used her Hispanic background to qualify her new $8.5 million company, Software Control International, for federal assistance granted to minority-owned businesses. Sharon Corr used all her start-up funds ($1,200) to make up samples of Ginseng Rush soda to take to a National Nutritional Foods Association trade show and financed the production of the orders she wrote up by offering a 4 percent cash discount for prepayment—the beginning of the now $10 million Corr's Natural Beverage Company.

17. Prioritizing

"My business (career, profession) is my child" is a common claim of many childless ladybucks earners who believe they could not have created their wealth while raising children. "I had to wait until my children were grown" is an oft-heard statement of women who waited to play out their moneymaking dreams. So is "I went for it, and it cost me my marriage (sanity, health, youth)." Again and again, the traditionally female "having it all dilemma" arises. Is it possible? Do some women manage it? How do they do it?

Yes, it is possible. Some ladybucks earners do have it all—impressive earnings, successful marriages, and happy children—all at the same time. It's very difficult, though. Generally they are lucky enough to have good health and cooperative husbands, children, and employers to begin with. Husbands pitch in with child care and housework. Employers provide flexi-time and worksite day-care facilities. Moreover, these women are exceptional prioritizers. They are godmothers of time, doling out their hours like pieces of gold. They want it all and run their lives off priority lists. Comedienne Joan Rivers, talking about her passionate drive to be successful and make money, recalls an incident where she flew home in the middle of the night from an exhausting engagement in order to be at a ceremony where her little girl would make the transition from Brownie to Girl Scout. She was depleted, but the little ceremony was a big event to her daughter, and she wouldn't have missed it for anything. It was a major priority.

Not all ladybucks earners are devoted mothers like Joan, but many are. They manage to put their families first, be present when their children need them most, be smart enough to have no more than two children, experience motherhood, and not become martyrs in the process. As they reach for their dreams, they don't chat much with neighbors and friends, and they don't keep their homes immaculate or serve their families perfectly balanced meals. They live with dust and sloppiness, thank God for fast-food eateries and take-outs, turn down invitations for social events they wish they could attend, and don't become Class Mothers (and thank God for the women who do). They know what's important for them and their families, what must be done, and what can be neglected. And they're not easily deterred from their priority lists.

18. Award-Winning

A large percentage of ladybucks hopefuls earn awards of recognition *while* they're climbing the ladybucks ladder. (Almost all are fêted with them *after* they've achieved fame and fortune.) They are "honored" with corporate sales awards, distinguished service awards, women of Smalltown USA, awards, women in law (medicine, engineering, fashion, technology) awards, minority businesswoman awards, or woman of the year (for this, that, or the other thing) awards. The list is long. We are a society that respects work-related achievement and that formally recognizes it by bestowing plaques, trophies, prizes, and certificates on individuals whose accomplishments are extraordinary.

Ladybucks hopefuls view award-winning as much more than an employer or professional association handing out a token of recognition to a woman who has done something of merit. It is an event that separates one female achiever from others. The award creates status; a decorator (dentist, store owner, consultant) is now an award-winning decorator (dentist, store owner, consultant) in everything that is written and said about her. The *award-winning* adjective has the power to push her up the ladybucks ladder. Corporations are impressed by recognized achievers. Customers and clients like to do business with an entrepreneur whose name is known because she's won acclaim in her area of expertise. Women who compete for awards, who engage in activities likely to gain them formal citations, don't do so for love of fondling trophies or hanging plaques. These wood and metal objects are cherished symbols of success—cherished because they applaud what has been done and accelerate what will be done.

Gessie Tassone, founder of A&T Iron Works of New Rochelle, New York, a company that designs and manufactures structural and ornamental railings, fences, and window guards for customers such as the New York City Housing Authority, Con Edison, and IBM, beams as she talks about an upcoming 1986 Westchester County Business Woman Award that she will receive from the Small Business Administration. With the current interest in permanent construction, security, and decorative grillwork, Gessie's company, producers of a high-quality line, thrives on revenues of close to $2 million. Nevertheless, Gessie sees her upcoming award as a kind of insurance, "formal recognition that my company does great work and is worth doing business with."

All the taste treats in Elaine Yannuzzi's Expression unltd. gourmet shop are carefully chosen from around the world. Elaine travels widely and selects exotic coffees, candies, pastries, cheeses, and patés from countries and producers whose goods are unequaled. She has always received customer and industry praise for her unique little shop. But praise and sales increased greatly when she was chosen New Jersey Entrepreneur of the Year for 1983. The award, which didn't affect the superiority of her offerings, gave her bankable celebrity status. Prior to it, she had received a Pacesetter Award for outstanding trend-setting contributions to the food service industry, an award that gave her recognition within her particular industry. The Entrepreneur of the Year Award expanded that status outside of her field into the retail business world at large. The fact that her sales are now on the $2 million level annually surprises no one who knows both how delicious her foods are and how consequential awards can be in the creation and maintenance of ladybucks.

19. Male "Trashing"

Whether women are trying for awards, sales, publicity, or promotion, much of the success or failure they encounter is related to how they deal with men. Though women have gained some clout in the business world, men still exert major influence. Often men are in a position to increase or decrease a woman's chances of attaining ladybucks. This is especially true in the corporate world, structured with male managers, supervisors, and bosses empowered to hold up green or red flags. The women who get the green flags are not necessarily more talented or better qualified than those who don't. But usually they are more skilled in dealing with male co-workers.

Misguided women like Ashley believe that the way to deal with men in a business situation is to behave like them, to adopt their macho mannerisms, language, attitudes, and humor. But this is untrue. Women who advance modify—but don't bury—their femininity. In her best-seller *Games Mother Never Taught You* (Rawson Publishers Associates, 1977), Betty Lehan Harragan, business consultant, job counselor, and lecturer on women's upward mobility, explains how men approach business relationships; their practices, ploys, inside jokes, and verbal and nonverbal messages; and how they speak the language of battle and sports and in doing so exclude women from their ranks. Women like Ashley read career-strategy guides of this sort and assume erroneously that the only way to survive in the male-dominated business arena is to act like a male. This is not Harragan's message. Harragan shows women how men interrelate so that they will understand what is going on, know what to expect, understand terminology and temperament alien to the female style of interacting, be able to correctly assess the men they work with, and gain a competitive edge.

In her book *Sweet Success: How to Understand the Men in Your Business Life and Win with Your Own Rules* (Macmillan, 1986) author Kathryn Stechert updates Harragan's findings, confirms the connection between understanding male colleagues and achieving career advancement, and gives practical advice on how to deal with specific office situations. Like Harragan, Stechert shows that women do best when they play by men's rules and make men feel comfortable around them but do not sacrifice their gender in the process. It's a tricky dilemma (to be or not to be feminine and how much is too much or too little). Readers are taught how it's done through stories of women who have managed it.

More and more, women are being told how to get ahead in a man's world. Instruction is given on how males use humor, conversation, and body language to express their emotions so that females can comprehend what's really being felt and expressed and use it to their own advantage. The women who get what they want, make it in a man's world, and reap ladybucks are either naturals in understanding how men operate—often they've grown up with several brothers around who've teased them into toughness—or have learned to play it right.

"Sure Brenda got the promotion I deserved," says one angry female division manager in a package design firm. "She looks like a man; sounds like one, too. If she were pretty, forget it." This division manager believes she was passed over for promotion because she is pretty and Brenda isn't. She is wrong. Unlike Brenda, the division manager consciously or unconsciously flaunts her prettiness, plays with her hair while talking, tilts her head in a flirty way, and giggles. Her work is as good as Brenda's, but men don't feel comfortable with her as an equal. Her "femaleness" is a distraction, an intrusion. When male co-workers tease her, she gets huffy, clams up, and refuses to cooperate on team projects. If they have to put up with a woman around or in charge, Brenda is more their kind of woman. She's a handsome, pleasant-looking lady who wears little makeup, conservative clothes, and sensible shoes. She doesn't come across as exceptionally feminine or masculine. "She's competent, confident, and fun to be with," says the vice president who promoted her. "She can take kidding and dish it back. She doesn't expect special treatment because she's a woman, nor does she try to be 'one of the guys.' "

When "the guys" talk about Brenda, they mention how she can "take and dish out the trash"—accept and give back the jokes and veiled insults that are a big part of the way male colleagues relate to each other. They admire the fact that Brenda doesn't appear sensitive or easily offended. And because they do, it is likely that

Brenda will continue to make the corporate climb, and that the disgruntled division manager will never achieve the ladybucks she believes she is worthy of.

20. Luck Making

Of all the golden methods used to reap ladybucks, luck making is the least rational. How does one make luck? The whole idea of luck is its flukiness, its randomness, its "accidental" advantage, right? Yes and no; women who attain ladybucks understand the contradiction. Luck can't be manufactured in the way a product is or created the way a relationship is, but it can be "encouraged" to stop on certain doorsteps.

"Ellen got the anchorwoman job because she was in the right place at the right time," says a miffed wanna-be.

"May always knows someone who knows someone," says an office rival who was hired as a trainee along with May and hasn't advanced as far.

"Christine had a bang-up year with her woolens because the weather was unusually cold. She lucked out," says a nearby shoe retailer, explaining why his profits were down and Christine's were up.

Are Ellen, May, and Christine just lucky; or is there something more operating here? Ellen got her chance to anchor a local news broadcast because the regular anchor took a maternity leave and then decided not to return to the station. May rose quickly from trainee to sales manager because a few important company clients put in a good word for her here and there. Christine's woolens were helped off the racks by freezing temperatures and chilled customers. An element of luck is apparent. However, Ellen chose to work at a station where, as she puts it, "it looked as though no one was going to be around for too long. . . . I had just left a station because everyone there had been around for years, and it looked as though they would die there."

Ellen didn't know that the pregnant anchor wouldn't return, but she invited luck by getting out of a setup where it looked as if no one would ever leave. May was fortunate that a couple of important clients took the time to praise her to her superiors; but, as she admits, "I really go out of my way for clients who seem to be credit-givers." Christine thanks Mother Nature for the wicked winter that urged her woolens onto customers' backs, but adds, "I also sell a cruisewear line my father manufactures that did much better last year than this year; I try to have a couple of things going at once."

These three women are luck makers. Ellen positioned herself in a place where she sensed she might luck into a good opportunity. May cultivates clients who will be likely to compliment her to company bosses. Christine handles a couple of dissimilar product lines—if one fails, there's always the possibility the other will succeed. Ellen might not have gotten the anchor job. May's cultivated clients could have remained mum. Christine's woolens might have done as poorly as her cruisewear, despite frigid temperatures. These women were all fortunate. But they all tickled the fickle finger of fate. They helped Lady Luck allow ladybucks.

Ellen, May, Christine, and all the women who are luck makers and moneymakers understand a fact that is unpleasant: Life is not fair. The deserving can remain poor forever, and the undeserving can make fortunes. There are no guarantees, no absolutes. But there are edges, ways to up the odds of luring luck and ladybucks. And the women who succeed up their odds by courting luck and by using the other methods covered in this chapter.

CHAPTER 6

Fail Smarts

In boxes at right, number on a scale of one to five (greatest to least response): Failure makes me:

a. angry ☐
b. freeze ☐
c. excited ☐
d. curious ☐
e. depressed ☐

This "number your response" question appears in a long, multi-part evaluation form used by a top career consulting firm to profile its clients. Filling in the form is one of several activities clients engage in to enable the firm to help them "find career paths best suited to individual temperament; choose work not in conflict with basic make-up; maximize interests and inclinations towards money making ends." The question about failure feelings is found in a section designed to determine whether the participant/client (the words *test* and *test taker* are never used) is better suited for "stress employment" or "security employment." There is no right or wrong numerical pattern; however, in the words of one of the firm's consultants, "the number-one answer of 70 percent of the females who go on to the highest earning level is *curious*."

Failure makes successful women curious? Yes, and they are thereby empowered to succeed. Failure is the trickiest ingredient in lady-bucks production. It can either start or stop the moneymaking process. The women who aren't stopped are wonderers. They examine their failures to death—and ultimately to life. They are like Thomas Edison, who, in response to a young reporter's question about how it felt to have failed 10,000 times with a new invention, replied, "Young man, since you are just starting out in life, I will tell you something of benefit. I have not failed 10,000 times. I have successfully found 10,000 ways that will not work."

Triumph in the Trenches

Ladybucks earners see failure as a means of eliminating impractical or unprofitable paths. They possess "fail smarts." Failure does not paralyze them into retreat; the response *freeze* is the least-popular answer of the 70 percent of females who go on to the highest earning level. They see hope in hell, opportunity in ashes. They pick themselves up again and again, each time curious to know why they failed and what they can do better. They eventually defeat failure by following up bad moves with improved ones.

Fail smarts is the secret weapon that turns defeat into dollars. Ladybucks earners know how to fail. *"Failure* is a word of losers," says one woman who worked for five different multilevel marketing companies before she made it big selling a canistered diet/energy supplement that increases productivity and decreases body fat. "I always thought of myself as a winner, whether or not I was making money. When I wasn't making money selling the other products [this lady has earned over $500,000 in commissions in the past four years], I kept asking myself, 'Why? What am I saying or doing that I shouldn't? Am I trying to sell to the wrong people? Am I selling the wrong product? Is my timing off for this product?' " She continually questioned herself and was curious for answers. She never thought of herself as a failure, "just as someone who had yet to succeed." Fighting back tears, she tells the story of her husband, who died in Vietnam two years after her marriage, while she was carrying their only child. "He used to write me long letters describing his different activities. I felt the filth and frustration of his daily existence. I didn't know some of the expressions he used, but he said something that explains to me why people keep fighting even when everything looks hopeless, why they go on even when victory seems impossible to everyone else. He used the words *I see triumph in the trenches.*"

There was no triumph in the trenches for this young soldier, but he passed on to his widow the spirit of winners—who don't always win but who fight the battle right. Winners, whether of wars or of ladybucks, see triumph as just a trench away. Of course, they're not always right, but they think and act in the way most likely to enhance the odds that are always against them. People are often amazed at the seeming ordinariness of the women who earn hundreds of thousands of dollars in short periods of time, who sell millions of dollars annually in goods and services. These women, often unrefined in appearance, speech, mannerisms, and education, are incredible in their approach to failure. They never see it as the end of something. It's part of the beginnng; it's built into the game plan; it's expected.

When Gessie Tassone talks about the $20,000-a-year ironworks company that she built into a million-dollar company providing security installations for major corporations and institutions, she says, "I knew it would grow; I had several plans figured out. If one didn't work, there was always another to fall back on." Gessie looks quizzically at those who question her about ventures in territory that few women enter, about the precision projects she undertakes, the large loans. Is she at all afraid of failing? "No, because I have more energy than most people," she explains. "I can keep going when everyone else is ready to fall asleep. If something doesn't work out right, I figure out what went wrong and try again." Gessie goes on to talk about the team spirit that keeps her company afloat through tough times. "Sometimes things seem slow or aren't working out well. Then everything will change; profits will really grow again." She sees her business as a continuum of triumphs interrupted by temporary setbacks. Gessie believes she and her company will always recover from problems or defeats. Failure isn't a negative event that leads to more failure; it's just part of the ladybucks equation, to be examined, understood, and corrected. That is so obvious—for the Gessies.

Failure Wisdom

"Failure is not falling down; it is remaining there when you have fallen."

"A failure is a person who has blundered but is not able to cash in on the experience."

"The only time you mustn't fail is the last time you try."

Today a huge amount of time, effort, and money are spent teaching and digesting failure wisdom. Women are particularly big customers of "failure therapy" because they put so much on the line in trying to succeed. Children, spouses, family life, and homes are compromised during certain stages of the golden grab. "It's got to pay off," says one young housewife/executive who is juggling job and children and justifying it with explanations of quality and quantity time and how her family will ultimately be better off. "If I fail to make it in my career, then everyone's suffered—for what? Where are the rewards?"

This woman, attending one of the dozens of success seminars currently being offered, writes down the above failure quotes. They are on the blackboard of the seminar room. The first half of the seminar is devoted to a discusson of failure; the second half to success. Basically, this housewife/executive is paying three hundred dollars to be told that failure is only failure when it is not followed by success. To sturdy females like Gessie who persevere through the bad times, the mistakes, the drubbings, and the aborted efforts and then emerge triumphant, it's three hundred dollars wasted. It's as old as the "if at first you don't succeed" advice given to children. Why pay to be told that money doesn't come easy?

The Gessies of the world don't go to seminars to acquire fail smarts. They get them growing up, in much the way street smarts are learned. They don't need professionals to tell them that it's fine to fail as long as you don't let it do you in. Life has taught them not to fear failure but to prepare for it, to stomp it out when it threatens to destroy. But life doesn't teach this to most women. It's everywhere to be observed, but it's not absorbed. Seminars are necessary. Inspirational pep talks are helpful. The obvious is not obvious, any more than common sense is common.

Fail Tales

Today some ladybucks earners are providing a tremendous service to new female hopefuls. They are telling tales of their failures, underscoring efforts that didn't work out, sharing their defeats and regrets. They are going way beyond the "I was so poor and struggled so hard but look at me now" saga. Honest and useful accounts are being given about the road to riches. "This is not for the fainthearted," says one mail-order millionaire. "I've gone through three husbands. My children think I'm crazy. I have no real friends. My lawyer is the only one who loves me—I keep him working." This mail-order maven strips away a lot of the magic and mystery of mail-order success. She talks about the hundreds of costly ads that don't pay off, the problems with purchasing and stocking low-cost imports, the competition, the lawsuits. She recounts explicit stories of product and service failures that were beyond her control, that cost her fortunes and almost undid her. She talks about how her children, spouses, and friends grew intolerant of her obsession with her business, with success, and with moneymaking, and how she now finds herself "living a life of lonely luxury." An inspirational recounting is given of how she has rescued her company and herself from ruin and defeat over and over again, "wondering often, 'Why am I killing myself like this?' " Lest she completely discourage her audience in the women's group she's addressing, she supplies a detailed, mouthwatering list of the golden goodies of success. She describes her beautiful homes, expensive cars, exotic vacations, designer clothes, jewels, and furs and adds, "If I had a wonderful husband, devoted children, and loyal friends and did not have all this, I would not be happier than I am now. My lifestyle is not the best, but for me it's a trade-off that works." To the question, "Can't one have the homes, cars, and vacations and still have a good family life and a few dear friends?" this woman answers by saying, "Yes, but so far that's where I've failed and haven't been able to turn failure into success."

Good fail tales inspire, inform, glamorize, and deglamorize. Whether they're told by mail-order mavens, corporate executives, fashion designers, or iron works owners, certain details are recounted frequently by successful women in every field. Again and again, there was a marriage that didn't work out. Either the ladybucks earner got divorced and then went on to discover her abilities and earn a lot of money, or she found herself driven toward moneymaking and in the process drove an unsympathetic husband away. Often the failed marriage was followed by a successful one because the divorcée realized that if she wanted a happy marriage, she had to marry a man sympathetic to her moneymaking drive, a supportive mate who would encourage her, who would not be jealous, who would understand her interests and goals and help her with children, house-work, and entertaining.

In November 1985, Gessie Tassone, founder and chief operating officer of A&T Iron Works, accepted the 1985 Businesswoman of the Year Award from the Contractors' Council of Greater New York with these words: "This is one of the most precious moments of my life as a woman in a field traditionally dominated by men. I feel great satisfaction in my achievements. As the saying goes, 'Behind every great man, there is a woman.' In my case there is a great man—my husband, Armando. Perhaps receiving this award will inspire other men to support their women in helping them attain the ful-fillment of their dreams."

Gessie went on to add that it is getting easier for women to succeed in businesses once run by men, "particularly when they are blessed with a relationship like the one I share with my husband." Those who knew Gessie before she became successful knew of an earlier marriage in which she was not so "blessed." Like many women of traditional Italian upbringing, Gessie had married fresh out of high school and created a family. Her marriage eventually soured and ended in divorce. Up to that point, Gessie had never had a paying job in her life and regarded herself as "just a housewife and mother." But this "housewife and mother" was determined to build a decent life for herself and her four daughters. She learned bookkeeping from her older sister, took part-time jobs as a bookkeeper and cook in a pizza parlor, and enrolled in night business courses at a local community college. She was twenty-nine years old before she stopped thinking of herself as a failure and began to try for ladybucks.

"I was unfulfilled with my part-time jobs," says Gessie. "A friend from years back offered me a full-time job as a bookkeeper/tele-phone answerer in his one-man iron works shop. I took it, and that's how it all began." What began first was a daily 120-mile round-trip commute from where Gessie was living to her new job. The iron-works shop was a rented two-car garage with only a telephone on the wall—no facilities, no bathroom, heat, filing cabinets, or type-writer—a gargage-based operation doing local residential railing jobs. "But I saw a chance to build it into something," says Gessie. She also saw a chance to work closely with her old friend Armando

Tassone, whom she had always considered "a wonderful human being" and who would eventually become her second husband. As friendship grew into love, Armando did the iron work, and Gessie escalated the tiny $20,000-a-year venture into a corporation that would acquire other iron works companies, bid on and win big contracts, and become a formidable million-dollar business, entering into joint ventures with overseas manufacturers. "Armando was very happy with things the way they were," stresses Gessie. "There were no debts, no loans, no charges, no checks; everything was paid on the spot with cash. I put Armando in debt," she says, "and he let me because he saw I had entrepreneurial ambitions. He didn't want or need any more than he had. But I did, and he encouraged me to play out my dreams."

Gessie's story is the story of many female moneymakers who fail in their first marriage, reach beyond the failed marriage and domestic activity toward a career or entrepreneurial goal, find a new and supportive second husband, and go on to attain happiness and ladybucks.

Some women achieve happiness and ladybucks within their first and only marriage. Some marry several times. Some build successful husband/wife enterprises with new spouses. And some never marry. But a very large percentage of the women who create successful careers and businesses have a history of failures in their first marriage (so too though do a large percentage of women who never go on to create successful careers or businesses)—failures that in many cases left them shattered, poor, and determined to build a successful life from the ashes of their mistake.

Along with fail tales of broken marriages are the "I wasn't making it as an employee (or I was fired), so I left and started my own company" stories. These are becoming more and more commonplace, with well over three million thriving female-owned enterprises now in existence. The employee-to-entrepreneur story often starts as a fail tale and becomes "the best thing that could have happened to me." Company policy, incompetent co-workers, an ineffective boss, low pay, or general job dissatisfaction prompts a woman to shed the shackles of corporate servitude and strike out on her own. She finds a marketable product or service, puts her unhappy-employee years behind her, and successfully parlays a good idea into a good income. Scores of unfulfilled workers look on, listen, and wonder if they too could find schemes to support their dreams of self-employment.

In 1980, Gail Chrystal was fired from her job as a management supervisor at a Chicago direct-marketing firm. She had been working happily at the firm for three years. Though in a corporate environment, she found ample opportunity for her creative ideas to materialize into productive systems. Then a prominent ad agency acquired her firm, and Gail got a new, narrow-minded boss who knew little about direct marketing. Happiness turned to hell. The boss was determined to inflict on her the stifling, nonproductive controls typical of large agencies. Gail could not live with the controls of her boss. Hoping to remedy the situation, she went to the chairman of the company seeking reassignment. The chairman promised to resolve the problem while she was away on vacation. He did. When Gail returned from vacation, she learned she had been fired. Then began a period of self-examination and soul-searching. Gail realized she did not fit into the standard corporate mold, that she didn't like taking orders, that she enjoyed being in control. New job offers were refused. Her next move had to be to a business of her own, to a marketing company where she could head the operation. Chrystal Direct Marketing Group, Inc., was founded in 1981. By the end of its first year, it had billings of $1 million. Two years later, it had increased its client roster, added large accounts such as Diners Club, GTE, and Montgomery Ward, and doubled its annual billings. Gail and the firm have won awards for excellence in the direct-marketing field. Chrystal Direct Marketing Group's client list and earnings are now growing steadily, and Gail looks back on her firing as the end of a bad employment situation and the beginning of an excellent one.

In addition to fail tales of "I couldn't make it as an employee," there are the failed-product tales. "I was sure it would sell," says Louise Berenson, talking about her purple worry stone. She had "developed a feel" for what her buying audience wanted. She knew what worked and what didn't. When something was selling slowly, she knew how to repackage it to enliven sales. Says Louise, "It was cutely packaged in a see-through box. It was attractive, novel—a great gift idea. It couldn't fail; I would have bet my house on it."

Fortunately, Louise didn't bet her house on it, because it did fail. "I've tried to figure out why," she says, "but I can't." Louise can't because certain failures can't be figured out—product failures particularly. Retail history is full of puzzling red-ink entries, of products that had everything going for them and died. The canister lady who lost her husband in Vietnam admits, "The diet/energy product I'm selling now is no better than some of the others I've sold with nowhere near the sales volume of this. Why did the others do poorly in comparison? I'm not sure, but I think timing has something to do with it. Right now, energy is very in. Everybody wants to increase their energy level. This product does that while decreasing body fat, cleansing the system, et cetera. People are hot to try it. If energy goes out and meditation comes in big, I hope someone invents a good, safe diet/meditation product, something that decreases weight and increases the ability to get into a trance. I'll rep it in a minute."

Fail tales often tell of products that should have succeeded but didn't. There is always speculation about why the buying public goes crazy for one product but rejects a similar or even better one. Females with fail smarts have many product fail tales to tell, but they weren't destroyed by products or services that should have sold and never did. Like Louise Berenson, their hunches tell them "it's a win"; they feel strongly enough to bet their house on their hunches. But they don't. Fail smarts hold them back. They test-market. They venture good amounts but not fortunes. Contrary to the dazzle tales that thrill armchair entrepreneurs, they rarely bet everything on a single product idea (unless they have very little to bet, in which case they have very little to lose). Says one woman who built a net worth of $3 million selling costume jewelry imported from several countries, "I kick myself whenever I don't buy enough of something and everyone wants it. But I'd kill my business if I started to bring in too many 'sure sells' that nobody wanted."

Letting Go

Part of fail smarts is knowing when to let go—when to write off a product, an idea, a person, or a job that will ultimately lead to failure. The above costume jewelry importer had an idea that delighted her.

She would set up a booth at the newly completed Jacob Javits Convention Center in New York City and display her pieces at the May 1986 Fashion and Boutique Trade Show. The Convention Center spans five city blocks. Built out of glass, it was termed a "crystal palace"—a radiant structure that would herald in a new era in trade show buying. At the May Fashion and Boutique Show, there would be over 1,700 booths; 2,500 lines would be displayed to a huge assembly of national and international buyers. The jewelry importer attended a reception held for prospective exhibitors. Booth rentals were expensive, but the investment would be justified by increased sales.

Or would it? A warning bell sounded in this lady's head. The shimmering, all-glass building was impressive—from the outside. But from the inside she saw a potential problem: a possible greenhouse effect—a show that could be disastrous if the scheduled May date turned out to be warm. She asked the center manager about indoor climate control, and he assured her that the building would be adequately air-conditioned. She was tempted to reserve space. She wanted to be at the show, particularly since it was the first boutique show to be held in the new building. "But my failure-prevention instincts stopped me from renting a stall," she says. "I liked the idea of being there. I told all my customers I would be there. I hated to change my plans. But something told me this might be a hard place to air-condition."

She was right. The show opened to press reports of exhausting heat, uncomfortable and irritable buyers, and angry and disillusioned exhibitors. "I hated to change my plans," says the jewelry importer, "but I'm glad I did. Sales were slow. The show would have been a financial loss for me. The building personnel were defensive, claiming that the building was air-conditioned but that with so many people, it was unreasonable to expect it to be any cooler. I don't know what it will be like there in the future, but right now I'm glad I didn't exhibit." (The climate-control problem at the Javits Convention Center has since been corrected.)

This lady let go of an idea she had initially embraced, that had enchanted her, but that would have failed to produce the sales and new business she would have needed to cover her exhibiting costs.

Many ladybucks yearners don't do this, and they suffer financially or emotionally or both. They hold an idea so close to their hearts, they can't examine it with their brains.

"Nothing could have stopped me from opening a café," says Cindy. "I dreamed of it from the time I was in college and visited Paris, until I was thirty and my last child was in school full-time. I saw it in my head for years: the red-and-white-checkered cloths, the hand-written menu, sketches on the walls, tables out front under an awning." Cindy tells of envisioning customers waiting for tables, eating, drinking, laughing, and spending. Her plan was pleasant, but it was destined to defeat. Cindy hates to cook, doesn't know Chablis from champagne, and dislikes record keeping. "I was in love with a memory, with the gaiety, with the idea of chatting and joking with the customers," she admits. "My husband, who's a businessman, had doubts from the beginning, but he financed my dream. Of course the café flopped, but not before it cost him $50,000 of hard-earned savings."

Cindy wouldn't let go of her dream until she had thrown good money after bad and had failed to establish the profitable café of her fantasies. No self-protective mechanism warned her that she was courting failure. Like a stubborn child, she was determined to pursue something that she wasn't equipped to handle properly and should have forgotten about—or become equipped to handle. Although persistence is sometimes a virtue, here it was foolishness.

"It's incredible how many women hold on beyond the point where it's admirable," says Cindy, who now, at forty, can look back dispassionately at her failure as "self-doomed." "It's written on the wall in front of them: 'Don't go ahead with this business the way you are; let go; modify; rethink.' But they don't see the wall any more than I did."

Not only are ideas clung to that should be discarded, people are, too. Successful women are often accused of abandoning old friends in their reach for ladybucks. "We were good friends until she got promoted (or made it big in business)" is a common claim. The person left behind is aggrieved—and understandably so. It hurts to lose a friend—to ladybucks or to anything or anyone. However, the callous side of the coin is that friendship takes time, and too much time spent maintaining friendships appropriate to an earlier period means too little time to create new careers, businesses, and relationships in keeping with new growth and goals.

"When our children were babies, Michelle and I were good friends," says Terry, who several years ago put her career on hold to be a full-time mother and has now resumed it as a successful marketing consultant. "Michelle was my closest confidante. I shared my problems, my hopes, my friends—everything—with her. I wouldn't think of having a party and not inviting Michelle. But it's different now. Our children are in high school, and we've developed separate interests. We don't have that much in common anymore.

"For a long time I felt guilty. I felt as though I were moving into a new world, meeting new people and leaving Michelle behind. Most of my time was spent building my consulting practice, making contacts, learning the ins and outs of the business. Any free time I had was spent with my family. I didn't have time for my old chats with Michelle. They were wonderful—then. But I had moved into a new life. Michelle wasn't very interested in my work, and I really didn't care about her tennis games, shopping trips, the petty neighborhood gossip that once interested me."

Michelle tells a different story—the story of the woman who is not driven toward career success and ladybucks. "Terry has become money-mad," she says. "She's not the sweet, caring person she used to be. All she cares about is her business, her accomplishments, her famous clients. If you're not making it big, Terry has no time for you. She's a changed person. I loved her the way she was."

Michelle may have loved Terry the way she was, and perhaps she was more lovable then. But as her children grew less dependent and she herself grew older, Terry no longer loved herself as she was. She wanted more in her life, to return to old career interests, to develop new ones. If she catered to Michelle's feelings and to the feelings of other old friends, she would have failed to realize her potential and her dreams. Terry now has "a few new Michelles in my life—businesswomen who like me for the same reasons I like them—because there is good chemistry between us and because we're interested in the same things, have the same goals." She admits there is a bit of "hardness" in "let go of (some) old friends" thinking, but she says, "If for some reason I were to sell my business and adopt Michelle's lifestyle, I'd be very unhappy. Also, I wouldn't expect my new friends to want to continue their friendships with me. Maybe I'd want Michelle as a close friend again; but that's not where I am now at all."

Certainly not all old friendships should be dropped in the name of professional progress, business building, or career climbing. Some old friends grow together. Some are undemanding and wonderful to keep in touch with periodically and should be cherished. Old friends are pieces of the past that permit a woman to touch the child or young adult that she once was. However, old friendships cannot be indulged to the point that they prevent new dreams from being realized. Fail smarts dictate this to the women destined to reap ladybucks. They feel pangs of guilt or regret, but they don't let the pangs prevent progress in new arenas or prevent them from undertaking new challenges.

Just as friendships must be modified in the reach for ladybucks, so too must employer-employee relationships. When Julia was named operating manager of a posh California department store, she was thrilled. The top executive job was the culmination of years of loyal service to the store in positions ranging from part-time salesgirl to assistant store manager. From her teen years on Julia knew she wanted a career in retailing. Before her big promotion, during her stint as assistant store manager, she had gotten her nephew a job in the store's auditing department. She loved her nephew, had babysat him, seen him take his first step, attended his college graduation. The boy had turned into a fine young man and would be an asset to the store. She had been pleased to recommend him for work there. Shortly after her promotion to operating manager Julia learned from her nephew's immediate supervisor that his work was slipping badly. She investigated the charge, spoke to her nephew, and fired him. Many of her family members were outraged. The boy was having problems, she was told. She could have tried to help him, to understand what was going on in his life.

Though family sentiment was against her, corporate sentiment was not. Julia sized up quickly that her nephew had developed a drug problem and was keeping company with undesirable friends. He claimed he was "working things out," but Julia couldn't afford to be sympathetic. "This is not Japan, where perhaps I could have buried him away in some remote location until he straightened himself out," she says. "He was ineffective at work and had been for a while, and I had to let him go. If I didn't, it could have affected my job."

Julia is correct. Her fail smarts told her that as a corporate boss she was vulnerable. Her years of striving for the success that was now hers could well have been wasted. It would have been hard to maintain her authority or advance further with her nephew to answer for. Julia protected herself from potential failure by letting go of an employee who could have damaged her reputation and dragged her down with him. She encountered criticism, as one often does in the firing process, but she made the right move for her goals and for maintaining her ladybucks earnings. Firing is hard, particularly the firing of a family member, friend, or loyal employee. However, to keep an unproductive employee who is a clear liability is to risk self-defeat—a risk too great for women intent on escalating their work into wealth.

Status Transference

Status transference is a voluntary shifting from one ladybucks situation to a better one in order to maintain and increase earnings and stature. A physical and mental relocation usually occurs. In April 1985, Wendy Rue went from entrepreneur to executive. She turned over her successful female networking business, the National Association for Female Executives (NAFE), to George Tunick, a seasoned corporate executive. Tunick took NAFE, which high-achieving women regard as a support system and which corporations see as a market for their products and services, restructured it as a subsidiary of a new company (Executive Female), and kept Wendy as chairman of NAFE while he assumed the presidency of Executive Female. The purpose of the restructuring was to market products to NAFE members and license the Executive Female name. Then a few months later, Rue and Tunick sold Executive Female to a holding company, Astro Drilling. Wendy signed a five-year executive employment contract with Astro. She received $5 million and 6 percent equity in Astro (with a potential $3 million more in the offing contingent on the future earnings of Executive Female). The female networking organization that she had begun in 1972 was now an established corporation with a growing corporate client roster—and Wendy was heading the operation.

Wendy went from NAFE founder to corporate head of Executive Female in order to become a millionaire. George Tunick, a male with corporate credentials and appeal, was a plus for Wendy's financial future. Corporations interested in marketing their products and services to executive females, but uncomfortable talking business with women, responded readily to Tunick. An increasing number of corporations signed up with Executive Female, and Wendy walked away with ladybucks that would have been unattainable to her had she kept NAFE as was. By moving from entrepreneur to executive, she enabled NAFE—and herself—to grow and to enjoy greatly increased earnings.

Fail smarts tell an ambitious woman, "You're doing well, but if you want things to get better, change your operating status." Wendy heeded the warning and left the entrepreneurial world in favor of a lucrative corporative opportunity. Usually ladybucks are earned in reverse: a woman leaves a well-paying (or poorly paying) job to become her own boss and multiply her earnings in the entrepreneurial world.

Lynette Spano Vives was twenty-eight years old and earning $52,000 a year when she left her job as a commissioned computer software saleswoman and began her own software company, SCI, which now, after two years in business, has annual revenues of $8.5 million.

Karen Fisher left her job as executive editor of *American Home* magazine to begin her decorator consulting firm; her first-year net profits were $150,000.

Janice Jones left a job as vice president of a banking and investor relations firm to found her own company that would structure stock offerings and that now, six years later, brings in annual revenues of $15 million and permits her equity in several quality companies.

The high earners who shift from entrepreneur to executive or from employee to entrepreneur see themselves as failing to maximize their potential in their present circumstances and thus unable to reap the ladybucks they could. By transferring from one money-making position to another, they increase their income. Their fail smarts alert them to pivotal opportunities and challenges that other women ignore or are reluctant to try.

Benefiting from Blunders

In addition to spotlighting new opportunities and challenges, fail smarts enable enterprising women to capitalize on mistakes. Rather than being defeated by blunders, they take what they have learned and apply it to more profitable ends within their area of specialization. In 1981, Barbara Adamak saw an unfilled market niche that could mushroom into a good business: the need for high-quality child care for the youngsters of career-oriented mothers who wanted their children attended to at home rather than at day-care facilities. The outcome was Nanny Pop-Ins, Ltd., an Atlanta-based corporation, begun with a partner and designed to match screened, trained nannies with appropriate clients. Barbara left a career in advertising to devote her business experience to the new operation. Earnings were very good. The company went from revenues of $25,000 in its first year to $250,000 in its third, with no slowdown in sight. Barbara was delighted with the results of her idea and decided to sell the Nanny Pop-Ins concept as a franchise package. Her plan was good, but it didn't work.

Barbara examined why the franchise plan was unsuccessful. Start-up costs and royalty fees for a Nanny Pop-In franchise were too high for most potential franchisees. Restrictive legalities dampened investor enthusiasm. Given the scandals that were erupting in the industry, the liability factor (against which it was difficult to insure), the difficulty in maintaining a high-level screening and training program in a franchise network, and the business's inherently low profit margin, a franchise arrangement added up to a lot of worry, work, time, and money spent before any gains would be realized. "I discovered that it was not an efficient way to market the concept," says Barbara. "The nanny industry does not lend itself to franchising; our business requires a hands-on approach, including constant contact with staff. It's virtually impossible to keep that kind of personal connection and control over franchises."

Barbara licked her wounds and decided to nurture an offshoot plan that has worked out well. Still believing in the need for professional at-home child care, she determined she would put her expertise to use as a consultant to nationwide nanny operations. She and her partner sold the Nanny Pop-Ins trademark to her then–office manager, and Barbara opened NPI Services, Inc., a management consulting firm that specializes in setting up and advising female-oriented and -operated small service businesses. These include domestic companionship services, domestic maid services, and tutoring services, but mainly nanny employment services, from which her consulting firm was a natural outgrowth. With 70 percent of the working women in the United States now mothers (compared with 23 percent in 1981), support services for nanny businesses are needed, and Barbara's flourishing firm is filling the need with a dedicated and rapidly growing client roster.

Unlike many women who have persistence but jump from one unrelated specialty to another at the first sign of trouble, Barbara stayed with her initial interest. She modified an unsuccessful child-care franchising plan into a successful domestic and child-care consulting firm. She extracted the best from a bad business move and funneled it into an improved approach that would work well. Many women don't display this kind of fail smarts. When a plan fails they become discouraged, which is easy to do and which Barbara did, too, but they abandon the whole idea instead of breaking it into segments, chucking what won't work and revamping the rest into ladybucks.

"I struggled three years trying to make it in the travel business," says Claudia, "but I kept falling more and more in debt. When I decided to bail out, I didn't want anything to do with the travel field. I'd had it." Claudia went to a business consultant to discuss her unprofitable stint as a travel consultant specializing in charter operations and to see what new business might suit her. The consultant analyzed her failed operation and determined that she had specialized in something that established local agencies had already locked in. Her competition was overwhelming. She could have battled it by undertaking certain marketing approaches, but she hadn't. He explained to her exactly what she might have tried and what she still could do to cash in on her travel expertise. He told her that if she was disenchanted with charter travel, she could focus on cruises, which could be very lucrative because of the relatively large fares charged, as opposed to plane travel (and particularly charter flights). Or perhaps, being young herself, she might enjoy specializing in the college market, setting up bases of operations at the two large nearby universities and locking in the still-untapped college trade.

Claudia wasn't having any of it. "The consultant's ideas were really good, but I closed my mind to anything he had to say about travel," she says. "I didn't care how much I'd learned about travel. I wanted to go into something new." The something new was catering. Claudia, a good and imaginative cook and baker, decided to tap the corporate conference market. She would supply hors d'oeuvres, wine, gourmet club sandwiches, and finger pastries for executive luncheon meetings. The food would be tasty and attractively presented. Her plan was fine. There was a need out there, and she could fill it with quality products and service. "It was an excellent idea," says Claudia. "Unlike in charter travel, there was little quality competition to worry about."

Claudia was correct. There was little competition to worry about. She could supply a needed service, sell her expertise to a waiting market, and make a lot of money. It looked good. But once again Claudia is failing. She hasn't benefited from the big blunder in her travel venture and has gone on to repeat the mistake: Again, she has no real marketing program.

"I didn't think it would be so important here," says Claudia. "Yes, I should have had one when I was selling charter travel because of the stiff competition, but here there is no stiff competition."

Claudia assumed, erroneously, that because she had no big competition, she had no need to concern herself with any major marketing of her service. She sent flyers to nearby corporate offices. That was enough, she believed. Requests should have poured in, and her business should have grown and prospered. This might have happened; she could have been lucky; but it hasn't happened. Again, Claudia didn't maximize her chances of success.

Says her business consultant, "Claudia is like a lot of entrepreneurs who could make it big but don't. She has talent in several areas, but she really thinks that talent triumphs over all. Minimal time and effort are put into marketing activities. I fully expect Claudia will forget about catering, jump into something new, and repeat her mistake."

It seems so simple. All Claudia has to do is let the business consultant advise her about marketing herself and her business. He could tell her how to get the kinds of publicity that would draw customers in large numbers, how to advertise for maximum results, how to build a large repeat clientele, and how to create the customer base almost any business needs if it's to produce high earnings. Why doesn't Claudia let her consultant guide her? She sought his analysis because she knows she's doing something wrong. He told her what it is. Now she should be all set to rectify her mistake and begin her climb for ladybucks—in travel, catering, or anything else she's qualified to pursue.

Shouldn't this all be self-evident? Claudia is a talented, hardworking woman, positively positioned to capitalize on her assets and ideas. Success could be hers more easily than most people's. But like a surprisingly large number of women, she is weak in certain fail smarts. She doesn't give up or fear failure. She's optimistic, even curious about why she's not doing well when she has so much going for her. But like the mother who believes her superior child should get into the college of his choice purely on merit, watches him get rejected, and doesn't suggest a wiser appoach, Claudia is a passive marketer who doesn't benefit from her blunders. Ten business consultants could say, "Wise up, lady; this is the real world; things don't sell on merit alone," but Claudia would continue her self-defeating pattern, believing that eventually she'll come up with a product or service that will sell itself.

"Claudia's reluctance to engage in a well-planned marketing program is no different from other entrepreneurs' inabilities to see their mistakes in undercapitalization or delegation of responsibility or time management," says Claudia's business consultant. "These people are not stupid. They understand they're making mistakes. But once shown their mistakes, they don't change what they're doing. They look for other explanations. Sometimes it's idealism; sometime it's stubbornness or subconscious conflicts about supersuccess. Whatever, it prevents them from cashing in on their abilities."

Women like Claudia spend a lot of time and money learning about cashing in on their abilities, about their business mistakes, about better operating strategies. They see consultants, attend seminars, read dozens of how-to books, and go on to repeat their mistakes, each time believing things will work out differently than before. They give credence to the saying, "A failure is a person who has blundered but is not able to cash in on the experience."

CHAPTER **7**

The Energy Link

It's 11:30 P.M. Gessie Tassone is designing a new piece of equipment for use in her million-dollar foundry. She's put in a ten-hour workday, stopped for dinner, and is now going strong. She'll keep working until the early hours of the morning, sleep for a few hours, and wake up refreshed, ready for another full day among her lolly columns, twisting machines, overhead cranes, and band saws.

Gessie, forty-two, is an attentive wife and devoted mother of four daughters. She fits everything into her life—family, friends, business, religion, and community activities. When people around her begin to collapse from fatigue, she is still able to operate at peak efficiency. Gessie has all the traits that lead to accomplishment (the four A's and three I's); she uses many of the golden methods that produce ladybucks; she has fail smarts. But she has something in addition that makes it all work, that is critical to her success: a very high energy level.

High energy is the link between all the pieces of the ladybucks phenomenon. It enables women like Gessie to simultaneously raise children, run thriving businesses, persevere despite disappointments, and bounce back from divorce, defeat, or disaster. It is the most obvious unifying element of the women who turn their dreams into dollars, who create wealth against all odds, who see their ideas grow into industries. Ladybucks earners don't look alike, sound alike, or dress alike. Some are sweet, humble, and low key, particularly outside their areas of specialization. Others electrify a room when they enter. Some are pedantic. Some are delightful. Some are amusing. But what comes across in almost all cases is a consistent, unebbing wealth of energy.

Gessie, an attractive but stout woman, moves through her 18,000-square-foot ironworks foundry like an elf on roller skates. One minute she's talking to a worker who is dipping a line of fencing into a paint bin. A few moments later, she is examining an arriving shipment of steel columns. Then, across the foundry to analyze the performance of a new thredding machine. Three minutes to consult with the Con Edison man about an electrical panel board that the utility company is installing at the entrance to the foundry. Out of the foundry and into a nearby trailer, housing an electronic machine that permits her instant access to a supplier in Italy. She reads an incoming communication, types in an answer, and feeds it back to the machine. Five minutes later, she's in her nearby office talking to a customer. The customer leaves satisfied after twenty minutes. Three phone calls later, she's ready to discuss a new job with her engineer. Lunch is eaten at her desk while she's perusing blueprints. The afternoon proceeds at this same pace, with Gessie moving from activity to activity, person to person, phone call to phone call, observing, absorbing, listening, questioning, making decisions. In the evening, Gessie is off to a Rental Rehabilitation Program she's involved in. From there she plans to . . .

Almost all of Gessie's days and nights are packed with activities, chores, meetings, and obligations. Seldom does she slow down. But like her successful counterparts in other fields, she doesn't realize she is supercharged. She accepts her on-the-move style and high energy level the way people with keen eyesight accept their vision—nonchalantly, a blessing taken for granted.

Joni Evans, forty-four, president of Simon & Schuster's trade book division, is considered a winner in the New York publishing world. She turns manuscripts into best-sellers—the name of the game in book publishing. Some people love her. Others hate her. Everyone who has ever worked with her is astounded by her energy, by her endless capacity to function with enthusiasm and skill on little sleep. "Built for speed," "works day and night," "can't sleep," and "has extra glands" are phrases used admiringly by colleagues to describe this woman, who has worked her way to the peak of publishing and ladybucks and shows no signs of slowing down. Joni is not unaware of her extraordinary energy, but like many ladybucks earners, she waxes ecstatic over her passion for the field she's in, her love of books, and work related to them. Authors who have worked with her have been impressed and amazed by how quickly and thoroughly she reads their manuscripts and calls them with comments. Editors at other publishing houses remark, "I wish I had Joni's endurance. I have the same passion for publishing she has; but I also have a need for eight hours a night sleep"; "I enjoy editing as much as she does, but I can't move the way she does. The woman never stops"; "She's always 'on'; it's incredible."

Gessie Tassone's and Joni Evans's counterpart in the professional world is Dr. Paula Moynahan. Here again is a nonstop woman who amazes colleagues and employees with her extraordinary stamina. Paula goes all day and well into the night, devoting long hours to patients, research, conferences, and seminars. Late in the day, this forty-four-year-old plastic and reconstructive surgeon looks as fresh as if she had just arrived at work and many years younger than her age. Like Gessie and Joni, she talks about her love of what she does as being crucial to her success. She does not dismiss her high energy level as insignificant, but having never been any other way, she doesn't focus on it as a major contributor to her success.

Genetic Green Lights

Women like Gessie, Joni, and Paula are often born with bountiful wells of energy. Their parents and grandparents were—and are—high-energy individuals. Superstamina is an inherited gift that they don't think much about unless fate intercedes in their lives and they lose it. They talk about their passionate devotion to their businesses, careers, and professions, their hard work, and the family and friends who accelerate their success. But they give only a passing nod to energy.

Certainly, abounding energy does not guarantee ladybucks. It could be put toward things having little to do with moneymaking. However, when women spilling over with stamina choose to build a business or pursue a lucrative career or profession, their natural vigor is a crucial ally.

"I don't move quickly; I don't get a lot done in a day; I can't move easily from one thing to another," says Rochelle, a conscientious thirty-three-year-old college graduate who took a secretarial job in a large advertising agency ten years ago and is still in the same position. "I have watched three women come into this company after I did and rise to top administrative positions. They're not smarter than I am or more ambitious. I can't even say they work harder, because I work as hard as I can. They just have enormous energy. They come in early, work late, and never get sick or tired. They can handle twenty different tasks in a day. I envy them; but if I tried to push myself to be like them I'd get sick."

Rochelle really believes what she says. Her boss considers her "a terrific secretary" and is delighted she has not climbed higher in the company. "It's not easy to find a good secretary today," he says. "A lot of young women come into this firm as secretaries, begin eyeing higher positions from day one, and within a few years forget they ever knew how to type." Rochelle listens and wishes she was one of those women.

It's easy to be critical of Rochelle. Says one of her co-workers, "Rochelle is a snail. She always complains about how her back aches, how tired she is, how much work she has to get done. She's like an eighty-year-old woman." This co-worker, like many supercharged young people in advertising, can't understand how someone only thirty-three years old can plod along day after day, year after year in the same entry-level job doing what she did ten years earlier. To an ambitious, young, single girl, or to an accomplished older career woman blessed with an abundance of energy, Rochelle is a bit of a loser—someone not to despise, but to dismiss as ordinary, unsuccessful, unworthy of time or attention from a would-be mover and shaker (or from the media, which helps elevate mover-and-shaker types to celebrity status and ladybucks).

Fatigue as Foe

Most women today are not movers or shakers. Often they're grateful just to be able to move their bodies out of bed in the morning. They are very much like Rochelle. The media that profiles female winners know this. But for their purposes the Rochelles fall into the "loser" category—they are losing out on the glamour, the gold, and the glory that a select group of women are attracting. The Rochelles are not newsworthy. Everyone knows too many of them. Print and air space is given to those successful female executives, entrepreneurs, and professionals who market products, services, and themselves, mother children, and become the measure by which other women evaluate themselves.

While successful, energetic women draw a lot of attention and admiration today, there are a growing number of scholars who are beginning to dissect the glitz, look beyond the traits and techniques that produce winners, and expose the lurking mega-enemy of female success—fatigue. Energy is the grease of achievement and affluence; fatigue is the foe. More women would accomplish more and earn more if they had more energy, say the glitz dissectors, who are very sympathetic to women like Rochelle. One such glitz dissector is Dr. Holly Atkinson, a thirty-three-year-old medical doctor and author of the book *Women and Fatigue*. Though successful and energetic herself, she views fatigue as a female crisis, as an epidemic among women—an epidemic rooted in physical problems and in psychological struggles that affect women exclusively.

Fatigue is an old problem under new scrutiny. The time is right to turn a spotlight on it. It's preventing ambitious women from achieving affluence. What causes it? What are its effects? How can it be treated? If it's largely a female problem, as Dr. Holly Atkinson believes it is, and if females now more than ever are seeking ladybucks, which they are, then women without naturally high energy levels must develop them.

IN SEARCH OF ENERGY

Understanding and acknowledging fatigue as a genuine ailment is the beginning of combating it and substituting energy in its place. There is a tendency to equate it with boredom, which is an oversimplification of the problem. "I'm always exhausted because it's boring staying home all day with two young children," says a twenty-five-year-old mother who looks forward to the day "when the kids will be in school and I can start a giftware business." She expresses the sentiments of many young mothers. However, though boredom does intensify fatigue, some young mothers with children acknowledge it but don't give in to the kind of exhaustion that leads others to put their entrepreneurial dreams on hold until their children are in school.

When Barbara Macaire began Skyline by Fabric Design in 1979, she was working as an elementary school teacher and struggling to get by as a single parent with two children to support. To supplement her teaching salary, she made and sold colorful kites and banners, working nights from her home sewing machine. "Sometimes I was bored; sometimes I was tired. But I really didn't think much about being bored or tired; I just kept going" says this art-educated businesswoman.

"I really didn't think much about being bored or tired; I just kept going."

Barbara Macaire experienced boredom and fatigue. She didn't draw either a connection or a nonconnection between them. She just kept working. Like the entrepreneurs who say, "I didn't know it couldn't be done, so I did it," Barbara didn't know that one couldn't accomplish much when tired, so she accomplished a lot despite fatigue, and whether or not it was boredom-related. When tired, she did routine chores that didn't require great stamina and saved more demanding work for more energetic hours.

Mothers of toddlers often talk about boredom and fatigue. So do unhappy wives, unfulfilled employees, and mourning widows. There is the assumption that when the kids are older, or the spouse is replaced, or a new job is found, or the depression subsides, the boredom will end and there will be an increase of energy and consequent success. This isn't just wishful thinking. There is potential truth here. When a monotonous lifestyle is altered, there is often an energy surge that can be applied to moneymaking activities. However, ladybucks earners usually don't wait for energy surges. Like Barbara Macaire they work through boredom and fatigue, allot their hardest work to peak energy slots, take short refueling breaks when necessary, and position themselves for high earnings. They don't wait for ideal circumstances to begin capitalizing on their ideas. Actually, by working through periods of boredom and fatigue, they increase their existing energy levels.

"I indulged my fatigue," says Pam, who admits to a bad case of "empty nest syndrome." "My children were no longer living at home. At first it was great. I loved the freedom. Then I found myself more tired than when they were home. I began to feel really old at forty-five. Friends of mine were going back to school, taking jobs, starting businesses. I got depressed and wished my children were little again and living at home. The dinner table seemed so empty with just my husband and me there. I felt as though I had to begin a career in order to justify my existence and show my face in town. I got so tired that I began sleeping fourteen hours a day. At the first sign of a yawn, I lay down for a nap." Pam went on like this for two years. The more she slept, the more sleep she needed and the worse she felt. Then things changed.

"It was just survival instinct, I guess," Pam says. "I felt miserable, but I began to hate myself for catering to my misery. I had reached the point where just getting dressed in the morning exhausted me." She had also reached the point where she was determined to help herself. She had always enjoyed shopping for smart clothes at a nearby department store and decided to apply for a sales job there. "It wasn't easy," she recalls. "The girl who interviewed me was the age of my oldest daughter." However, she got through the interview and got the job. At first she was drained by lunch hour. She liked being around the attractive designer outfits, showing them to customers, and helping customers make choices. "But was I weak!" she says. "However, I liked my work, and slowly I began to feel better." Pam's manager admired her. Unlike some younger salesgirls in the store, Pam was conscientious, considerate of customers, and hardworking. "It's interesting," says Pam. "Salesgirls half my age complained about exhaustion. Two of them were fired because they were too lazy to hang up some shipments that came in."

Instead of getting fired, Pam got promoted to assistant buyer. "I was thrilled," she recalls. "One day my boss came in and said the department buyer was going on a buying trip to New York and needed an assistant; would I be interested?" Pam was very interested. As a teenager she had considered the idea of becoming a buyer but had gotten married a few years out of high school, had children, and forgotten about a career.

"It was incredible," says Pam, remembering and clearly fighting back tears. "All of a sudden, I felt twenty-five. Everything seemed as though it were just beginning."

A lot of things were just beginning for Pam. She loved the buying trip, came home, enrolled in some retailing courses at a local college, and joined a fitness program. Says Pam, "I had gone from sleeping fourteen hours a day to sleeping four, just to fit everything in. My days and nights were filled with work, classes, homework, new friends. I didn't have time to think about being tired. I just kept going, and I loved it."

Two years have passed. Pam is now head buyer of a new boutique in her store. Her department has become the most popular and profitable one in the store. She does a lot of traveling, receives several "tempting" job offers a month, is considered "indispensable" by her employer, and says, "I think I'm going to celebrate my fiftieth birthday by opening my own shop." On her desk is a lavish engraved plaque that reads, "A live wire makes hay with the grass that grows under other people's feet." "A gift from the head of the store," she says, smiling and looking radiant.

Energy and Physical Health

There is much truth to the notion that a woman can fight fatigue with work, overcome it, and go on to an exciting and lucrative career. Too much rest and relaxation can increase, rather than decrease, exhaustion. However, not all fatigue is caused from an unsatisfying lifestyle and not all can be successfully treated in Pam's "stop indulging it" manner. Dr. Holly Atkinson points out that first women must rule out possible physical causes when dealing with fatigue. Conditions such as anemia, urinary tract infections, neurological disturbances, and cardiac problems can rob energy and have serious consequences. She advises visits to one or more physicians and having blood analyses and tests for mononucleosis, thyroid functioning, and glucose tolerance. In addition to emphasizing the importance of investigating fatigue as a symptom of a critical disorder, she stresses that many women increase their fatigue levels in attempts to decrease their weight. They deprive themselves of the complex carbohydrates (found in whole grain breads, cereals, potatoes, and pastas) that provide energy and stamina. When the body lacks sufficient carbohydrates to fuel itself, it begins to burn the muscle tissue that makes energy, she says. Women must build muscle, not burn it, if they are to combat fatigue.

In the search for energy to keep going from day to day, from dream to deed, the most touted solutions are continually ignored.

Fad diets that sap energy are resorted to over and over in a desire for svelteness (which often outweighs the desire for energy). Vitamins are carelessly used as substitutes for sound eating habits. Smoking, which reduces oxygen delivery and consequently energy supply, is used to curb appetite and tension, despite the fact that it also curbs energy. Aerobic exercises, which build muscle, help the body eliminate waste, and increase endurance, are often ignored in favor of exercises that improve appearance more than general health and fitness. The more challenges women undertake and the more they try to juggle career and motherhood, the more energy is required. The searches for ladybucks and for energy need to go together. It is very difficult to achieve one without the other. Even women gifted with genetic green lights in the energy department admit to having to work to maintain their high energy levels as they get older.

Mental Energy

"I believe you can be anything you put your mind to," says sports marketer Carol Jenna. Physical and mental energy must be combined, believes this athlete who devotes time both to aerobic workouts and to creative visualization. In addition to working her way to success, Carol thinks her way to success. "I concentrate on what I want. I see myself achieving it and enjoying it, and that makes the process easier," she says.

"Energy, like happiness, is a state of mind," says Dr. Paula Moynahan. "I'm a big believer in the power of positive thinking for getting things done." The doctor side of Paula admits the importance of proper exercise and diet in building and maintaining exercise. She talks of a childhood of "excellent nutrition, adequate rest, and good exercise," of "no illness or sickness except for an occasional slight cold." "Mom and Dad did everything right," she says. Now forty-four, she takes a calcium supplement and vitamin C and does "occasional aerobics, swimming, and trail riding." But what does she recommend most for energy-deficient people? "A positive mental attitude. . . . Of course physical health is important," she says. "But mental energy can work miracles. I can improve a woman's appearance; she can be in good physical condition. But if she doesn't use her mental power to feel good, to believe in her abilities, she won't get what she's after."

"When you implement a thought, you set energy into motion, which then builds its own energy. That's why it is important to think about what you want instead of what you don't want, because you get what you think about." So believes Bonnie Prebula, a Honolulu-based astrology consultant who receives up to five hundred dollars per consultation, offers monthly seminars, sells cassette tapes, furnishes a telephone consulting update, and employs four part-time astrologers to help her handle the high demand for her services. Bonnie markets her services to the business community of Hawaii because "I like to help people make money, and I like to make it myself." She emphasizes that she is "a facts-and-figures, not a crystal ball, astrologer" and underscores that "success is in the stars and in your head; you can make things happen by believing they will happen and acting in accordance with your birth sign and an astrological chart."

Bonnie, Paula, Carol, and scores of other ladybucks earners are involved in some form of mental science. They believe in a connection between thought, attitude, energy flow, and success. Meditation of one kind or another, formally or informally practiced, is considered essential to accomplishment. Generally, physical and mental energy are viewed as a holistic, synergistic, interactive trigger to goal fulfillment, with mental energy considered the prime force.

Phyllis, an electrical engineer who considers herself "a low-energy person unless I feel challenged and excited," underscores the essence of mental energy. "It's self-generated, cerebral vitality," she says. "It's stimulated by an opportunity, vision, dream, problem that won't go away, that demands immediate response. In my case it's an adrenaline flow that continues until the challenge ends, the job is completed." This award-winning engineer, who built up a net worth of $2 million before her thirtieth birthday, adds, "Mental energy works differently for different people. I work in spurts. For a few months I'll go nonstop, day and night. I work through meals, get by on almost no sleep. My mind won't quit; my body keeps going. Then when a project is completed I collapse."

Phyllis "collapses" and "spaces out into stupidity." She watches sitcoms on television, reads "silly" magazines, visits friends, and "babbles about nonsense." "I lie around on a beach and let my mind wander. . . . I doze off all day long," she says. Though she talks about "spacing out into stupidity," she's really letting her mind and body regenerate from an intense spell of unbroken, singleminded concentration. After a month of this regeneration, she's usually back working at the same intensity on a new job, again drawing mental energy from "an opportunity, vision, dream, problem that won't go away."

A bit of probing reveals that Phyllis usually eats sensibly and rides a stationary bike every night while watching the eleven o'clock news. But she dismisses this with, "Of course you can't abuse your body too much if you want your mind to work, but without mental energy you can easily be just an aerobically fit fool."

Phyllis, like several ladybucks earners, pushes her mind and body to the limit but instinctively protects herself along the way. She doesn't necessarily think of her nightly bicycle exercise or her "spacing out into stupidity" as self-protective mechanisms that enable her to function when she wishes to at a fever pitch, but that's what they are. Women like Phyllis don't thrive for long without these safeguards.

Unlike Phyllis, Edith, a very successful freelance technical writer, "budgets my mental energy the way people budget money." She knows Phyllis and describes her as "a crazy, wonderful, self-indulgent genius." "I could never live like that," says Edith. "Phyllis couldn't either if she had a husband or kids to think about."

Edith, a wife and mother of three grade-school children, says, "I have no problem with household work. The girls help; Ralph [her husband] is terrific; I have someone who comes in once a week; that's not what's hard. My problem is keeping my brain working well enough and long enough to write six or seven pages a day, help the girls and Ralph with what may be bothering them, read, attend seminars, maintain the relationships that are all part of my work."

Edith keeps her brain working "well enough and long enough" by "respecting my brain and trying to relax." She doesn't push her mind or body to the limit. She meticulously allots herself "a few hours a day at the typewriter, a daily meditation break, a couple of afternoons a week in the library, a couple of hours a week attending seminars or networking on the telephone, and a few hours a day I devote to talking to my family."

Edith is amazingly efficient. Her mind works like a well-oiled machine that's programmed for a certain amount of work daily or weekly, gets it done, and stops. "She's a nice woman, very smart," says Phyllis, talking about Edith, "but the most constipated person you'll ever meet."

From Meditation to Masturbation

Edith doesn't see herself as constipated. She is very proud of the way she operates. She talks (a bit piously) about the significance of meditation in maintaining her mental energy. Phyllis, though she doesn't like the word *meditation,* also meditates to some extent when she "spaces out into stupidity," but she doesn't think of it that way. Like Edith, she too must regenerate her mental energy. A spontaneous type, Phyllis says, "Women like Edith plan their lives in energy segments and fear losing control—a few hours at the typewriter, a few hours talking to their families, an hour meditating. Three times a week they go from meditation to masturbation."

Phyllis talks liberally and lightly about masturbation, unlike most enlightened and enterprising women who do masturbate but aren't comfortable exploring the subject. A large percentage admit (in anonymous surveys) to masturbating regularly as a substitute for regular sexual intercourse or in addition to it. They know it can serve as a tension valve, but they don't publicly analyze its benefits or advocate it as a means of increasing mental energy.

The relationship between masturbation and mental energy is interesting. Masturbation releases negative physical and mental energy that prevents concentration and thus permits positive physical and mental energy to take over. Its effects are not very different from the effects of physical exercise, but because of masturbation's sexual aspects, it's not a topic of conversation widely explored by accomplished women intent on maintaining and increasing their professional image. The medical community examines it with a scientific and detached eye, but their clinical reports, couched in technical jargon, make boring reading.

"I don't think about masturbation," says Phyllis. "I just do it when a certain edginess comes into my body. I get myself going on some sexual fantasy, and I come. It's fast, safe, and private. If there's a great man around that I want to go to bed with, then I do. If that helps, terrific. If not, I'll still masturbate."

"Masturbation doesn't work for me," says an investment banker.

"I wish it did. Maybe I'm doing it wrong. Maybe my sexual fantasies aren't arousing enough. Maybe it's my religious upbringing. I don't know."

"It doesn't do enough for me," says a well-known fashion designer. "My life is a fast-lane existence. Like a lot of women today, I need fast and good service. A refreshing lay from the right man, with no strings attached, is wonderful. But it's not always available on my terms, so I masturbate. It helps, but it's not like the real thing."

"It's better than the real thing if you're married to a husband like mine," says a sporting goods retailer. "He really tries to please me. I adore him. I love talking to him, being with him. But I can do more for myself in five minutes with my hand than he can do in an hour with his whole mind and body."

"I need the emotional warmth that comes from physical contact with a man I care about," says a college administrator. "I try masturbation periodically, but it intensifies my aloneness. Before my divorce I resorted to it regularly. It helped a little, but it hurt my self-esteem. I wanted my husband to want me, but he didn't."

The role of masturbation in the lives of successful women is significant. The approach to it is pragmatic. Generally it is neither glorified nor condemned. To the degree that it helps to reduce negative energy and increase efficiency, it is considered a valuable work aid. A Texas criminal litigator puts it well when she says, "Who does it hurt? If it makes you feel better, why not? It's not like engaging in antisocial activity where you feel better at someone else's expense. It's too bad more attention isn't given to this subject where women are concerned. Men have always masturbated freely, talked and joked about it."

Stress

Stress is bad; it leads to fatigue and health problems. True or false? It's both true and false. Now that there are over 50 million women in the workforce, with the numbers increasing, a lot of attention is being focused on women and stress. Sometimes stress is terrible for women. It destroys their physical and emotional health. Dr. Holly Atkinson points out that women are now breadwinners as well as breadmakers. It is a dual role defined by self-denial. Stress and fatigue follow. The body pumps out too much adrenaline, becomes depleted, and breaks down. In her book *Women and Fatigue,* she emphasizes that current social conditions cause chronic fatigue for women. This can be corrected, she says, by challenging the traditional roles of motherhood and fatherhood. She calls for paternity leaves in addition to maternity leaves, more and better day-care facilities, and flexible work schedules.

Dr. Atkinson's approach to stress is sound. If you spend too much energy without repletion, you become stressed out and break down. It makes sense and is the foundation of all stress theories. However, now stress is being examined and qualified as good stress and bad stress. Recent studies on women and stress expand on the "limited pool" theory, which says each person has a limited amount of energy and each additional role a woman takes on drains more energy from the pool. The new energy-stress theories hold that when a woman does something that excites and challenges her, she increases her energy supply, despite the fact that she may also be a married mother dividing her time between home and office. Crucial here is not how hard a woman works but how she feels about what she's doing— at home and at the office. If husband, children, and community are supportive (in keeping with Dr. Atkinson's recommendations) and work offers ego rewards and self-esteem, a woman's energy supply will be continually replenished and her overall health enhanced. If her family resents her career and she's working at a job where she feels powerless, frustrated, and bored, she's likely to experience constant exhaustion and health-threatening stress.

Though *stress* is a word with negative connotations, latest reports emphasize that bad stress must be distinguished from good stress. Stress is more than pressure or tension. Women who feel the least influence over their lives suffer damaging stress. Their home and work lives put them under pressures they can't cope with. They don't have the power to make decisions or demands that can reduce anxiety. Decision-making women, women with authority, ladybucks earners who have clout and control usually have enormous stress in their lives, but they don't suffer from it. They are vitalized by it.

Sometimes situations that are stressful and draining to one woman will be stressful but stimulating to another. One executive is done in by cocktail party chitchat and despises it; another finds it tiring but loves it. Stress is personality-linked. However, for all women, good stress, nondamaging stress, is that which is combined with freedom to act. Repressed stress is dangerous. Stress must be vented—through confrontation, conversation, exercise, pleasing hobbies. The woman who keeps her stress inside, who does not take action, who feels forced to apologize for actions she's not guilty of, can easily find herself nervous, nauseous, depressed, and headed for ulcers, psychological disorders, high blood pressure, and heart disease.

Fight or Flee?

Women in search of energy, careers, and ladybucks should some-times fight stress and sometimes flee it. Stress is the body's mental and physical response to events that annoy and excite. It is almost impossible not to experience it. It enables the body to handle conflict, challenge, and change. The trick is not to eliminate stress but to manage it correctly. The women who capitalize on their interests and ideas, who create employment situations and earnings people envy, have learned when and how to fight or flee stress. Usually they deal daily with large amounts of stress and have become skilled in handling it in order to keep going and keep enjoying what they're doing.

One master of stress is marital litigator Doris Sassower, a pros-perous New York lawyer in her fifties who approaches stress with a combination of philosophical detachment, hard-nosed management strategies, and self-discipline. "My days are filled with the unexpected, the emergency, the draining," she says. "Marital litigation is even more stressful than regular litigation. Overall I believe, in light of eternity, What difference does it make? Keep as calm and unemo-tional as possible; maintain poise under pressure. But I do know that stress has its place in success and must be handled properly.

"Too little stress is nonproductive; too much is self-destructive. There is the age-old dilemma of seeking the middle of the road. The best way to avoid damaging stress is to take preventive steps before coping becomes an issue." Her preventive steps include fleeing stress that causes unsolvable anguish and grappling with that which can be harnessed and directed toward constructive ends. Says this pedagogic lawyer who practices what she preaches:

- "Confront problems immediately. Don't let stress escalate. Unresolved stress is the worst thing. Do something with a problem, don't just worry about it.
- "Organize time well. It leads to a feeling of control.
- "Being helpless, passive, or trapped causes stress. Avoid these feelings whenever possible.
- "Distinguish imaginary problems from actual ones.
- "Relinquish self-imposed expectations that cannot be accomplished. Take on problems where you can see a light at the end of the tunnel."

A hardworking fighter, this award-winning attorney admits that much of what she advises is difficult to do. Speaking of women who dream big and reach far, she says, "If one chooses a competitive, stressful life, one must be able to stand the heat. Self-discipline is essential. Sometimes you must force yourself to maintain control, optimism, energy when you're low on all three. Panic or depression can't be revealed; the show must go on. Acting through stressful situations can revive the spirit."

Energy Preservation

Too much negative stress, too much spent energy. Too much spent energy, too great the potential for negative stress. It's a threatening circle of concern that can sap the emotional and physical strength needed to create and enjoy life and ladybucks. Despite excellent advice from professionals such as Dr. Holly Atkinson and attorney Doris Sassower, and from expert studies on the subject of stress and energy, the starting line is preserving whatever energy exists—maximizing what's there—before support systems, nutrition, exercise, power, and coping skills.

Ideally, the quest for ladybucks begins with a nurturing family structure, good health, a fit body, a satisfying amount of authority, and survival systems all worked out—everything in place. It's a nice picture, but seldom are ladybucks built from ideal circumstances. More often than not, the ideal circumstances evolve along with the ladybucks. A woman likes the goals she's achieving, the money she's accumulating, the admiration she's attracting. If she's to hold on and gain more, she realizes she must develop the support systems, the health, and the coping skills that increase energy and ward off fatigue.

Before anything is developed, however, whatever energy already exists must be preserved. This is accomplished in several ways. Home-basing is a big energy preserver, though it is not often thought of as that. Besides its obvious conveniences and money-saving benefits, it permits ladybucks seekers to save time and energy traveling to and from job locations. Traveling, particularly during rush hours, is tiring. Two hours of travel time saved are two hours of energy preserved for product or service marketing, networking, record keeping, and performing tasks more directly related to the moneymaking process.

"I would hate working from an outside studio," says nationally acclaimed watercolorist Linda Perlmutter, who lives and works in a spacious home in Westchester County, New York. "My house is designed for my work needs as well as my family's living needs. Why waste valuable time and energy traveling somewhere to do what I can do here? Many artists do it, but I can't see it."

Much of Linda's success in a field where money is difficult to come by is related to her ability to maximize her energy by eliminating activities she regards as needlessly draining. Though she enjoys recreational travel and does a lot of it, daily commutes to an outside work location "would gain me nothing and cost me on several levels," she says. "I don't know why more women don't work out of their homes. So many jobs and businesses today can be done beautifully from a carefully planned at-home work area. Maybe it has something to do with ego. Perhaps some women feel they're not building a real business or career unless they're commercially located. It's so silly. It's hard enough trying to juggle a family and a career. Why make it worse by battling traffic, dealing with crowded trains, late buses?"

Although Linda's art creations are often abstract, Linda is a logical, ego-sturdy, pragmatic individual. Her days are filled with a variety of personal and professional commitments. She wakes up early and goes to bed late. Her energy level, though high, is stretched to its limits. Activities that could eat up her stamina supply and give nothing worthwhile in return are shunned. "If I didn't guard my time and strength," says Linda, "my career wouldn't be thriving the way it is."

In addition to home-basing, Linda does something else that preserves energy and that she, like many ladybucks earners, does automatically and effortlessly. Linda is a two-things-at-once person; whenever possible she combines two or more chores within a single time and energy slot. If she's talking on the phone, she's sorting papers. Her mouth and hands can work at the same time. She doubles up on whatever tasks can effectively be done together in order to preserve energy for other jobs she wants to accomplish.

Two-things-at-once women are often amazed and annoyed to learn that many women (often their own employees who fantasize about gold and glory) don't double up whenever possible. "I hate to sound like a dragon lady," says a supermarket owner and mother of three young children, "but I can't stand check-out cashiers who stop packing when someone talks to them. Does it take great skill to carry on a conversation and put cans of soup into a bag at the same time? No wonder they don't rise to better-paying positions!"

Delegation is another important energy preserver. Today, enterprising women are learning to become effective and comfortable delegators. They recognize the value of delegation not just as a crucial management tool but also as a prime way to conserve physical and mental energy. Though often there is a feeling of "I can do it better and faster," authority is relinquished.

Linda Perlmutter says, "I simply can't afford the time and effort it takes to frame my pictures. Fortunately, I've found a wonderful framer [also a home-baser like herself] who does the job as well as or better than I could. I'd be foolish not to use her." Linda would also be foolish to attempt to answer her numerous telephone calls herself or to do laundry and cleaning without help—and she doesn't. She has a first-rate housekeeper/assistant whom she has trained to relieve her of certain routine, energy-draining chores.

When-To's

Sometimes fun is poked at people who build their work lives around astrological forecasts, biorhythm charts, and other quasi-scientific sources of when-to advice. Women who readily devour all other sorts of questionable how-to advice will dismiss sun signs and body cycles as nonsensical guides to moneymaking.

Says corporate astrologer Bonnie Prebula, "Skepticism is to be expected. Business-minded people have to be shown the accuracy of these sorts of approaches, but when they are, they become the biggest believers. Of course there is an optimum time to initiate activities for success, to push for your objectives, to go for it." Dozens of conservative and initially skeptical business and career women have come to agree with her. She has proven to them that important activities must be timed—and they pay her well to tell them when to spend their energies.

Prime-time planning, whether formally followed Prebula-style or self-regimented based on night person/morning person–type thinking, is an energy approach to moneymaking. Clients pay Bonnie to analyze when they should advertise, market, invest, or attempt to generate capital. People who don't believe in the stars but in themselves plug into their own hunches. In either case, emphasis is on "When shall I spend my energy—what time of the day, day of the week, week of the month?"

"I don't need an outside adviser to tell me to plan business meetings at nine A.M., or to avoid business trips at certain times of the month, or to do donkey chores in the evening and undertake mentally demanding work in the early morning when my mind and body feel refreshed," says Roseanne, a systems analyst and software inventor. "Anyone can tune into herself and realize that the best use of mental energy is when you feel the most mentally strong. I would never schedule a dinner meeting with a new client because I know I'm at my worst in the evening. I love breakfast meetings because I can accomplish in one hour what it would take me three to cover at dinner, and with less impressive results."

"I need assistance in working into my prime time," says Roseanne's sister, Dorothy, a successful lyricist who disagrees with her sister's "I can tune into myself" approach. "I have two teenagers and a husband who is not all that supportive. It makes a big difference when a professional determines the days and times when you can use the least amount of energy and get the most amount of productivity. Marla [her psychic] uses special charts and feelings to tell me when I am most likely to work well and without fatigue. She's almost always right."

There are no scientific studies that prove whether Roseanne's do-it-yourself or Dorothy's get-help approach is more effective. But there is irrefutable evidence that whether a time-to-push/time-to-pause schedule comes from self, psychic, stars, or any other source, the search for energy must include an analysis of one's individual time clock.

MAGIC ENERGY

The story of the hundred-pound mother who lifted a two-ton car off her dying youngster is often told to demonstrate that the undoable can be done under certain circumstances. Fear triggers adrenaline flow, and a frail mother is transformed into superwoman. There's a magic to it because it sounds improbable. Adrenaline or not, how can someone so small and powerless move something so heavy with her tiny hands? It's difficult to picture exactly what transpires in a severely frightened mother's mind and body. But it has been shown again and again that, stimulated by emotions such as intense fear, anger, love, or hate, people accomplish feats that require exceptional energy and that could not be accomplished in the absence of certain extreme emotions. Magic energy is born from intense positive and negative feelings.

Denise, who worked her way to a net worth of $2 million in the dry-cleaning business, recounts how hatred of her stepmother played a big role in her success. "I was sixteen years old," she says, talking about the energy that can come from hate. "My father and I had always been close. When he divorced my mother and married Bea [the stepmother], he promised things would never change between us. Bea had other ideas. She disliked me from the beginning, wanted all my father's attention and money to go to her and her own child. In my second year of college, Dad had a stroke and died. Bea took over his bankbook. She put her daughter in an expensive private high school and ended all support to me and all payments toward my college education."

Denise goes on to discuss the battling that ensued over her father's $750,000 estate, "how Bea lied and maneuvered to make sure I didn't get anything left to me in Dad's will." Denise didn't receive anything, quit college, and, with the financial backing of a friend of her father's, bought a tiny dry-cleaning store. Three months later, Bea learned that her late husband's estate was $100,000 larger than she had believed. Due to a series of technicalities, the money would be divided between herself and Denise (unless Denise were deceased), and she could not get her share unless Denise signed certain papers. Denise, who admits she was being spiteful and hurting herself in the process, refused to sign the papers "because I knew Bea was drooling at the mouth waiting for me to do so. I eventually would have signed because I was desperate for money at the time, but this was the first little bit of revenge I could get. I missed my father terribly, and this bitch who was able to laugh, love, and forget just days after the funeral was over and who had been my bitter enemy before and after Dad's death, now wanted something from me. No way!"

Bea saw a way: Get Denise out of the picture and get the whole $100,000. With the (paid) assistance of a boy working in a store adjoining Denise's, Bea devised a chemical-poisoning scheme. It was poorly planned, and Denise discovered the plot. Fury combined with hatred. "I didn't know how I would get even," says Denise, "but I knew it would take money and power." So began an eighteen-hour-a-day business expansion program that saw Denise triple the size of her original store, add three delivery trucks and two drop stores (little shops that don't have dry-cleaning equipment in them), and eventually go on to repeat the same process in twelve other towns with excellent results.

"I was operating on a unique kind of energy that comes from pure hate," says Denise. "Fortunately, I put the energy toward money-making ends. I think I could just as easily have turned into a criminal myself." But Denise didn't become a criminal. She used her self-made wealth to prove that Bea was. Once she had a few prospering stores and enough capital to comfortably hire a good lawyer and take Bea to court for fraud (relating to her father's estate) and attempted murder, she proceeded to go after her. "It took eight months in and out of court, talking to lawyers, filling out papers, et cetera, and $80,000, but it was worth it," says Denise. "I no longer needed money, but it lessened my anger to see Bea ordered to pay me $200,000 and told she would not share in the additional $100,000 she was willing to kill me for. Bea actually came to me crying, saying how her daughter would have to quit college because of the court's decision. I looked at her, smiled, and said, 'I had to quit college because of your decisions,' and walked away. It was the first time since Dad's death that I felt the hate draining from my body."

Denise goes on to say that it took a year after that episode before she could muster sufficient energy to continue building her dry-cleaning empire. "As the hate subsided after I got even with Bea, I found that my energy level did, too. I still wanted to acquire more cleaning plants, but I no longer had the same stamina for hard work—that horrible hate-driven energy that enables you to concentrate so intensely, function on almost no sleep, go and go and go without any relaxation."

Undiluted, throbbing, emotionally triggered energy, whether hate-driven, fear-driven, or driven by any powerful feeling, is strong and consequential. It can be harnessed and directed to several ends, ladybucks being one of them. Today, compelling stories are emerging of women fired by passions, both pleasant and unpleasant, to create income far greater than they ever imagined. The energy needed to keep them going through disappointment, dilemma, and disaster seems to surge from a bottomless well—a well that begins to empty only when the emotion behind the energy begins to subside, as in Denise's case.

The most cherished ladybucks are those created by the magic energy of love. They are happy earnings facilitated by the most positive of human emotions. "I love what I'm doing!" "It's so exciting!" "I'm working hard, but I'm having fun!" "I've never been happier!" These sentiments are expressed again and again by female moneymakers attempting to explain the source of the energy that sustains them.

When the gold is gained, the glory granted, often what still remains is a bubbling bundle of energy like sixty-seven-year-old Edna Hennessee, chairman of the board of Cosmetic Specialty Labs, Inc., who, when asked about retirement, smiles and chirps, "Oh noooo. My work is one of my hobbies. I plan to expand my business activities."

CHAPTER 8

Behind Every Woman

When Gessie Tassone accepted a Businesswoman of the Year Award with the words, "Behind every great man, there is a woman. In my case there is a great man, my husband," she wanted her audience to know that women, like men, need spouse support to happily fulfill grand dreams and goals in the commercial world.

Olivia Buehl, editor of *Working Mother* magazine, a McCall-chain publication for women trying to excel at work and at home, says of her husband, "He's a fabulous father, and he's always there for the children. He takes the kids to doctor appointments more than I do, makes many phone calls, and takes care of school appointments." She wants husbands and wives to know that working mothers like herself often succeed largely because their husbands are eager to pitch in with child care.

When watercolorist and art entrepreneur Linda Perlmutter says, "I wouldn't be making the money I am if it weren't for David's total encouragement, his legal and business know-how, willingness to help me market my work, my classes, myself," she's explaining that even talented, ambitious, hardworking women (like herself) need help and can benefit tremendously if they're fortunate enough to have husbands (like her David) who provide it wherever and whenever they can.

More and more, successful women are publicly making it clear that the female moneymaker is not a self-made or self-sustained phenomenon—that behind her, along her road to riches, are people who silently but solidly provide tremendous support. High among these people are low-profile spouses who cheerfully act as sounding boards, help with housework, advise, instruct, finance, and encourage.

This Spouse Ain't No Mouse

"Carl was a hostile wimp," says Trish, explaining why she changed husbands after her promotion to vice president in a major corporation. "He talked a great game, always saying how proud he was of my career, my promotions, telling his friends he would hate to be married to a woman who didn't have ambition, who wasn't independent. Maybe he would have liked to believe what he was saying, but there were no actions to support his words. When I had to work late, he whined. When I had to travel on business, he pouted for days. When I got business calls at home, he was annoyed. When I took him with me to important business affairs, he sulked around, mumbled when people spoke to him, complained about the food. I loved him when we married, but as the years passed and I began to advance in my career, he started to look and act more like a mouse than a man. It was at this time that I met John."

Trish met John, an international investment banker, during a business trip to China. He was intrigued by her insights, her ideas, her energy. She was impressed with his understanding of the international business scene, with his contacts, and with his compassion for some of the problems she was dealing with. Friendship slowly grew into love. John advised Trish on a few crucial negotiations and gave her behind-the-scenes constructive sympathy and encouragement when things looked bleak. He helped her through two difficult deals that resulted in her rise to the vice-presidency level. Meanwhile Carl, thirty-seven, was going to drive-in theaters with a teenage girl who worked in a local amusement park. After her promotion, Trish divorced Carl and married John.

In the six years that Trish and John have been married, both their careers have thrived. Says Trish, now in line for another major promotion, "John would be doing great with or without me. He's really a citizen of the world. But I couldn't have gotten to this point without him. He has a global perspective that I'm just beginning to develop. My income has doubled since we met, largely because John has guided my thinking from a national to an international plane. He's always interested in what I'm doing. Whenever something good happens to me, he comes home with champagne and flowers and insists we celebrate. When things don't work out, he cheers me up by helping me to look beyond the immediate, to step back from my disappointment."

There was a time not long ago when husbands like John were seldom found. Women were entering the workforce in increasing numbers, and many spouses, realizing the family's need for a two-person income, pitched in with domestic chores, child-rearing, and sympathy for the on-the-job tensions their wives were experiencing. Some husbands shared and cared more equitably and cheerfully than others. But for the most part, that's where it ended. Then, within the last decade, the working wife started to become the working woman, the career woman, the entrepreneurial woman. No longer was she working just to help maintain and improve her family's lifestyle. Often she was working to maintain and improve herself, too, to satisfy an internal longing for self-expression and for ladybucks. Spouses were challenged into a new type of support—to be the soulmate and helpmate behind the enterprising female executive, professional, entrepreneur, to work at their own jobs, help at home, and contribute happily to their wives' career growth and goals. Some husbands have managed to provide this new support. Others haven't. It hasn't been—and isn't—an easy situation for husband, wife, or marriage. Marriages fall apart under the strain. Those that last and get better often do so because a husband becomes a valuable contributor to his wife's career and is genuinely pleased to see her fulfilling herself and capitalizing on her abilities.

Spouse Faith and Financing

Trish didn't need money from John to advance to the executive suite. She benefited from his sophistication in world markets, not from his financing. Often, though, ladybucks are created by women whose husbands believe in their abilities and provide them with the hard-to-come-by funds to launch product lines, cookie companies, and retail stores, ideas and dreams that would never see the marketplace were spouse faith and financing not forthcoming.

Debbi Fields doesn't attempt to hide the fact that her first Mrs. Fields cookie store, which opened in 1977 in Palo Alto, California, was financed with $50,000 borrowed from her husband, Randy, a businessman and financial consultant. Similarly, Dalia Ratner, founder of the All My Muffins franchise, would have found it difficult to go into business without the financial support of her husband, a trucking executive for a family-established business. Today, Lina Lee Lidow's three apparel boutiques (two in Beverly Hills and one in New York's Trump Tower) bring in $22 million in sales annually, but it took a $35,000 loan from her husband—an employee of a publicly held company begun by his family—to open her first Lina Lee shop on trendy and costly Rodeo Drive.

Undercapitalization is a major cause of enterpreneurial failure among women. Stories are told of women who parlayed a few hundred dollars into million-dollar enterprises; it happens. But often a personal backer, such as a spouse, steps in at a crucial point with a $30,000 or $50,000 or $80,000 loan—a loan that could not easily be obtained from outside sources. The business bursts into recognition and banks line up to offer future financing. But it was the initial spouse faith and financing that enabled the business to grow beyond its start-up stage and not become one of the four out of five new ventures that fold within three to five years.

Often, along with faith and financing, a husband pitches in as a jack-of-all trades to smooth and accelerate his enterprising wife's transition from ambition to affluence. Such is the story behind *Women's News,* an informative, inspiring monthly newspaper that focuses on women's issues, women's problems, and women who reach beyond ordinary challenges to accomplish extraordinary feats. Merna Popper, publisher of *Women's News,* had owned an art gallery in New York City. Though she had a good liberal arts education, nothing in her background prepared her to become a publisher and businesswoman. However, she had studied the women's movement, had a talent for writing, and was eager to do "something important that would make a difference." The "something important" was *Women's News,* a publication that has had a profound influence on many women and has won Merna national acclaim.

Merna's dream to create "something important that would make a difference" came about "largely because of a woman who put us into action; because I'd been able to round up a superb editor, advertising sales manager, and business manager; and because of my husband." Merna, who says financing came from personal money and wasn't too big a problem because she started out as a tiny home-based business, credits her husband with believing in her idea and being "supportive and proud and doing just about everything he could to help, from installing air-conditioning, to writing restaurant reviews, to finding advertisers."

Coupling for Love and Money

Merna's husband believed in his wife's idea and gave his spare time and know-how to help *Women's News*. However, he is not a partner in Merna's venture. He is a partner in a marriage, and he helps out at *Women's News* whenever and wherever he can. Today, though, many husbands partner up with their wives to do together what neither of them could successfully do alone, to capitalize on separate skills, interests, talents, and temperaments, to develop unique products, services, and businesses that never existed before. Spouses share fantasies, fears, foul-ups, fun, and fortune. They support each other in the creation of not just ladybucks but "couplebucks."

In 1980, Felice Willat, a busy thirty-six-year-old wife and mother, longed for a systemized plan to simplify her activity-filled days. Her longing led her to devise Day Runner, a fashionable, functional, multi-section time organizer. It solved her problem. Impressed, her husband Boyd used his marketing skills to introduce her time-management product into the marketplace. With $12,000 of family savings, Felice and Boyd began Harper House in their West Hollywood, California garage, where they manufactured and distributed Day Runner locally. Harper House broke even in its first year and then took off when the national Yuppie market discovered the effectiveness of this elaborate datebook and skyrocketed its annual sales to the $11 million range. The company now occupies a 40,000-square-foot factory facility, employs 227 workers, and sells 600,000 Day Runners annually.

Due to the joint talents of Louise and Dwight Minkler, computers, which do just about everything today from controlling companies to flying planes, are doing one more thing: composing poetry, for million-dollar profits. The co-creators of Computer Poet of Incline Village, Nevada, Louise and Dwight combined their respective literary and technological talents to create a machine that has found a home in card stores, airports, casinos, gift shops, and college campuses all over the United States and promises to revolutionize the American greeting card industry.

In 1978, Patricia and Mel Ziegler began the Banana Republic apparel chain with $1,500, a thin, hand-stapled pamphlet, and a vision of exotic places, experiences, and fashions. A husband-and-wife team, Mel was a journalist, Patricia an artist. Together they created a whimsically written and illustrated pamphlet that tickled the imaginations of thousands of would-be adventurers, attracted famous literary contributors, and soon became one of America's most enchanting and profitable catalogs. Today, it is a sixty-two-page production that reaches 12 million customers through the mail and through Banana Republic's forty-one stores, which generate annual sales of approximately $60 million.

Parental Support

Spouse support and participation in the production of ladybucks is substantial. However, ladybucks are often produced by single women aided by other support sources. Among these sources are parents who, like spouses, provide capital that might otherwise not be obtainable, who bolster confidence, who encourage with words, who pitch in with labor, and who sometimes partner up with their children.

"I couldn't do this without her," says Annie Hurlbut, speaking about her mother, Biddy, with whom she is a fifty-fifty partner in the Kansas-based Peruvian Connection. Annie had gone to Peru as a Yale sophomore, fallen in love with the country, and in 1976 returned there as a graduate student. At Christmas, when she came home for the holidays, she brought with her a soft, silky Peruvian-made alpaca sweater for her mother's fiftieth birthday. "My mother loved it and her friends went crazy over it," says Annie. "They thought I should consider importing alpaca sweaters." Annie went back to Peru to continue her doctoral research. Her mother took her gift sweater to a nearby department store and came away with an order for twenty of them. A mother-daughter wholesale operation began. Annie returned to the United States to work on her dissertation, sold alpaca sweaters in her spare time, discovered she didn't like wholesaling, and eventually moved into direct-mail sales. As the operation grew, Biddy managed the books and handled the shipments while Annie designed the garments that would be featured in the Peruvian Connection catalog and traveled back and forth to Peru to oversee production and export. The relationship has continued with this division of labor, and the mother-daughter union thrives, both financially and personally.

Among the most powerful and enduring forms of parental support is one that involves not parental work, but words—particularly the words of a proud father to his young daughter. The father providing the support doesn't think, "I am saying or doing such-and-such so that one day my little girl will earn ladybucks." It's an unplanned act with long-lasting effects. Dad makes a casual statement or behaves in a particular way, and a positive pattern is set into motion. Confidence, activity, and education combine to glide the young daughter from childhood into happy prosperity.

Today Lynn Johnston is a cartoonist, whose strip, "For Better or Worse," ranks high in polls of America's favorite daily comics. It appears in over five hundred newspapers, in seven books, and in a television special that aired Christmas 1985 and is likely to be repeated in 1986. When Lynn was a child, her father used to tuck her into bed every night with the same joking words: "See you in the funny pages!" Recognizing Lynn's cartooning ability and humor, he always told her she would one day be a comic-strip artist. But it's not something she planned or even thought much about. In those days little girls didn't grow up to become cartoonists—unless they had fathers like Lynn did, in which case they might grow up to be anything extraordinary. Recently, Lynn Johnston became the first woman to win the Oscar of daily cartooning. The National Cartoonist Society presented her with its annual Reuben Award.

When Susan Porcelli's father brought his young daughter on carpentry jobs with him and encouraged her to do various repair jobs, he didn't know that one day his little girl, at just twenty-five years old, would be a top mechanical engineer for Con Edison—a boss out in the field, directing crews of men almost twice her age. "I was his chief assistant," says Susan, talking of her father. "My brother couldn't hammer a nail. . . . My father encouraged me a great deal. Whenever he said to do this or that, even if I had never done it before, if he said it, then I could do it."

Paternal support such as that received by Lynn and Susan isn't less significant than maternal support, but usually, when it exists, it is of a different nature. Frequently, a mother's praise and support carries a message of general, unconditional love: "I know you can do it; I love you. When you put your mind to something..." Such support gives a little girl a cushion of security. It's lovely. It fortifies her for the real world. However, more often than not, it is Dad whose opinions are more valued, who is believed to offer the important, specific, objective judgments. Says an award-winning architect who speaks for many ambitious young daughters with good parental support behind them, "I love my parents equally, but if Dad says something I do is good, it means more to me than if Mom says it; his focus is different."

As women achieve greater executive, entrepreneurial, and professional success, parental support and encouragement will be more unisex in nature. The future generation of mothers won't be as likely to have daughters who believe "if Dad says something I do is good, it means more to me than if Mom says it." Mom's focus will be honed and hardened by marketplace experience. Mothers will have a realistic, clear vision of where their daughters' financial futures might lie and will be behind them with specific and savvy words and actions.

Nonsupportive Spouses and Parents

When ladybucks stories are recounted, an amazing number of accomplished women tell of parents and spouses who were strongly nonsupportive, who belittled their dreams, instilled fear, or forced them to leave home early, end their marriages, and turn to grandparents, aunts, uncles, or siblings.

"My husband was fine as long as he felt my business was a part-time diversion," says Grace, who slowly but steadily built a prospering music and dance academy for talented children. "When the school got some good publicity and started to show a profit, I needed Steven more than ever. I wanted to share everything that was happening to me with him, hear his opinions, get some help around the house. He would turn on the television whenever I began to talk about my business. He was a plumbing contractor but refused to inspect a new building I was interested in leasing. He took all the joy out of my accomplishment." This woman, who has since divorced her

husband, got some of the help she needed and a lot of encouragement from her kid brother, who "has helped in dozens of big and
little ways," and from her grandmother, who "was the only one who
believed in me enough to lend me money to expand."

Says attorney Doris Sassower, who was always at the top of her
class in grade school, college, and law school and early on was at
the top of her profession as a marital litigator, "I had no parental
support, emotional or otherwise. If I hadn't gotten a scholarship to
law school, I wouldn't have been able to go. My parents were against
the idea. They wanted me to be a teacher, have long vacations, more
time for a husband and family." Doris goes on to explain that her
mother had always assisted her father, a businessman, and felt that
Doris should get married and assume a similarly subordinate role.
At nineteen, during her first year in law school, Doris married a lawyer
and got the career support she hadn't received from her parents.
Her husband was a workaholic who passed on his habit of working
long hours, weekends, and holidays to his promising wife. Unlike
Doris's parents, he didn't discourage her professional ambitions, but
he let her down in other ways. "There was no emotional support,"
says Doris, who admits that her husband's workaholic ways that
rubbed off on her "may have enriched me professionally," but "left
me without emotional support until my life was half over." Now
divorced, Doris has found another man, also an attorney, who is
proud of her successful career and who "has introduced the idea
of relaxation into my life, who insists we enjoy life together away
from our work."

"If one door closes, you try to open another one," says Elizabeth,
who at twenty-eight earns a six-figure salary as a portfolio manager
for a multimillion-dollar stock fund. "When my parents heard I wanted
to leave home and move to New York, they were furious. They were
counting on me to go into the family food business. They told me
horrible things about New York and predicted I'd fall flat on my face.
So much for warm and encouraging parents." Elizabeth says she
might have fallen on her face had she not had an aunt in New York
who loved her spirit, taught her about investment strategies, and
helped her get a trainee position at a utility fund. "Sometimes you
need a fairy godmother to make it," says Elizabeth, "and Aunt Mary
was my fairy godmother. She had a big account at the firm, and

when she told the fund manager she hoped he could find a place for me, he wasn't too thrilled, but he agreed to give me a try." Elizabeth made her Aunt Mary proud and is in the process of making herself a hatful of ladybucks before her thirtieth birthday. Her parents refuse to talk to her and have told her they have no desire to have her come home to visit at Christmas.

Some women earn ladybucks because they are fortunate enough to have parents and/or spouses who stand behind them and support their dreams. Others earn them despite—or perhaps because of—parents and spouses who let them down, who don't come through when they could, who say and do the wrong things, who force their daughters and wives to turn elsewhere for encouragement and support. There is no evidence that women with warm, loving parents or spouses behind them are more likely to earn ladybucks than women without them. However, there is abundant evidence that behind many a ladybucks earner, there is more than a combination of winning traits and a series of golden operating methods. There is someone, or a group of people, who has made a significant difference, who was around at the right time with the right words and deeds—an individual or individuals about whom it is said, "I couldn't have done it without . . ."

OUTSIDE SUPPORT

"I couldn't have done it without my high school business math teacher," says Jeanette, now a partner in a prestigious accounting firm. "I was headed for a commercial high school diploma. In those days that meant you didn't go to college. Mr. DeWitt asked me what I planned to do when I graduated. When I told him I would probably become a secretary, he shook his head and said, 'No, you can do more than that with your future; you should go to college.'" Jeanette explains that as one of four children and the daughter of immigrants, she was expected to get a job upon completing high school and contribute to the family. "My three brothers hadn't gone to college. No one in my family had gone to college," says Jeanette. "When I told my parents what Mr. DeWitt had said, they were uninterested. I remember my father saying, 'Good, you go to college and tell DeWitt he can help put food on our table.' "

Jeanette told Mr. DeWitt what her father had said. "I thought that would end it," she says. "But Mr. DeWitt asked if it were possible that he talk to my father. It wasn't easy, but I got them together at an Open School Day event. Mr. DeWitt told my father about the Baruch School of Business, a branch of the City College of New York. This was before it was fashionable for anybody to study business, but he explained to my father that I had more ability than any of his other students, that I could make a lot of money in business, if he permitted me to get more education. He explained to my father that I could get into the college based on merit. It would not cost him anything, and eventually I would really be able to help out the family. I didn't think he could pull it off, but he did. My father did a lot of grumbling, but I did complete college and go on to live out Mr. DeWitt's predictions."

Teachers, Mentors, Therapists

Jeanette's story is not uncommon. Schoolteachers, though not high earners themselves, have had a major impact on the later earnings of many women. Girls who were for one reason or another unable to confide their dreams to their parents or muster parental support have turned to sympathetic teachers for advice and encouragement. They have been spurred and motivated to excellence and eventual achievement by an English teacher who said, "You have what it takes to be a great writer," or a science teacher who said, "You're brilliant; you can go far in this field," or a college professor who put an A+ on a term paper and added the words, "I see a brilliant career here." No long-term, crib-through-college, deeply felt handholding, but critical input at a critical time.

Many women have earned ladybucks without any long-term, continuous, I'm-always-here-for-you support. But when they reflect on the beginnings of their paths to prosperity, they remember clearly one individual who was very important in their success. "Mrs. Stinson liked me from the moment I came into the company," says Noreen, now president of a division of a large electronics company. "She was a cross between a mentor and a mother. She was my manager, but she went beyond her role to tell me who to watch out for, what to avoid, what to aim for. She introduced me to important people in the company and got me invited to meetings that I otherwise would have been excluded from. I worked under her for only four months before I was moved up and into another division, but in those four months I felt a support I have never experienced before or have had since. She was a special lady at an important time in my life. I'll never forget her."

"If I had waited for a support system, I'd still be earning two hundred dollars a week." says Meryl, a nursery school teacher-turned-film producer. "I loved the children, but I loved a lot of other things that I wasn't doing because I was afraid. The nursery school was safe, a hideout, a way to keep from challenging myself into exciting projects that I dreamed about." Like many women, Meryl had entered teaching because her parents told her it provided security, good vacations, and a steady salary. She wasn't unhappy "as much as unfulfilled," she says. "I was always the one at the school putting on the plays, designing the costumes, persuading the administration to go beyond blocks-and-easel play. When I turned thirty, it was a watershed time for me. I wasn't married, I wasn't seeing anyone, and I saw myself growing old in a two-room building surrounded by three- and four-year-olds."

Meryl decided she needed "real help." "When you're leading a routine or boring life, it's interesting that everyone you're friendly with is doing pretty much the same," she says. "I had no role models, no spunky friends who urged me to get out of my rut, to take chances. I didn't know anyone in the film industry. My family talked about pensions and saving for their old age. Anyone they ever knew who broke away from the traditional or went into some interesting business venture always ended up poor. Whenever I mentioned anything related to theater or filmmaking, my parents rolled their eyes, shook their heads, and told me the dangers I would be letting myself in for." Meryl realized it was dangerous to continue as she was and found a therapist who "spent three years walking me through my fears and into a new career."

Meryl's therapist was an older woman who urged Meryl to work in summer stock, take courses in drama and filmmaking, join organizations related to her interests and talents, become an apprentice. "She didn't say anything I couldn't have thought of myself," says Meryl, "but she enabled me to allow myself to go for my dreams, to break out of my narrow lifestyle, to not be intimidated by my parents' warnings. For two years I juggled teaching with a whole new world, knowing I had this one lady to talk to, consult with, draw strength from. I was like Clark Kent/Superman. I'd leave the nursery school, let out my hair, change into jeans, and fly into another life. When I finally left teaching to take a job as a production assistant, I broke out into a rash that covered my entire body. But my therapist was there to turn to."

That was five years ago. Today, Meryl is an independent producer of documentaries and corporate training films. She is bicoastal, in demand, and averaging an annual income of $200,000. She has dozens of contacts within the industry and in peripheral industries, is branching out into "experimental projects involving new technologies," and will be married at Thanksgiving to a record producer she met at an awards dinner. Meryl and her fiancé have invited two hundred guests to their wedding. "A very important one is my therapist," says Meryl. "None of this would have come about without her."

Friends as Support Systems

When Meryl was teaching, she had friends who liked her and cared about her happiness. But as she said, they were as undaring as she was and not the type of people to inspire her to play out her dreams. Some women are more fortunate than Meryl in the friend department. Like her, most of their closest contacts may not be set-the-world-on-fire people, but they have relationships with a couple of accomplished women who inspire or encourage them; or they meet or know other women with whom they partner up, each bringing necessary qualities into what will become a moneymaking arrangement; or they have friends who believe in them and their moneymaking ideas and who are willing to show it with financing. They are blessed with not just the right stuff, but the right friends.

Sharlyne Powell and Sharon McConnell of Yakima, Washington, had some important things in common. They were both overweight, were interested in joining an exercise program where they felt comfortable, and were unable to find a fitness center with routines and workouts designed for the two-hundred-pound woman. Trained as saleswomen for a multilevel firm, they were both experienced in promotion and decided to join together and use their training to promote a fitness program catering exclusively to large-size females. They would support each other commercially and emotionally. Their business, Woman-at-Large, was begun with a couple of hundred dollars, a rented Grange hall, and a tape player; it closed two months after it opened because Sharlyne and Sharon had made the mistake of hiring thin aerobics teachers. "People came, but we looked like any other exercise class, so they didn't stay," says Sharlyne. "Large ladies do not feel comfortable with skinny instructors. They are not realistic role models." Unable to find ample-size instructors, the two friends studied up on exercise and fitness, designed a program for the heavy woman, became instructors themselves, and reopened two months later.

Sharlyne and Sharon realized that though their start-up costs were small, to make their venture really work they would need some solid capitalization. Surprisingly, this was an easy step for them. Four friends pitched in and loaned them $70,000. "They believed in our dream and were willing to help out," says Sharon. "They knew if we became a success, they would, too. In fact, we had more people interested than we had a need for money."

Sharlyne and Sharon supported each other in turning a good idea into a profitable reality, and their friends supported them with financing. Because of this friends-as-support backing, Woman-at-Large, now franchising, will help thousands of overweight women come to feel good about their bodies and themselves. Sharlyne and Sharon will feel good about this—and about the ladybucks they will be earning.

Women's Organizations and Networks

Sharlyne and Sharon had each other and their friends to turn to for support. Sometimes a woman beginning a business, profession, or career has no one with whom to share her problems or pleasures. The people she is friendly with don't understand what she is doing, or she doesn't have enough people with whom to brainstorm, or she's new in town and has nobody. Starting out, relocating, or making it can be an anguishing experience for the lone venturer. As women are beginning to make significant strides, they are taking steps to ensure that they don't feel adrift and that other women going it alone will have people to turn to for support in their endeavors.

Females whose career climbs are hitting detours now have places to turn to for help and encouragement. Organizations and networks have formed, many with local chapters, that provide valuable information and contacts for professional, business, and career women. (See Appendix for a listing.)

Anne Breckenridge has a Master of Arts degree in interior design and a background as an interior designer and as a freelance entrepreneur specializing in corporate design work. Since 1979, she has worked as an interior designer for Coca-Cola. She is manager of the Interiors Group, which is responsible for making sure that the thousands of employees in the Atlanta offices of the company feel comfortable and thus are able to work at maximum capacity. This is Anne's first executive position after a career that has taken her through over six jobs and four states, after two divorces, and after several setbacks. She perseveres and thrives largely because she is a believer in women's support systems. She acknowledges that women in demanding work often need sympathetic peers in order to keep going. Anne meets twice a month with other working women. They talk about what they're reading, share their intellectual thoughts, and discuss what may be troubling them. She also belongs to a church group that has meetings on subjects such as gender and power— a church group that she considers very much in the mainstream of what's currently happening and in touch with women's career problems.

In addition to intellectual and emotional support, women's organizations and networks provide financial support often otherwise unobtainable to females. They put women who are in need of funding in touch with women and men who have funds to invest. They sponsor conventions, trade fairs, and seminars that unite female entrepreneurs with cooperative government agencies, private corporations, and banks. They provide last-resort loans to women who have been turned down by other funding sources. They permit women who would give up to stay in business and women who would take years to see large profits to realize them quickly. Says one woman who is certain her company would be nowhere near its $10 million annual level were it not for the backing of a women's network she belonged to, "My image consulting firm was making $2 million in annual revenues and needed capital to expand. I had a thorough business plan and was turned down by eight banks. They just glanced at the plan and told me their banks didn't like to make business loans to women, that they were wary of service businesses which are low in assets and too commonplace. They were awful, deriding women for having poor credit histories, no ability to work with figures, no understanding of the basics of what makes a business grow."

Backers and Bankers

Commercial loan officers claim innocence in their treatment of women. They state that they are rarely approached by women or are approached incorrectly. Venture capitalists say few women come to them with requests for backing, and when they do come it is with inadequate business plans that don't warrant attention or financing. Investment bankers say most women are bad risks and seldom take their companies public. The overall statement is that there is no sex-based discrimination against women. If they approach a lending institution for assistance, have what it takes, and are loan-worthy, they will be provided financing as readily as a man would be.

Not so, claim credit-worthy women who have tried and come away disillusioned and disgusted. Professional and entrepreneurial women, they claim, are not only discriminated against but treated shabbily, are quoted interest rates many times higher than those charged to men, and are asked for their husbands' signatures, even though their husbands have nothing to do with their professional or business endeavors.

The truth lies somewhere between the two claims. Often women are treated unfairly, but often it's because they do come across as poor credit risks. However, things are changing and will change more in women's favor. According to the Bureau of Labor Statistics, the number of self-employed women increased by 76 percent between 1975 and 1985, with woman-owned businesses becoming the fastest-growing segment of the small-business economy. If these businesses currently don't have what it takes to attract major backers and bankers, if they do not appear promising enough, if they are too focused in the competitive service sector, this situation will improve as women gain experience in the male-dominated business world and receive increasing support from women's organizations and networks. As child-rearing responsibilities become divided equally between spouses and as more female-founded ventures succeed, mature, and become formidable forces in the business sector, the sharp distinction between male and female ventures will fade and financing will become gender-free.

Bookkeepers, Accountants, Business Managers

Sad stories abound of creative, bright women who could have earned ladybucks and didn't because they refused to become figure-savvy, preferring to focus on the creative aspects of their businesses, on promotion and marketing activities, and on what they like doing to the exclusion of problems that should have been addressed and weren't.

"I was sure I had everything in place," says Gloria, a leather goods importer. "I had excellent suppliers in Brazil, excellent markets in the United States. No one could compete with my prices or the quality of my merchandise. I had worked hard to put together a beautiful line, to establish my contacts in both countries. Sales had multiplied each year to the $4 million level; net profits were high on paper. I thought I was doing everything right. My employees loved me. My customers loved me." Everyone loved Gloria and her leather goods. No employer could have asked for harder-working, more loyal employees.

But when Gloria's bookkeeper talked to Gloria about customers who were late in paying their bills, Gloria's response was always, "Don't worry; they'll pay eventually; they're good for the money." They may have been good for the money, but they were bad for Gloria's business. Gloria didn't want to think about initiating penalties for late payments, about offering prepayment discounts. "Anything having to do with percentages, figures, things like that, I hated and put off," she admits. So began a cash flow problem that forced Gloria into high-interest float loans and eventually forced her out of business. "By the time I started listening to my bookkeeper, it was too late," she says. "Our accounts receivable seemed to have mush-roomed overnight, and it became harder and harder to meet our loan payments and pay our creditors."

As women seek to establish profitable businesses and professional practices, they realize that behind their dreams and derring-do there must be a bookkeeper, accountant, or business manager—some down-to-earth facts-and-figures person or people who force them to think about percentages, operating capital, cash flow, production costs, and interest rates. The fired-up entrepreneurial or professional woman may not want to hear that an enterprise with annual sales of $4 million can easily be operating at a deficit and headed for bankruptcy, or that sales is only part of the success equation. She may not want to think about numbers, profit margins, or percentages, but she hears and heeds if she's determined to attain ladybucks.

"Thank God for a conservative accountant!" says Joann Crawford, owner and manager of Tigerlilies, a thriving Boston restaurant widely praised by reviewers. When Joann drafted her business plan that became the foundation of her success, she had underestimated payroll expenses. Fortunately, her accountant had provided her plan with a cushion for such mistakes. He had a fund marked "other" in every cost category for unforeseen expenses. This allowed her some leeway for mistakes.

"I love our publication and I love the editorial side of publishing," says Merna Popper, publisher of the acclaimed and award-winning *Women's News* that services the New York metropolitan area. "But I do not enjoy the business side. My business skills are not good. Fortunately, I have a great business manager. She makes sure everything is in order and scolds me if she feels I'm negligent."

Says Patti McVay, who built Fifth Season Travel, a money-losing travel agency, into a prospering $100 million operation, invested over $500,000 into the start-up of two out-of-town branches, ran short of capital, fell over a million dollars in debt, and was forced into bankruptcy, "We were striving, striving, striving for greater growth, but we didn't have the controls in place. . . . We thought we could do it all by ourselves. We were wrong."

Too-Late Support

Patti's agency was rescued from extinction by a buyout. A wealthy family took it over and assumed its debts. Patti made no money on the sale but has been asked to stay on as manager and was offered expansion funds. What she does remains to be seen.

Variations of Patti's story are heard frequently. Many disillusioned ladybucks aspirants echo her "We thought we could do it all by ourselves. We were wrong." Whether they talk of lack of financial assistance, peer assistance, spouse assistance, or any other type of backing, it becomes clear that the scarcer the backing, the less the likelihood of ladybucks.

As women continue to carve out a female economy founded on good ideas, implemented by good management, supported by hard work, and measured in billions of ladybucks, the words "Behind every woman..." will become more and more significant. People will want to know who was behind the female winner, will applaud those who were and question those who could have been and should have been but weren't.

CHAPTER **9**

Twenty-One Ladybucks Myths

Nontruths and nonsense surround the ladybucks phenomenon. It's a new economic movement. Most women do not earn ladybucks, and the quest for them has escalated into a significant trend within just the past five to ten years. Also, nontruths and nonsense always surround the creation of wealth and the individuals who manage against difficult odds to parlay good ideas into extraordinary income. Following are twenty-one major ladybucks myths that exist, persist, and should desist.

Myth 1: Female moneymakers are not money-motivated.

Untrue. They have to be money-motivated in order to attain and maintain ladybucks. There is much talk about women being less interested in expansion and wealth than men, about their being concerned mainly with satisfying creative urges. They are not out to become CEO's, or create large companies, or build million-dollar professional practices, it is said, but to be self-employed, self-supporting, and self-satisfied. This is true of many women. It is also true of many men. But it is not true of the women who earn exceptional amounts of money. These women are interested in earning large sums, along with being self-employed, self-supporting, and self-satisfied. They want to succeed on a grand scale, and they learn fast that in a capitalistic economy, success is measured by earnings.

Money is the major means of evaluating how well an individual or company is doing.

Initially, a ladybucks earner may intend only to capitalize modestly on an interest, supplement family income, or escape the demands of marketplace employment, but once the potential for ladybucks presents itself, things change. Potential does not turn into profit without a strong interest in bottom-line figures. Some ladybucks earners say, "I never dreamed I would make this much money; I was never that interested in big money." But they admit that when they began to do well and found themselves presented with opportunities, they enjoyed the feeling, the power, and the new self they saw emerging, and then they became money-motivated.

Sandra Kurtzig, founder of ASK Computer Systems, Inc., who at thirty-nine has recently retired to enjoy the things she put aside to build her company, speaks for many female tycoons when she says she was not out to make huge amounts, that she never planned to create anything so large; but once it looked as though it were possible, she put aside all else and drove herself to work twenty-hour days to build her now multimillion-dollar corporation.

Other ladybucks earners admit to being money-motivated right from the beginning. "I wasn't particularly interested in travel," says Patti McVay, talking about the travel agency she built. "I was interested in establishing myself in a big way in the Indianapolis, Indiana, business community."

"When I tasted the money and power of Wall Street I was hooked," says Janice Jones, who upon completing college got a job on Wall Street, learned the ins and outs of the financial world, and in 1980 founded Chartwell & Co. "I love building equity in companies which I target as winners," she says.

"Of course I'm money-motivated," says Louise Berenson, creator of Purple Panache. "I love the color purple; I love the products we sell. But I want to make a lot of money, too. That's why I'm working so hard."

After ladybucks are earned and safely invested, their creators often echo the sentiments of Lane Nemeth of Discovery Toys, who says that money is no longer personally important to her, that it's not what keeps her going, that she doesn't "need twelve houses, fifteen cars, ten fur coats." But like Lane, they also acknowledge that it's easy to be unmotivated by money after huge sums of it have been amassed and safely tucked away.

Myth 2: Ladybucks are earned by women who think and act like men.

Almost never. Usually they are earned by women who understand how men think and act and use this understanding to advance their own careers and businesses—but who don't force themselves to think or act in an unnatural manner. Eventually, women will run a powerful economy that is uniquely their own, that acknowledges and applauds values, skills, and inclinations different from those underlying the male economy, and that functions unidentically but equally as effective. At that point it will not be so critical that women analyze the male business culture and gear their behavior toward it. Now it is.

The women who attain wealth and its accompanying power don't expect the men they work with to understand that at certain times mothering is more important than marketing, or that competitiveness can be a vicious trait, or that the bottom line is not always facts and figures but often faces and feelings. They suspend their own personal convictions, seek sympathies elsewhere, and talk to male colleagues in terms they quickly comprehend and about problems they can easily identify with. Says one woman who heads a top personnel agency, "When I was forced to let go of a certain employee [for cutback reasons], I was sick inside. I liked the woman a lot; I knew her family well. But I didn't express the emotions I was struggling with to the guys in the office. Instead, I talked about the new computer system we were installing and the new division we were planning." This woman, who is widely respected by her male co-workers, saved a discussion of her emotions and feelings for a women's network group she belonged to—a very wise move.

The woman who believes she will achieve ladybucks by focusing on earnings more than people, or by becoming a fierce competitor, or by pushing aside child-rearing concerns is headed for disillusionment and defeat. It doesn't work. Conflicts emerge that cause harmful stress. Most women are constituted differently from men and have different priorities and different responses to situations and events. Ladybucks come not from forcing a priority or response change but from realizing that men don't have the same priorities and responses as women and adjusting conversation accordingly to gain an operating advantage.

Though ladybucks are earned by women who simultaneously maintain their feminine inclinations and adapt their behavior to the male-dominated business culture, certain skills are developed that permit them ease of function in the male economy. The three basic ones are number skills, networking skills, and negotiating skills.

"I realized early on I would be stupid to talk to my suppliers about the importance I felt because of the health food chain I'd built or confide to them my worries about my son seeing too little of his mommy," says an owner of five popular stores catering to nutrition and fitness aficionados. "But it took me awhile to get good at talking about what they talked about comfortably—numbers, prices, discounts, amounts, not feelings and conflicts about success."

"Networking was something I shied away from," says an oil company executive. "I hated the schmoozing and boozing that went on between the men. I preferred to work alone. I wasn't sensitive to their constructive criticism, but I was to the joshing and teasing. It wasn't my style." This woman realized that if she were going to advance to where she wanted to be, she had to build a tolerance for the schmoozing, boozing, and joshing that often lead to important contacts and promotions. "It wasn't easy," she says, "but I treated it like a part of the job that you do efficiently and get over with as quickly as possible. Eventually, I got good at it. I hate to make this comparison, but in a sense I became like the wife who marries a wonderful, wealthy man whom she loves and admires in many ways and learns to tolerate sexually."

"You can use agents, business managers—all sorts of people to do your negotiating," says a ten-year soap opera veteran. "But you have to know how to negotiate for yourself, too, and negotiating with some of the men in this business can be horrible." This young woman, who plays a conniving vixen on television, has learned on and off the screen that "women and men negotiate differently. Men enjoy the fight, the game; women prefer to work things out in a more polite, less direct manner." Though it was hard for her, she observed the confrontational techniques used (in reel and real life) by successful male negotiators and trained herself not to be thrown by them, to see them as how men operate, and to introduce similar strategies into her maneuvers when necessary.

Myth 3: The "Work as Play" philosophy leads to ladybucks.

Not so. Because female moneymakers often explain their endurance and accomplishment by saying, "I love what I do," it's assumed they view their work as play. They don't. They view their work as work—some of which they love doing. Successful men, more than successful women, regard their work as play, as a game that they're expected to play and that they usually win at. Women are compartmentalizers. Their work, whether or not they ever achieve ladybucks, is consciously broken down into pleasure parts and problem parts; segments that fulfill, segments that frustrate; times of guilt, times of glory. Work is not viewed as a singular whole. Ladybucks hopefuls tread on particularly fragile ground here. They're new at the game of self-made real money. They feel the contradictions that all working women feel, but more intensely.

When Sandra Kurtzig recently quit ASK Computer Systems, she said, "I was in such a hurry, I never had time to smell the roses." She made it clear that her original goal had been a part-time job while raising her two children and that she got sidetracked by success into working harder and harder to generate more success. Now she says it's time to play, and her idea of play is to spend more time with her children, travel, go to plays, study French impressionist painting, and visit museums.

"I like my work," says Sharon Corr, "but it's not my play or way to relax." Sharon puts in sixty- and seventy-hour work weeks (which she's trying to shorten) to expand her beverage corporation, which she predicts will have sales in the $100 million range by 1990. But for pure fun she turns to passions, hobbies, and interests that include scuba diving, photography, and a Listen to Dolphins research project that seeks to improve communications between the Atlantic bottlenose dolphins and humans.

Many male millionaires claim they have no hobbies or interests, that their work is their love and passion, that they hate Sundays, that they got to where they are because their work was their play: Ladybucks earners rarely make such claims. (Frequently, they say they

achieved their success by sacrificing play.) They have interests outside their work and don't believe they achieved their wealth by viewing
their work as play. Says Dr. Paula Moynahan, who has a passion for
animals and a large collection of them, "I enjoy my work. It makes
me feel good to help people. But it's not recreational. I put in long
days, and when I'm not working, I relax on my farm with my horses
and other pets."

Myth 4: Ladybucks are most likely for the woman who sees opportunities other women miss.

This is part of the "myth of the hidden opportunity." Most women
today are not missing opportunities. They are aware of them. They
read magazine article after magazine article about ways to make
money, how to build a business, and how to find and cultivate marketplace niches, about what's hot and what's not. They are aware of
fields that are ripe for moneymaking, of women in their communities
and throughout the United States who are cashing in big on opportunities, ideas, and talents.

Opportunity does not present itself to a chosen few. It's up for
grabs. Rare is the woman who doesn't know that if she has a talent
for preparing some unusual food treat, or for helping people look
and feel better, or for satisfying any marketplace love or need, an
opportunity exists for her to make good money. Rare is the woman
who hasn't said to herself, "I could do what so-and-so is doing, if I
wanted to," or, "I thought of that idea long before she did," or, "I
could make a fortune doing ——— or ——— or ——— if I could
just get myself moving."

Ladybucks come not from a woman spotting a concealed opportunity but from her grabbing an opportunity visible to many,
imprinting it with her own personal style, gearing it for consumer
acceptance, and marketing it effectively.

When Christine Martindale began Esprit-Miami in 1980, she didn't
know she would end up with a $6 million flower importing business,
but she did recognize an increasing marketplace interest in unusual
varieties and colors of flowers. Consumer tastes and fashions were
changing frequently and dramatically, so why not provide a changing
assortment of dramatic, colorful flowers to complement clothing,
furnishings, and the fantasies of the moment?

Christine had worked as a sales manager for one of Miami's largest flower importers, had learned the business, and decided to begin her own company. She saw money to be made from offering wholesalers rare and attractive flowers to coordinate with varying color tastes and trends. She subscribed to a New York service that forecasts colors likely to be in style a year or two in the future, contracted with growers to create appealing flowers in those colors, hired an ad agency to design a brochure highlighting her specialty, took a booth at a florists' trade show to convince retailers to pressure wholesalers to stock her high-fashion flowers, and became a formidable force in the floral industry. Had she seen what none of her competitors saw? Were her competitors unaware of a growing interest in new and unusual flowers? "No," says one of them. "Martindale sensed what we all sensed, but she acted on her instincts."

Myth 5: The ladybucks earner is a superwoman.

She appears this way *after* she has made her mark. She does have traits (see Chapters 3 and 4) that maximize her chances of earning ladybucks. She does use methods (see Chapter 5) that maximize her chances of earning ladybucks. But she is not a superwoman. Her income is what is super; thus, a mystique develops around her. Were she to possess the same winning traits and use the same golden operating methods but not reap any gold, she would not appear to be a superwoman. Ironically, she would evoke pity. Observers would say, "Poor Susie, she has so much going for her; she works so hard; she does everything right. It's a shame she's not making any money."

Susie becomes superwoman if she makes that magic leap from great potential to great prosperity. At this point a celebrity is born. The media are drawn to her. The public is intrigued. Susie goes from pitied toiler to heroine and role model. She appears larger than life and much more special than she really is. Reports flow of how she struggled against incredible odds, endured what few women could endure, sacrificed everything imaginable, juggled career and family, seldom slept, tolerated the intolerable, and ultimately was rewarded with exceptional earnings. Susie is quoted selectively, misquoted widely, and what emerges is a portrait of an awesome breed of woman—a wonder woman, a superwoman.

"It can happen very quickly. You can go from superschlep to superwoman almost overnight," says an inn owner who received some good local press in relation to her popular, profitable little resort, tripled her revenues, was profiled in a trendy magazine, was invited on a couple of morning television shows, and found her inn and herself very "in." "One month I was changing linens and serving dinners; the next month I was sitting in 'green rooms' preparing for television appearances and being questioned about what it takes for a woman to succeed in America," she says. "People who barely noticed me before went out of their way to talk to me, treated me like a celebrity. It's very interesting; you might gain more self-confidence, but you don't really change because your income and image improve. People see you differently, but you're no more a superwoman than before."

Most women who suddenly find themselves earners of incomes they never expected and objects of adulation do not see themselves as superwomen at all. The superwoman myth persists because of media hype and incorrect public perceptions. The woman who achieves ladybucks finds that other women can identify with her problems but not with her prosperity. They know what it's like to have a difficult teenager or an unsupportive husband. But they don't know what it's like to be able to purchase anything they want, travel anywhere, or put their children in the best schools. Thus the self-made woman able to do this seems different, stronger. Yes, she suffers, too, but she's assumed to be better equipped to handle pain, to have greater control over her destiny. Sometimes this is a correct assumption; just as often it's not. The ladybucks earner is no more a superwoman than before she earned her ladybucks, or than other women who have a lot going for them, work hard, do everything right, and are never rewarded financially.

Myth 6: It takes bucks to get ladybucks.

This is a variation of the myth, "It takes money to make money." Many believe that women who create wealth, particularly in the business sector, do so because they have money to start with. Most don't. They usually start with less than $1,500, create ventures that show great promise, and then, a couple of years down the road, borrow money for expansion activities that take their successful start-ups into the national marketplace and ultimately to the ladybucks level. Initially they begin humbly, from garages, gyms, and Granges, with friends and family as sole employees, little equipment, and no cash flow.

Annie Hurlbut and her mother Biddy began—and still run—The Peruvian Connection from the family's Kansas farmhouse. Their start-up funds were five hundred dollars. Three years later, seeing a steady, growing demand for their goods, they decided to move out of wholesaling and into direct-mail sales. A $50,000 Small Business Administration–guaranteed loan enabled them to publish an attractive color mail-order catalog and build their sales to the million-dollar level.

Sharlyne Powell and Sharon McConnell began their Woman-at-Large fitness center in a Grange hall with a few hundred dollars, a tape player, and a strong conviction that overweight women needed workouts tailored to their needs and provided for them in an accepting environment. When they saw the popularity of their concept and sensed a national market for it, they borrowed $70,000 and structured their Washington-based exercise business into a national franchise operation.

Sharon Corr began Corr's Natural Beverages with Ginseng Rush (a ginseng-based natural soda beverage), her husband Bob, and $1,200. The $1,200 made up six cases of the beverage that Sharon believed would take the health food field by storm. Retailers at the National Nutritional Foods Association Trade Show, where Sharon and Bob distributed one-ounce samples, loved the product and gladly accepted a 4 percent cash discount for prepayment. (In this industry 1 percent is standard.) This prepayment financing provided the cash flow that led to a business that today, seven years later, has annual sales of $10 million.

Myth 7: The biggest ladybucks are earned by women in prestige professions and executive positions.

Many female doctors, lawyers, and CEO's enjoy good incomes, but the largest ladybucks are earned by successful female business owners. Advanced educational training and corporate employment provide impressive status bucks. But women with excellent marketing skills, who head companies providing in-demand services or products, make the most money and have the best chance of seeing their net worth escalate into the millions of dollars.

"My accountant, doctor, and lawyer are all women," says Carla, who owns three fast-food franchises. "Together they earn less than I do, and they all get top dollar for their services." Carla admits that these three professional women may get more satisfaction or status from their work than she gets, but when it comes to bottom-line earnings, "degrees and dedication don't bring in the dollars that good, greasy french fries can," she says.

Carla, like many ladybucks earners, does not have high-visibility income. People assume she's doing okay because most food franchises do well, but few know for sure. She is not particularly attractive or articulate, has not drawn media attention, and does not engage in conspicuous consumption. Carla engages in church functions, bowling tournaments, baby-sitting for her grandchildren—and in saving and investing her fast-food profits, which have given her a net worth of over $7 million.

There are a good number of Carlas who earn and amass unpublicized ladybucks, who are not first-choice media material, who don't become entrepreneurial celebrities. They operate quietly and live modest lives. With more glamorous moneymakers garnering publicity, theirs are the unheralded—but often the largest—ladybucks.

Myth 8: Ladybucks earners live lavish lives.

Most don't. The type of woman who achieves ladybucks generally feels her reward is having done it, having built a profitable business, career, or profession. The joys and toys she purchases may be expensive, but they are are not excessive. There is little squandering or splashiness. Most ladybucks are funneled back into the businesses, careers, or professions that sprouted them, or into investments. Press stories and photo layouts sometimes depict the ladybucks earner as living in a mansion, driving an $80,000 car, wearing huge diamonds, or always vacationing in exotic places. Very few female moneymakers live on this "movie star" scale. They selectively choose a special car, or a piece of jewelry they love, or a trip they always dreamed of, but not the whole package. They don't regard themselves as rich, and they don't indulge themselves with pleasure after pleasure.

Says a Wall Street stockbroker who has a picture on her desk of herself and her family on an African safari, "I thought when I earned my first million I'd get over my thriftiness. I'd buy a sports car or a bigger house. But my old car was working fine, and I had become attached to the house we had." This woman added a spacious extension to her home and treated her family to a costly safari vacation, but she didn't purchase anywhere near what she could have or change her lifestyle in any dramatic way. Like many women who earn six-figure incomes and build net worths of over a million dollars, she does not covet an array of material possessions or an endless series of dazzling experiences. Nor does she see herself as being able to live lavishly if she chose to do so.

Once a woman begins to make a lot of money, she starts to meet other people with larger earnings and discovers not only that they live middle- or upper-middle-class lives, but also that they often have very little disposable wealth. "Most 'rich' people have a few million, not many, many millions, and that's not a lot today," says a thirty-five-year-old female radiologist. "You're trying to save for your future and your children's futures, and much of your wealth is paper wealth. Most of our friends and associates are very well off in comparison to most people, but none of us can afford to live lavishly."

"If I were to win a fortune in a lottery, perhaps I could suspend my 'depression mentality,'" says a fifty-three-year-old female real estate investor who has accumulated twenty high-income commercial properties. "But my money didn't come windfall style, and I can't spend it that way." This woman lives in a pleasant suburban neighborhood. Her neighbors have no idea that she is worth several million dollars. Her possessions, pleasures, and pursuits draw admiration and interest but not envy. Like most American millionaires, female and male, she believes that a million dollars is not big money today, does not see herself as wealthy, enjoys her work, and lives beneath her means.

Myth 9: Ladybucks earners are born winners.

Nonsense. They are born babies. There is no such thing as a moneymaking chromosome. Intelligence, energy, and creativity can be linked to genetic green lights, but not moneymaking, not female or male moneymaking. A girl may appear to be a born winner intel-

lectually, athletically, or artistically, but she is not born to be rich—
or to be poor. Unlike eye color, hair color, and skin color, income
is not determined at birth. Circumstances combine that teach a girl
how to capitalize on whatever gifts she may be born with—and until
recently this hasn't happened very much.

Most women of today were not introduced to marketplace wheel-
ing and dealing or encouraged to capitalize financially on native
abilities. They were taught to play with dolls, cultivate feminine mannerisms, help around the house, look pretty, be neat, attract males,
and be mothers. There has been little direction toward activities that
might provide the foundation for females to comfortably cash in on
native inclinations and talents. Orienting a young girl toward moneymaking possibilities has been regarded as vulgar—and still is in
many places.

Things are beginning to change, though. With the divorce rate
and two-income families a necessity, parents, schools, and businesses are becoming more enlightened in their treatment of females
as potential ladybucks earners. Sometimes the poor are leading the
way and demonstrating that hands-on experience is the best approach toward turning a young girl into a financial winner.

When Natalie Tong was eleven, she worked afternoons in her
parents' grocery store. On weekends she helped her father sell nuts
and dried fruits at a large Sunday flea market. She was a slightly
below-average student. Her teachers believed she wasn't interested
in academic pursuits because her parents made her work so much.
Some of her friends' parents whispered that she wasn't being raised
properly, that she was being deprived of her childhood. Upon completing high school, Natalie took a job as a gal Friday for a T-shirt
manufacturer. She learned silk screening, record keeping, product
distribution. At nineteen, she was writing up orders and distributing
hundreds of her boss's T-shirts to vendors at the flea market where
she had worked with her father, as well as at several other markets.
At twenty-one, she was in business for herself, both as an independent distributor forging contracts with different manufacturers
and as the owner of four permanent flea market stalls run by high
school girls whom she trained.

At twenty-four, Natalie linked up with one of her T-shirt suppliers
and became a flea market organizer, setting up indoor and outdoor

markets in three states. Today, at twenty-eight, she has expanded into exposition ownership and management, bringing in revenues of over $14 million. She pays herself an annual salary of $150,000 and owns several of the sites that house her public events. Recently, at the tenth reunion of her high school graduating class, one of her former teachers said, "I can't believe it: a least-likely-to-succeed student has succeeded the most, and some of our most-likely-to-succeed pupils are still finding themselves."

How does this happen? Why has Natalie so outearned her former classmates? Is this the immigrant experience in America playing itself out with its daughters? What enabled Natalie, the daughter of poor merchants, to become a millionaire before her thirtieth birthday?

Natalie was not a born winner in any way. She was an ordinary child and a less-than-ordinary student. But because her parents needed her help in their store and stall, she learned early how money is made, how to pitch a product, and how to negotiate with customers. Her parents didn't plan to create a ladybucks earner. Circumstances combined that taught her how to make a buck, circumstances that provided her the know-how and confidence to later turn ambition into affluence—circumstances that many "luckier" young girls don't encounter.

Myth 10: Ladybucks are service bucks due to lack of start-up capitalization.

Most ladybucks are earned in the service sector, but not because women are financially blocked from entering the product sector. It is harder for a woman to get start-up capitalization than for a man, but women gravitate to service businesses and professions because they derive greater satisfaction from selling services than from selling products. Many women enjoy manufacturing, importing, product development, and retailing, but many more like to deal with people, help, nurture, motivate, and communicate. These later preferences lead women into service fields such as health care, travel, catering, public relations, advertising, and counseling.

Often ladybucks are spawned in the service sector but are swelled by the addition of a product line to a service offering. A woman starts an exercise program, does well, franchises it, and expands into selling warm-up suits, leotards, and workout cassettes. Or she begins a travel consulting firm and branches out into the manufacture and sale of carry-on luggage. Or she runs a successful catering firm and decides to wholesale some of her specialties to restaurants and retail shops. The successful service business prompts its owner to introduce tie-in products. It also provides her the financing to continue doing what she enjoys most while simultaneously venturing into new offshoots.

One caterer with a thriving local business doubled her earnings by making, freezing, and selling to restaurants, hotels, and supermarkets hundreds of gourmet quiches and cheese pastries weekly. This woman had found that her quiches and pastries were favorites with the guests at the affairs she catered. She did a bit of amateur market research and determined that if she produced a commercial line through a bakery she worked with and had it distributed by a good sales rep, she could match the net she was getting from her catering services. Her catering profits were funneled into her new venture, and it worked out as she had hoped. Currently, she is test-marketing two of her other popular specialties for wholesale manufacture and distribution. If they work out as she expects, her income will be well over $100,000 a year.

Myth 11: Ladybucks demand real risk taking.

Not really. It depends how one defines ladybucks. Real risk taking may become necessary if a woman wishes to skyrocket already-high earnings. Should the above caterer decide to open several branches, or franchise her operation, or develop an extensive product line, certain large risks might have to be taken. She could make a fortune, but she could lose everything, too—particularly if she moves too fast.

Many a woman earning in the $50,000-to-$150,000 range could possibly skyrocket her income by expanding her company into a franchise operation, or opening another professional office, or moving from employee to entrepreneur. Sometimes the courage to move on an idea of the moment or to borrow heavily turns a thriving enterprise into a formidable multinational corporation, or an exceptional income into an incredible one; sometimes such courage proves to have been misdirected. And sometimes very little courage or risk taking is required to leap into larger ladybucks.

Sandra Boynton, thirty-two, is the artist behind the greeting cards with elephants clutching balloons, hippos and sheep singing happy birthday, and cats grinning best wishes through toothy smiles. Her rise to fame and fortune was safe and steady and required little risk taking. In her words, it "proceeded step-by-step, inexorably, everything always seeming to fall into place." Sandra entered the greeting card business by accident twelve years ago. In an attempt to raise financing to attend Yale Drama School, she created whimsical animal cards and sold them to several East Coast crafts shops. To her surprise, they moved briskly. More were ordered; she paid her expenses and began to build a bankroll. With demand growing rapidly, she went to a New York trade show and found a greeting card company, Recycled Paper Products, Inc., that would distribute her cards in exchange for a royalty agreement and artistic control. After this agreement proved successful, she licensed her artwork for use on clothing, mugs, stationery, and other items. This year, Recycled Paper Products, Inc., plans to sell 25 million of Sandra's cards in the United States alone. Currently, her licensed products are among the biggest sellers in gift shops all over the country.

Modest, careful, well-planned risk taking can bring a woman revenues and earnings in the millions of dollars. Sometimes, though, in order to move above the $1-million-to-$5-million level, serious decisions must be made—decisions that demand increased degrees of risk taking. At this point one of two things happens. The ladybucks earner stays where she is, enjoys her work, funnels her savings into equity positions, and pursues personal pleasures—the path chosen by successful professional women more intent on personal and professional growth than on multiplying ladybucks. Or she tastes the glory, touches the gold, and wants more—frequently the wish of entrepreneurial women who have founded and nurtured marketplace niches into sizable, prospering businesses that they believe have far greater potential. Rarely do the women who take real risks in the attempt to multiply their ladybucks positions do so blindly. They know what they may be letting themselves in for, but they proceed, believing in their ideas and in their abilities to survive should their ideas prove unworthy of the risks taken. Sometimes their gambles pay off splendidly. Sometimes they don't.

When Patti McVay laid out over $500,000 to open two out-of-town branches of the $100 million Fifth Season Travel Agency, which she had built from the ground up, she knew she was taking a big risk. Profit margins are paper thin in the travel business; cash is dear, and $500,000 is a lot of money. If her expansion idea worked out, her agency could double and triple its already excellent revenues. If it didn't work out, her entire business would be jeopardized. She had an ambitious plan, gave it her best shot, but couldn't bring it off. She needed more funds than she had planned on and was forced to file for Chapter 11 bankruptcy (a reorganization strategy that permits a debtor to agree on a negotiated settlement with her creditors in an attempt to save a failing venture for the benefit of all concerned).

Myth 12: Ladybucks begin with a novel idea.

This could be called the "hot product (or service) myth"—a woman makes money because she hits upon a clever product or service whose time has come, sells it to a ready public, and makes an excellent profit. It sounds appealing and could keep a lot of women waiting to stumble upon that one novel idea that would reap them ladybucks. But it seldom works this way. There are very few novel ideas around that dozens of women haven't already discovered, acted upon, and, in many cases, found unprofitable. Usually, if anything, the ladybucks earner gives a novel twist to an old idea—such as Debbi Fields's selling of *warm,* just-baked cookies.

Ladybucks are rarely generated from the sale of novel products or services. Generally, they grow from the cultivation of marketplace niches, from proving one's superior abilities, from the help of the media, from the execution of ordinary ideas with extraordinary skill. Despite abundant evidence to the contrary, the myth persists that consumers are waiting for the next Pet Rock. They aren't. They are waiting for quality work, superior service, relief from problems, and guidance.

When a woman makes a fortune with an "I wish I'd thought of that" product or service such as Dalia Ratner's All My Muffins shops or Carole Jackson's Color Me Beautiful workshops or Louise Berenson's Purple Panache pushcarts, thousands of other women nod and say, "That's what I need—a really clever idea." Not so. Clever or novel ideas are not what earns ladybucks for 95 percent of today's female moneymakers. Most ladybucks today are earned by women who meet perennial needs, or perceived needs, better than their competitors do. Many women run fitness programs; only a tiny fraction of them reap ladybucks. Many women sell baked goods; only a tiny fraction of them reap ladybucks. Many women sell cosmetics; only a tiny fraction of them reap ladybucks. Many women sell clothing. . . .

Lina Lee Lidow sells expensive clothing to a young, sophisticated, well-to-do clientele. Her three Lina Lee boutiques, opened within the past eight years in fashionable locations, have among the highest sales volume rates of any clothing store in America. While most retailers are currently struggling along, Lina's sales are in the $22 million range and growing.

What is Lina doing right that other ritzy retailers aren't? She stocks only imaginative designs from unknown designers who offer her exclusive contracts. But other less successful retailers who stock famous names also support unknowns on exclusive contracts. She knows her customers and caters to them with special courtesies. But other upscale retailers also keep in touch with favored customers through "we just got in something for you" phone calls and "thank you for your patronage" notes. Her stores are exceptionally welcoming, and her sales help are nonintimidating. But many upscale retailers have inviting surroundings and employ the "don't hover" policy, too. What then is her secret? There isn't any. Lina just does a combination of "right" things better than her competitors do. Her clothing is more interesting. She specializes in promising fledgling designers to the exclusion of the big names. Her service is especially attentive. Her offerings aren't novel nearly as much as they are on the highest possible level that her type of customer could hope for.

Myth 13: Mentors make the difference in ladybucks production.

They don't, simply because few successful women have actually had mentors. They have had support systems—husbands, parents, friends—who have cheered them on with words, deeds, and financing; but they have not had the traditional mentor that women hear about and hope for but rarely encounter. Ideally, mentors are selfless, sincere individuals who devote themselves to advancing the career of a woman whom they feel could make it to the top with the right guidance from someone experienced in the field. They're there from the starting gate to the finish line, making sure that the path up is as painless and perfect as possible. It sounds nice, but it almost never happens. At best, a woman meets a few influential colleagues who provide her with specific and time-limited assistance at major crossroads or crucial moments.

Anne Sadovsky became a top seminar speaker and a successful business owner by working in sales and learning from trial and error how to appeal to customers, interest them, and motivate them to buy. She credits people such as Mary Kay Ash, for whom she worked at a critical time in her life, with inspiring her to reach higher and giving her helpful how-to tips, but no one took her hand and walked her to the top. She did this herself.

Similarly, the Aden sisters, renowned financial analysts and newsletter publishers whose predictions of major financial trends are followed by millions of investors, were inspired but not mentored to their present ladybucks level. Pamela and Mary Anne Aden worked as bilingual researchers for a wealthy American investment banker. The man taught them his unique system of forecasting trends. After several years, the women decided to strike out on their own. They expanded on what their boss had taught them, built a global network of contacts alert to developing market fluctuations, created their own forecasting system, and guided, with remarkable accuracy, their clients and newsletter subscribers to highly profitable opportunities. As their clients began making large sums, they themselves did, too. The sisters are grateful to their former employer for introducing them to a lucrative service possibility—but they turned possibility into prosperity.

Myth 14: If you believe you can do anything you want to do, ladybucks can be yours.

Ladybucks earners are known to say, "I believe a woman can do anything she wants to." Questioned about their successful ventures, they talk about hard work and persistence and wax philosophic about the importance of positive thinking. They genuinely believe a strong link exists between believing and achieving. But they are right only conditionally, for a very important reason that they usually fail to acknowledge: Positive thinking works for them because they are very realistic about what they think about. They analyze their abilities and limitations and pursue businesses and careers that they have a good likelihood of succeeding at.

When Carol Jenna talks of the $5 million sports marketing agency she founded, she credits her belief in herself with her success. But this lady was always a sports enthusiast, a believer in physical fitness and athletic competition, and a wheeler-dealer. Today, at forty-three, she wakes up at 5:30 A.M. for a three-to-five-mile run, follows it with a free-weight workout and meditation, and then prepares for a day that often ends late at night. Carol looks like a champion. She loves talking sports and business. She delights in competition. Clients are impressed with her ability to profitably match their corporations with high-visibility athletic events and competitions. Beaming health and happiness, Carol says, "This agency was an ideal way for me to marry my love of sports and fitness with my strong business acumen." This is lovely, but it's very noteworthy that Carol set her sights on making it in a field that she was well-qualified to pursue. She didn't believe she could be successful in an out-of-the-blue venture that caught her fancy, something that sounded appealing but that she knew nothing about and had little likelihood of succeeding at.

Like Carol Jenna, Dr. Paula Moynahan talks about the role of positive thinking in making her one of America's top plastic and reconstructive surgeons. But here again is a woman who had good reason to believe in herself, to feel she could be a successful physician. Paula was always an excellent student, with a keen interest in, and understanding of, science. She had excellent powers of concentration and abstraction, loved working with her hands, and had a great sensitivity to beauty and proportion. She also had solid family support in her endeavors and the type of rejection-proof disposition that enabled her to persist against the prejudice that women of her day experienced in getting into medical school. Had Paula believed she could be a prima ballerina instead of a doctor, she probably would have given it a good shot, but it is unlikely that she would have succeeded. Like Carol Jenna, Paula knew her abilities and limitations and dreamed in the right direction.

Myth 15: Luck has little to do with ladybucks.

So stresses a well-known women's rights advocate who hammers away on the theme of passionate pursuit as the road to prosperity. "You struggle your way to success; you don't luck your way to success!" emphasizes this die-hard, who is well-intentioned but incorrect. Of course struggle is part of the success formula. But so is luck. The woman fortunate enough to have a naturally high energy level or a good mathematical mind or a pleasant face enters the money game with a stronger hand than the woman without such advantages. Similarly, the woman who has ready sources of financing or a loving husband cheering her on or an abundance of family connections has the odds of success more in her favor than many other female aspirants.

"You make your luck," advise the pedagogues, and they are correct—to an extent. Women who network, maximize opportunities, and provide themselves escape hatches lure Lady Luck to their corners. They actively set themselves up to be lucky, rather than passively hoping for a lucky break. However, to deny the role of plain, ordinary luck in the creation of ladybucks is foolish. Some women definitely have more of an advantage than others. This doesn't mean they will do better—simply that their journey will probably be easier, all other things being equal.

The saga of the ladybucks earner who has everything against her, no luck to bolster her, and every reason to fail but nevertheless defies impossible odds to turn grit into gold is especially inspirational and appealing. But many, many ladybucks earners do start out with some lucky assets or get some lucky breaks along the way. Sandra Kurtzig put in long hours to create her computer corporation, but she was lucky enough to have a mathematics and engineering background at a time when such training was being translated into successful high-tech industries in Silicon Valley where she lived.

Paula Moynahan studied hard to become a successful surgeon, but she was lucky enough to be born not just with an excellent mind but to adoring parents who were willing to work hard and sacrifice in order to finance their daughter's expensive education.

Debbi Fields put a lot of effort into creating her cookie empire, but she was fortunate enough to be married to a financial consultant who supported his wife's dreams with solid advice and financing.

Today Lane Nemeth's Discovery Toys looks as though it might soon become a multinational company with annual revenues of over $100 million, but it could well have faded into oblivion had Lane not been rescued from impending bankruptcy by a venture capitalist who by chance accompanied his wife to a Discovery Toys sales party. The man was intrigued by Lane's company, its products, and its prospects, wanted in, and got his firm to invest $90,000 in the operation and help Lane secure a $250,000 Small Business Administration loan.

Myth 16: Ladybucks are the result of a clear, singular, long-range vision.

This is the myth of the "straight career path." It assumes that the self-made woman had it all worked out from the beginning. A woman enters a company, sees the boardroom, learns what she must do to get there, and proceeds. It's an acceptable way to begin. The goals are good. However, more often than not, this is the stuff of successful soap operas, not of successful women. Indirect routes are much more likely to lead to ladybucks. The highest earning entrepreneurial and corporate women have had unplanned jobs and experiences en route to their achievements. A woman enters a company with high hopes and qualifications, strives to reach the top, realizes she'll never get beyond middle management, quits her job, and goes on to build her own moneymaking company. Or she starts out with her own business and decides after a few hard, lonely, stressful years that she'd like to try the security, socialization, prestige, and power that can come from a good executive position with a major corporation. The path to ladybucks is a crooked one. A steady input of ambition and action combine with generalized goals and flexible dreams.

Anne Breckenridge, who now enjoys a top corporate position with Coca-Cola, came to her job by what she calls a "winding staircase." Like most businesswomen, she did not finish school, knew exactly where she wanted to be ten years down the road, and headed toward that end. Actually, her basic plan was to get married, work for a few years, and have a baby. Like Sandra Kurtzig, who was interested in motherhood more than a career (but nevertheless turned part-time technical work into the $80 million ASK Computer Systems), Anne found herself divorced and was forced to reorganize her thinking. She went back to college to get an M.A. in design, took a job in the design field, suffered a layoff and a second divorce, took another job in the design field, worked for herself as a freelancer, and then took a job as an interior designer of Coca-Cola's 673,000-square-foot Atlanta facility.

Even when an executive woman has spent her employment life with a single company, her success is rarely the result of an early vision of herself running the corporation. In 1959, Janice Stoney took a job as a service representative for Northwestern Bell. She planned to work a couple of years and then return to college. Things didn't work out this way. Instead of completing her college education, she put in a few years here and there in different departments of the company, moved from service representative to labor negotiation, recruiting, and marketing, and ultimately became vice president in charge of a five-state district. Last year, she became Northwestern Bell's chief operating officer. Talking about crooked career paths, she says, "People who are most effective have usually had a variety of experiences. . . . What we look for [at Northwestern Bell] is whether a candidate's plans make sense now."

Myth 17: Ladybucks earners are born users.

"Show me a woman who has made a fortune, and I'll show you a born user," says one male investment banker, who claims this statement is complimentary, not critical. Whatever this man's sentiments, his contention is wrong. Yet many share his view. Whether it is considered mandatory or malicious, people-using is frequently regarded as the root of ladybucks. A woman turns an idea into an industry because she instinctively knows how to manipulate bankers, suppliers, associates, employees, and clients.

Just as ladybucks earners are not born winners (Myth 9), neither are they born users. Most ladybucks earners learn, often with great difficulty, to network and exchange favors, but usually they are reluctant people-users initially. Often they fail to adequately use individuals to whom they pay good salaries and whom they should use *more* effectively.

Female moneymakers frequently need training in people-using in order to maximize their ladybucks potential. They turn for advice to business consultants and psychologists because they find it hard to ask for assistance, to master tasks such as delegation and discipline. They are well-positioned to profit and prosper but need guidance in giving commands, controlling people, and directing others for the purpose of fulfilling their own goals. They know the importance of "connecting and using" (see Chapter 5) and work to become polished networkers.

There is a thin line between people-using and people-abusing, and ambitious women are usually very interested in staying on the good side of that line. Says one industrial psychologist, "It's amazing how overconcerned these successful women are with pleasing employees and customers, rewarding good work, being fair. Often they could go much further much faster if they were just a bit more ruthless, perhaps a bit less guilty about their positions. Successful men have much less difficulty in this area."

Myth 18: A ladybucks earner develops a callous veneer as she advances in the money world.

Not so. If anything, she mellows out as she achieves her dreams and becomes comfortable with her wealth and power. Ladybucks achievers are nonabrasive women, as a whole. Those with brusque exteriors are often among the biggest supporters of other women trying to make it. Occasionally, an aloof, self-centered cold heart achieves ladybucks because she is exceptionally proficient in an in-demand field. But mostly the perception of the female tycoon as callous is a misperception.

Carol Jenna surprises new associates with her soft voice and gentle manner. She deals professionally with hardened executives and athletes in punishing sports without becoming hardened or punishing in her manner. One expects to encounter a female jock with a good business head, and one encounters just this; but the female jock with a good business head also has a tender heart and a caring approach.

Similarly, Gessie Tassone could be called "An Iron Lady with a Gold Heart." Many of her business associates and employees are as hard and unrefined as the raw materials in A & T's shops; but Gessie is callous neither on the outside nor on the inside. This woman in a predominantly male industry is proudly caring and kind. She learned the business from the ground up and is at great ease talking equipment, specifications, and regulations with macho industry giants, and no one dares to take advantage of her softness.

Sometimes a ladybucks earner appears to be callous or hard-hearted, but the veneer fades away upon knowing the woman and learning of her contributions to other female aspirants. Attorney Doris Sassower initially comes across as the tough, self-confident fighter that she is. But beyond this facade is a woman deeply concerned about advancing the prospects of women entering the legal profession today. Doris gives time, encouragement, and the benefit of her experience to many young female lawyers who adore her and consider her to be their role model.

Muriel Siebert is Doris's counterpart in the world of finance. She is a "don't mess with me," street-savvy discount broker, but she is also a generous supporter of women's rights and has had a positive impact on Wall Street and on women eager to make it there.

Edna Hennessee, now well into her sixties and still heading Cosmetic Specialty Labs, a multimillion-dollar manufacturer and supplier of cosmetics to private-label companies all over America and the world, remembers well her poverty beginnings, and she tours American business conferences encouraging women to reach beyond their roots to enjoy the American Dream. She has a no-nonsense "determination, not dreaming, gets you there" approach. But her beyond-the-podium, one-on-one discussions with would-be imitators leave listeners knowing they, like she, can be both sweet and successful.

Myth 19: Ladybucks are related to position in family.

A little bit of research about entrepreneurship has revealed that first-borns and only children are more likely to create moneymaking enterprises than are their younger siblings. This is interesting but inaccurate in relation to ladybucks. It may be factual for the relatively small number of males studied. However, these findings can't be generalized to female entrepreneurs, who have hardly been included in the research—because until recently there have been so few of them—or to female corporate executives and professionals, who also have been little studied in regard to where they fall in a sibling lineup.

So far, empirical evidence suggests that entrepreneurial, professional, and corporate ladybucks are unrelated to position in family. Some firstborns and only children have enjoyed the attention, independence, and leadership that their rank can provide and have carried this advantage into the commercial world. Some have been handled too delicately, have been catered to too much, have received undue adulation, and have been unable to deal with the pressures and privations that often accompany the quest for ladybucks. Sometimes last-born females of large families outearn their older siblings and go on to head big businesses or build prosperous professional practices. They've learned to observe, listen, and fight for their rights. They've benefited from the wisdom and the mistakes of their older brothers and sisters. For the first twenty years of their lives, they may never have worn anything but hand-me-downs, but they figured out what they had to do if they wanted to put new outfits on their own babies' backs. And they went out and did it—and went on to do a lot more.

Gessie Tassone's mother had seventeen children. Nine of them died at birth. Gessie was last-born—the youngest of the eight who remain. All her siblings look up to her. Her oldest sister works for her in the A & T Iron Works offices.

Doris Sassower is the youngest of five children. From the time she was twelve, she knew she wanted to be an attorney. Her parents discouraged her ambitions, but she persisted. None of her siblings are professionals.

Dr. Paula Moynahan is the younger of two children. Her older brother and closest friend is a successful lawyer and a great admirer of his sister's accomplishments. A list of hundreds of ladybucks earners contains many similar last-born stories. It also contains many firstborn and middle-children ladybucks stories. No pattern emerges that points to a connection between ladybucks and position in family.

Myth 20: Ladybucks require a readiness to relocate.

This is the "relocation myth." It assumes that a woman must be willing to move in order to advance. Often relocation does enhance moneymaking opportunities, but it is not essential, and it is becoming less and less so. Ladybucks are created in the most unlikely locations. Entrepreneurial women devise ways to bring their offerings to distant consumers (see Chapter 1). Small-town professional women accept lower fees than they might receive in prestigious big-city locations, but often their overheads are less, and thus their net profits are still high. Corporate women set up new divisions in old flagship locations or travel frequently rather than leave communities they like and in which they've established roots.

When Coca-Cola executive Anne Breckenridge talks of the "winding" career path that took her through many jobs and states in several years, she reflects the experience of many upward-bound executives who determine where they live by where their companies move, or want to send them, or where they believe they can maximize their chances of career success. However, today more than in years past, even corporate women have solid choices. They don't have to relocate in order to rise. Compromise situations are available. With relocation costs spiraling, the increase in the number of two-income families, and the number of couples who refuse to move and jeopardize their spouses' careers, many corporations have been forced to modify their relocation policies.

Myth 21: Ladybucks do not bring happiness.

This is related to the "money can't buy happiness" philosophy and is fostered by reports of severe conflicts in the lives of ladybucks earners. Top fashion designer Donna Karan, whose clothes are the biggest sellers in 120 of America's most prestigious stores, talked to *The New York Times* about the tensions of being a designer and a chief executive officer. She revealed her fear of creative burnout and said, "I'm not happy right now. I wish I were. A part of me is really looking for the quality of life that works for me. What's happening now is ripping into everything I hold dear—my husband, my child, my mental time. I'd like to have another child. It's tough. It's much bigger than I thought it would be."

Millions read this and similar quotes from women successful on a less spectacular scale and wonder if it's all worth it. Here is the newest star in the fashion industry, a woman whose company industry analysts estimate has the potential of bringing in annual retail revenues of $250 million—and she's not happy. Everything is open-ing up for her. Her future looks golden and glorious. Shouldn't she be at the peak of pleasure?

No. Donna Karan and other female achievers cracking into the ladybucks lane shouldn't be happy during their skyrocket phase. The stakes are high, the pressures are great, and the limelight is un-yielding. Serenity and family life must be put on hold. This is not a time of happiness. It is a time of eighteen-hour days filled with work and worry. However, once the ladybucks earner is established, has found capable assistants, has tucked away a few million dollars, has sold her business if she finds it too much, and has regained her balance and sense of priority, she is more likely to be happy than the woman who has never amassed ladybucks. The ladybucks earner experiences problems, pains, and an array of negative emotions, but she also experiences the splendid self-satisfaction that comes from cashing in big on dreams, ideas, and talents, that comes from being self-sufficient, defying difficult odds, achieving what few women manage, and creating wealth in a society where income is a major measure of performance and success. Life is too complex for lady-bucks alone to bring happiness, but their creation permits positive feelings and pleasures that would not exist in their absence.

TRUTHS IN LADYBUCKS MYTHS

Many myths surround the ladybucks phenomenon because it is relatively new and has not been studied widely. The absence of solid information has led to speculation and beliefs that have yet to be proven or disproven. As more research materializes about women and moneymaking, ladybucks myths will begin to fade. Emerging in their place will be a fact that applies to all myths: they might contain touches of truth, but for the most part they are inaccurate and should be ignored.

CHAPTER **10**

Your Likelihood of Ladybucks

In a large New York City hotel, hundreds of women are assembled to hear cookie queen Debbi Fields talk about her success and how they too can become successful. An audience member whispers to the woman on her right, "I don't know why I keep coming to these things. I do everything these moneymakers talk about, and I'm still just barely getting by." She is probably telling the truth. Like thousands of women today, she pays a good amount to hear female entrepreneurs, executives, professionals, business consultants, and industrial psychologists talk about success and moneymaking; she takes copious notes; she tries everything she learns that's applicable to her situation; and nothing much happens. Maybe she does a bit better, but considering the time, effort, and money put into income improvement, she is disillusioned.

Today, women are doing better than ever before. How-to seminars do help, but overall, ambitious women are not earning great amounts, despite the fact that they often work hard, sell needed services and products, and sacrifice many things. For every Debbi Fields grossing $70 million a year, there are millions of women who would be delighted if they could sell $100,000 worth of cookies, or anything else, a year. Actually, most ladybucks hopefuls do not even fantasize about astronomical sales or salaries. They would just like to earn some decent money.

If you fall into this latter category, would be pleased to achieve some reasonable level of ladybucks, and wonder about your likelihood of doing so, a Likelihood of Ladybucks Quiz follows. It is designed to let you know how likely you are to earn a lot of money in the future. For each question, circle the answer that best describes how you are, feel, act, and think. Don't choose what you believe is the "right" answer. When you've completed all twenty-five questions, compare your answers with the LOL answers, and score yourself four points for every LOL answer you circled.

Lest you become easily discouraged, be careful how you judge your score. An LOL score of 50 percent, for example, means that your chances of earning ladybucks are one out of two—good odds. An LOL score of 75 percent indicates that your chances are three out of four—very good odds. Even a score of 25 percent is nothing to fret about—one out of four is not bad. Don't take a low LOL score to mean that you will never earn ladybucks. Review the questions that you did not give an LOL answer to. Consider them as representative of areas that need attention, rethinking, and restructuring if you are to increase your likelihood of ladybucks.

LIKELIHOOD OF LADYBUCKS QUIZ

1. I feel best when I sleep
   a. six hours or less a night.
   b. at least eight hours a night.
   c. four to six hours at night and take a one-to-two-hour afternoon nap.
   d. eight hours a night and take a brief afternoon nap.

2. At a party, professional meeting, or social/business get-together, I tend to
   a. seek out a couple of people I know and spend most of my time with them.
   b. be a people-watcher.
   c. circulate as much as possible.
   d. zero in on people I believe could be most helpful to me.

3. My ideal chief assistant would be someone who is
   a. loyal, fairly intelligent, and hardworking.
   b. very intelligent, very conceited, fairly lazy.
   c. imaginative, skillful, and very energetic.

4. Home-basing (working from home) strikes me as

a. a pleasant, low-pressure way to combine moneymaking and parenting.
b. fine for earning pocket money or beginning a sideline business.
c. a low-risk, low-overhead way to test out several different business interests.
d. an excellent way to begin and operate certain types of businesses or professional practices.

5. My ideal ladybucks role model is a woman who
   a. earns a lot of money and also has a loving husband and happy children.
   b. is the master of her destiny.
   c. is personable, powerful, prosperous, and kind.

6. The women who make the most money excel at
   a. coming up with creative, clever ideas.
   b. marketing themselves and their ideas.
   c. getting others to execute their ideas.
   d. raising the capital needed to turn good ideas into good income.

7. The most successful corporate women in male-run organizations are those who
   a. think and act like men.
   b. worry about getting the job done well.
   c. understand how their male colleagues think and act and use this understanding to their advantage.

8. You get fired from your job. The first thing you do is
   a. request an explanation.
   b. arrange a severance package.
   c. take solace from the fact that 70 percent of female firings lead to greater career happiness and success.

9. The best way to capitalize on a media interview is to
   a. subtly change subjects to cover areas you want to emphasize.
   b. set the ground rules.
   c. ask the program manager for a preview list of questions and topics to be covered.

10. The relationship between formal education and ladybucks is
    a. significant in professions such as law and medicine but not in business.
    b. significant in many fields, including business, but is less significant than the relationship between hard work and ladybucks.
    c. not significant at all, judging from the large number of female college graduates who can't get good jobs, must still live at home, and earn less than their uneducated friends or acquaintances in blue-collar trades.

11. Positive thinking can lead to ladybucks, provided it is
   a. geared to moneymaking.
   b. combined with ambition and action.
   c. realistic.

12. Many ambitious, action-oriented women fail to make ladybucks because they
   a. are figure-phobic.
   b. are unlucky.
   c. can't come up with the right product or service to sell.

13. I believe there is a time to be assertive; but aggressiveness
   a. is going too far; it turns people off.
   b. though unladylike, is often the only way to achieve ladybucks.
   c. is also necessary and must be used cautiously and cleverly.

14. Visualizing oneself as earning ladybucks is
   a. like daydreaming—it's fun but gets you nowhere.
   b. very important; it helps program a person for wish fulfillment.
   c. a frustrating waste of time that could be spent working toward wealth.

15. Banks and professional investors base lending decisions primarily on
   a. the potential profitability of a business plan.
   b. their response to the individual seeking the financing.
   c. an applicant's employment, financial, and credit history.

16. The highest-paid professional women run their practices
   a. like businesses.
   b. for personal satisfaction and growth, and the money follows.
   c. with an entrepreneurial slant.

17. Intuition is too chancy; the decisions that lead to ladybucks must be based on
   a. facts and figures.
   b. cold, clear logic.
   c. intuition tempered by intelligence and experience.

18. Ladybucks come from working hard and working smart, but also from
   a. lucky breaks.
   b. risk taking.
   c. personal support systems.
   d. all of the above.
   e. b and c

19. Failure is
   a. part of the experience of all ladybucks winners.
   b. sometimes the foundation of success but best avoided if possible.

   c. neither negative nor positive; it depends upon how a ladybucks hopeful handles it.

20. I can cope with hard work; stress
   a. does me in.
   b. doesn't bother me, provided I'm in control.
   c. upsets me, but it's part of the price of ladybucks.

21. Most ladybucks earners
   a. rely on others to bring them to the winners' circle.
   b. get much behind-the-scenes support.
   c. rely on themselves to make it to the top.
   d. b and c
   e. all of the above.

22. Ladybucks earners enjoy
   a. the quest more than the money.
   b. the money more than the quest.
   c. the quest and the money.

23. The ladybucks earner is usually driven to
   a. have it all—career, family, money, status.
   b. cash in big on her ideas and skills.
   c. work to the exclusion of almost all else.
   d. become rich in any legitimate way.

24. Ladybucks are earned by women who want to
   a. be rich.
   b. create something that never existed before.
   c. earn some spare cash.
   d. a and b
   e. all of the above.

25. The surest way to earn ladybucks is to
   a. work your way up in a big company with a proven record of promoting women to high positions.
   b. build your own business.
   c. study an in-demand profession.

ANSWERS TO THE LIKELIHOOD OF LADYBUCKS QUIZ

   1. a. Ladybucks require time. The more hours a day that can be devoted to the moneymaking process, the more likely a woman is, all other things being equal, to generate wealth. Most ladybucks earners do not require large amounts of sleep. They function all day and well into the evening on six hours or less sleep a night. Although some sleep as few as four hours a night and refuel with an afternoon nap, the American marketplace does not

work on a siesta schedule; and the woman who can go from morning to night without tiring has a definite edge.

2. c. Though some ladybucks earners dislike networking, they recognize its value in the moneymaking process and train themselves to be good at it. Generally, the philosophy is the more contacts, the better. There is nothing wrong with zeroing in on a few people who could prove helpful; however, the ladybucks earner learns quickly that help often comes from the least likely sources, and she uses large gatherings to meet several new people, selectively handing out business cards and following up potentially good contacts with phone calls.

3. b. The ladybucks earner learns quickly that she is best off relying heavily on key personnel who are very bright and sure of themselves but too lazy to go into competition with her or drain her energy and creative juices with their own high energy levels or excessive zeal.

4. d. The woman most likely to make ladybucks may view home-basing as attractive for reasons ranging from lower overhead to proximity to family, but she tends to analyze work styles mostly in terms of their effectiveness in creating income.

5. b. Although kindness, power, family, love, and money are important to ladybucks earners, these women think first about controlling their fate. They believe that if they can take charge of their destiny, they will survive and thrive; and then they can properly direct their attention to other concerns.

6. b. Good ideas, good helpers, and good financing are important, but the women who turn ideas, assistance, and financing into high income are excellent at marketing themselves and their products or services to begin with. Their ability to convince potential customers and clients of their personal superiority and the superiority of their offerings is the biggest contributor to their ladybucks status.

7. c. Most women, even highly successful ones, do not naturally think and act like men, and when they try to, they often make themselves uncomfortable and come across as offensive. The women who climb to the top of the corporate ladder are a very small group with a very unique ability to understand how men operate, and they use this insight to get along well with their male colleagues and consequently accelerate their own advancement. They don't worry about getting the job done well. They know they can do it and realize that promotions for quality performance are usually granted by men.

8. b. If fired, the ladybucks earner knows to think first of what she will get from the situation. Later she finds out why she was let go and, if applicable, what she can do to prevent a similar mistake in the future. Eventually, she will probably look back on the firing, as do 70 percent of women who have been dismissed, as one of the best things that could have happened to her financially.

9. a. It is always wise to request the opening question and a list of subjects

that an interviewer plans to cover and to inform the program manager of questions you don't want asked. As it is in a show's best interest that you be prepared and pleased, your requests will usually be granted. However, in order to maximize a media interview to sell yourself and your products or services, you're best off steering questions that won't enhance you or your offering toward areas that you wish to highlight. For example, if you sell a matchmaking service and the interviewer asks if you've ever matched two people who hated each other and you have, you might respond, "Most of our clients take a few tries before finding a match that fully pleases them, but they keep coming back, so we must be doing something right. We matched one fifty-five-year-old woman with . . . "

10. b. Formal education is crucial and required in many professions. Though it is not mandatory to operate most businesses, it is useful to study how the marketplace functions, how records are kept, and how best to market particular goods and services. However, all the best formal business training available won't lead to ladybucks without hands-on experience and hard work.

11. b. The ladybucks earner not only evaluates her abilities realistically and adapts them toward moneymaking activities, she charges her positive thinking with "let's get going" ambition and much action. Without such charge, all the positive thinking in the world can't create wealth.

12. a. Ambition and action are essential to the creation of ladybucks, but the woman who is afraid to deal with numbers is likely to doom herself to defeat in the financial world. A mastery of mathematics is not critical, but a woman who delegates all numerical control of her business or professional practice is likely to find herself standing by helplessly as it declines into bankruptcy. Selling a "right" product or service means nothing if a woman doesn't know how to figure costs, prices, fees, mark-ups, cash flow requirements, and gross versus net profits.

13. c. Most ladybucks earners are masters of aggressiveness without necessarily realizing it. They act and react forcefully when they must; but they focus their aggressive behavior only on those situations that demand a peremptory response. They combat threatening events as swiftly and thoroughly as possible and then resume a cordial demeanor. Usually they are applauded as self-protective, decisive, take-charge individuals, not as offensive or unladylike.

14. b. Visualization is an important step toward putting a moneymaking plan into action. Ladybucks are built by women who envision themselves successfully selling goods and services and who gaze into their own futures and see their target customers buying, using, and rebuying their offerings for profits that make hard work worthwhile.

15. b. A woman's economic history and the potential profitability of the business plan she proposes are taken into consideration, but professional lenders are most interested in the person to whom a loan will be made: Is

this individual capable of executing the idea she proposes? A woman can appear responsible and offer a well-thought-out business plan, but if she doesn't impress the lender as having the derring-do to make her idea work in a big way, financing will not be granted.

16. c. The professional women who make the most money generally enjoy their work and are interested in growth within their field. However, it is their ability to sell their offerings with an entrepreneurial flair that gives them an edge over their competitors. One engineer, for example, has a business card designed in the shape of a T-square. Her name and phone number are at the top of the T. The base offers a table of popular linear metric conversions. She tells clients and prospects to use her card as a bookmark— a bookmark that, of course, is intended to keep her name and phone number close at hand.

17. c. Many of the best ladybucks decisions have been based on intuition and sometimes on intuition that has overridden facts, figures, and cold, clear logic. However, ladybucks earners tend to examine their intuitive impulses before taking action: Does my experience support the probable success of this intuition-based move? Does my intuition make any intellectual sense at all?

18. d. There is no simple ladybucks equation. Several important ingredients blend in a unique way to create a moneymaking business, career, or profession. Without any one of them, things might not work out at all. A woman can work hard and work smart, but without some cautious risk taking, or a lucky break, or some well-timed personal support, or one of several other variables, her work could amount to nothing.

19. c. One woman's defeat is another woman's drive. Failure can be negative if it is viewed as the death of a dream. It can be positive if it is analyzed, understood, and used as a springboard for a new plan of operation. Ladybucks winners, like everyone, hope to avoid failure; but they triumph over it when it occurs because they handle it as a detour, not a disaster.

20. b. Stress, like failure, is not something a ladybucks winner enjoys. However, here too its negative or positive value is determined by how it is handled. Women who create profitable businesses, careers, or professions often experience great amounts of stress, but it is stress over which they have control and which thus is unlikely to endanger their physical or mental health. They are not powerless victims of situations they can't deal with or change.

21. e. Seldom is the ladybucks earner a completely self-made winner. She definitely relies on her own abilities in her quest for success. But almost always she has some important assistants and solid behind-the-scenes support that enable her to reach her peak of prosperity.

22. c. Once a ladybucks aspirant amasses a large amount of money and knows she is set for the rest of her life, future earnings may be merely a means of measuring how well her business, profession, or career is pro-

gressing. The quest for new accomplishments may well outweigh the quest for more wealth. However, until this time, both quest and money are enjoyed.

23. b. Women who create ladybucks often hope to have it all (career, family, money, status), usually work very hard, and would like to become rich; but they are driven to capitalize on specific ideas and skills that they believe to have great commercial worth.

24. e. Generally, ladybucks are earned by women who are determined to build new and unusual businesses or make a lot of money in a high-paying profession or career. However, a surprising number of women create fortunes from kitchen table operations begun with the humble hope of earning a little spare cash to make life easier for themselves and their families.

25. b. A few women earn several hundred thousand dollars a year working for big corporations. More and more are crawling up the corporate ladder to salaries previously denied to female executives. An increasing number of women are collecting ladybucks in certain lucrative or timely professions. But most ladybucks earners own and operate their own businesses and earn larger amounts than their counterparts in executive jobs or professions.

Postscript: From Garage to . . .

And then there is the story of the very practical ladybucks earner who runs a multimillion-dollar business from a garage. When a real estate broker tried to sell her "a home befitting your grand accomplishment," she said, "A home? I was born in a hospital, educated on the streets, courted in a car, married in a church, divorced in a courthouse. I eat breakfast at my desk, lunch at a restaurant, dinner at my health club. Evenings are spent with customers; weekends on the golf course. I seldom sleep. When I die, I'll be in a cemetery. Why do I need a home? All I need is a garage."

Appendix

Following is a list of large and small women's organizations, networks, and sources of help that can provide ladybucks aspirants with valuable information, assistance, loans, and referrals. There are over 1,000 such operations nationwide. This is a sampling of the more prominent ones from around the country. A few have membership restrictions based on kind of business or income level. Some have local chapters.

American Business Women's Association
P.O. Box 8728
9100 Ward Pkwy.
Kansas City, MO 64114
(816) 361-6621

American Council for Career Women
P.O. Box 50825
New Orleans, LA 70150
(504) 468-5665

American Society of Professional and Executive Women
1511 Walnut St.
Philadelphia, PA 19102
(215) 563-4415

American Woman's Economic Development Corporation
60 East 42nd St., Rm. 405
New York, NY 10165
(212) 692-9100

Business and Professional Women's Federation
3310 Alginet Drive
Encino, CA 91464
(818) 789-3855

CATALYST
250 Park Avenue South, 5th floor
New York, NY 10003
(212) 777-8900

Committee of 200
500 North Michigan Avenue
Chicago, IL 60611
(312) 661-1700

Displaced Homemakers Network
1010 Vermont Avenue N.W., Suite 817
Washington, DC 20005
(202) 628-6767

Minnesota Women's Network
1421 Park Avenue
Minneapolis, MN 55404
(612) 375-9496

Minority and Women's Business Division of the New York State Department
of Commerce
230 Park Avenue
New York, NY 10169
(212) 309-0440

National Association for Female Executives
1041 Third Avenue
New York, NY 10021
(212) 371-0740

National Association of Women Business Owners
600 South Federal St.
Chicago, IL 60605
(312) 346-2330

National Council of Career Women
1629 K St. N.W.
Washington, DC 20036
(202) 775-8199

National Federation of Business and Professional Woman's Clubs
2012 Massachusetts Avenue N.W.
Washington, DC 20036
(202) 293-1100

National Forum for Executive Women
1101 15th St. N.W., Suite 400
Washington, DC 20005
(202) 857-3100

Network for Professional Women
15 Lewis St.
Hartford, CT 06103
(203) 247-2011

New York Chapter of the National Association of Women Business Owners
604 Fifth Avenue
New York, NY 10020
(212) 489-9236

Small Business Administration
26 Federal Plaza
New York, NY 10278
(212) 264-9488

Woman Business Owners of New York
322 Eighth Avenue
New York, NY 10001
(212) 206-8250

Women's Economic Development Corporation
1885 University Avenue West
St. Paul, MN 55104
(612) 646-3808

Women's Employment Network
109 Lexington Avenue, Suite 300
San Antonio, TX 78205
(512) 224-3002

Women Entrepreneurs
2030 Union St., Suite 310
San Francisco, CA 94123
(415) 929-0129

Women's Information Exchange
1195 Valencia St.
San Francisco, CA 94110
(415) 824-6800

Women's International Network
1887 Grant St.
Lexington, MA 02173
(617) 862-9431

Women's International Resource Exchange
2700 Broadway, #7A
New York, NY 10025
(212) 666-4622

Index